French Cities in the Nineteenth Century

Grève des midinettes à Paris en 1910 (Collection Viollet)

French Cities in the Nineteenth Century

Edited by John M. Merriman

Holmes & Meier Publishers, Inc.
New York

First published in the United States of America 1981 by

HOLMES & MEIER PUBLISHERS, INC.

30 Irving Place, New York, N.Y. 10003

Library of Congress Cataloging in Publication Data
Main entry under title:

French cities in the nineteenth century
  Bibliography: p.
  Includes index.
  1. Urbanization – France – History – 19th century.
  2. Municipal government – France – History – 19th century.
  3. France – Industries – History – 19th century. I. Merriman, John M.
  HT135.F76   307.7′6′0944   81-2520

  ISBN 0-8419-0464-2   AACR2

Manufactured in Great Britain

Contents

Acknowledgements   6

List of illustrations   7

List of contributors   9

1 Introduction: Images of the nineteenth-century
   French city *John M. Merriman*   11

2 Restoration town, bourgeois city: changing
   urban politics in industrializing Limoges
   John M. Merriman   42

3 Charivaris, repertoires and urban politics
   Charles Tilly   73

4 Proto-urban development and political
   mobilization during the Second Republic
   Ted W. Margadant   92

5 Industrialization and republican politics: the
   bourgeois of Reims and Saint-Étienne under
   the Second Empire *David M. Gordon*   117

6 Industry in the changing landscape from
   Daubigny to Monet *Robert L. Herbert*   139

7 Three faces of capitalism: women and work in
   French cities *Louise A. Tilly*   165

8 Decazeville: company town and working-class
   community, 1826–1914 *Don Reid*   193

9 Urbanization, worker settlement patterns and
   social protest in nineteenth-century France
   Michael P. Hanagan   208

10 Mayors versus police chiefs: socialist municipalities confront the French state *Joan W. Scott*   230

Notes and references   247
Select bibliography   287
Index   294

Acknowledgements

I first became interested in French towns and cities while doing research for my dissertation exactly ten years ago; and, despite some rather grim times in Limoges, have subsequently spent as much time as possible exploring France's urban world, though not necessarily always for scholarly reasons. Teaching a course on the urbanization of Europe with Charles Tilly, Miriam Cohen, Michael Hanagan and Kingsbury Marzolf at the University of Michigan, 1971–3, left me with an appreciation of an interdisciplinary approach to the topic. Reading Richard Cobb has always provided a different kind of important inspiration. John Brewer first suggested that I put together such a collection for Hutchinson; subsequently, Claire L'Enfant, Leonie Hamilton and Emily Wheeler of Hutchinson Education have been unfailingly encouraging and helpful. And so have all of the authors, as well as Peter Gay, Susanna Barrows, and Carol Payne Merriman for reading my two essays. During the inevitable final crunch, friends Alan Forrest, Rory Browne, Simon Reeve, Joe Mandel and Monsieur and Madame Charles Bonis provided encouragement at the latters' *Le Petit Berri*, across from the Archives Nationales. And finally, but not at all last, thanks to the John Simon Guggenheim Memorial Foundation whose grant funded my research on French cities this year; their generous support meant that there were a few francs left over for M. Charley's *rosés* and for the Mati Hari *flipper* machine.

11 Rue François Miron
15 September 1980

Illustrations

Maps

French cities with at least 40,000 inhabitants, 1896   10

Le Chambon-Feugerolles, 1887   228

Plates

1 *The Belfry of Douai*
Oil on canvas by Camille Corot (Musée du Louvre Paris)   13
2 *The Road to Sèvres*
Oil on canvas by Camille Corot (courtesy of Musée du Louvre, Paris)   141
3 *The Sèvres Road*
Oil on canvas by Alfred Sisley (courtesy of Musée du Louvre, Paris)   141
4 *La Vapeur*
Etching by Charles Daubigny for the 1851 edition of Pierre Lachambeaudie's *Fables* (photograph courtesy of Yale University Photographic Services)   144
5 *Les Deux Rivages*
Etching by Charles Daubigny for the 1851 edition of Pierre Lachambeaudie's *Fables* (photograph courtesy of Yale University Photographic Services)   146
6 *The Bridge between Persan and Beaumont-sur-Oise*
Oil on panel by Charles Daubigny (Sterling and Francine Clark Art Institute, Williamstown, Massachusetts)   148

7   *Le Départ*
    Etching by Charles Daubigny from the album
    Voyages en Bateau, 1861 (Baltimore Museum of
    Art, George A. Lucas Collection on indefinite
    loan from Maryland Institute College of Art)   148
8   *The Railroad Bridge at Argenteuil*
    Oil on canvas by Claude Monet (Stavros S.
    Niarchos Collection)   151
9   *Railroad Bridge*
    Oil on canvas by Claude Monet (John G. Johnson
    Collection, Philadelphia Museum of Art)   151
10 *Sailboats on the Seine at Argenteuil*
    Oil on canvas by Claude Monet (Fine Arts
    Museums of San Francisco)   156
11 *Gladiolas*
    Oil on canvas by Claude Monet (courtesy of
    Detroit Institute of Arts)   156
12 *In the Garden*
    Pastel on paper by J. F. Millet (Shaw Collection,
    Museum of Fine Arts, Boston)   157
13 *La Gare St Lazare*
    Oil on canvas by Claude Monet (courtesy of
    Musée du Louvre, Paris)   160
14 *A Socialist Baptism*
    (from Jules Guesde and Paul Lafargue, *L'Egalité*
    – *Le Socialiste: Collection Complète*, vol. 4,
    1887–91; Paris: Editions Hier et Demain 1974)   243

Contributors

John M. Merriman is Associate Professor of History and Chairman of the Council on West European Studies at Yale University. He is the author of *Agony of the Republic: The Repression of the Left in Revolutionary France, 1848–1851*, and editor of and contributor to *1830 in France* and *Consciousness and Class Experience in Nineteenth-Century Europe*.

Charles Tilly is Professor of Sociology and History at the University of Michigan and the author of *The Vendée, From Mobilization to Revolution, The Rebellious Century: 1830–1930* (with Louise Tilly and Richard Tilly), and *Strikes in France, 1830–1968* (with Edward Shorter). He has also edited and contributed to *The Formation of National States in Western Europe, An Urban World*, and *Historical Studies of Changing Fertility*, among many other publications.

Ted W. Margadant is Associate Professor of History at the University of California, Davis. He has recently published *French Peasants in Revolt: The Insurrection of 1851* and is the author of several articles.

David M. Gordon is Assistant Professor of History at the University of California, Riverside; his doctoral dissertation at Brown University was a comparative study of the bourgeoisie of Reims and Saint-Étienne.

Robert L. Herbert is Lehman Professor of the History of Art at Yale University. He has written extensively on the social history of art, including *David: Brutus*, and published the catalogue of the Millet centenary exposition of 1975 in Paris.

Louise A. Tilly is Associate Professor of History at the University of Michigan; she is co-author of *Women, Work and Family*, and author of *The Rebellious Century* and of many articles.

Don Reid is Assistant Professor of History at the University of North Carolina, Chapel Hill. His dissertation at Stanford University was a study of Decazeville in the nineteenth and early twentieth centuries.

Michael P. Hanagan is Assistant Professor of History at Vanderbilt University. His *The Logic of Solidarity: Artisans and Industrial Workers in Three French Towns, 1871–1914* was recently published.

Joan W. Scott is Professor of History at Brown University. She is the author of *The Glassworkers of Carmaux* and co-author, with Louise Tilly, of *Women, Work and Family*.

French cities with at least 40,000 inhabitants, 1896

1 Introduction: Images of the nineteenth-century French city

John M. Merriman

France, like England, Germany, Belgium, the United States and other western countries, urbanized during the nineteenth century, but France alone remained essentially a nation of peasants at least until well into this century.[1]* In the familiar movie scene of August 1914, peasants, hearing the rapid ringing of church bells, leave their fields to go to the village to be mobilized into the army. But urbanization had profoundly changed the economy, society and politics of France in the nineteenth century for both urban and rural dwellers; as a process its impact was as great in France as in the other seemingly more urbanized nations that fought in the first world war.

The growth of Paris dwarfed all other French cities and has dominated the awareness of contemporary observers and historians, just as Paris dominates France. The population of the capital swelled by five times from 548,000 in 1801 to over 2.5 million at the beginning of the twentieth century. Its suburbs, hardly more than villages in 1800, became large towns by the *belle époque*: Asnières grew from 1200 to over 23,000, Boulogne–Billancourt from 2400 to almost 40,000. Montmartre had long ceased to be a rural village on a hill characterized by its famous windmill. The urban experience of Paris has been described frequently and unforgettably: one cannot think of the capital without recalling Balzac's Rastignac waving in challenge towards the financial quarter of the Chaussée-d'Antin from the heights of Père Lachaise cemetery; Zola's Gervaise and her wedding-day trip to the Louvre from the slum of the Goutte d'or, and her eventual drunken prostitution on the boulevards to the north; Delacroix's highly romanticized but still stirring painting of Liberty leading the people in 1830; or the Goncourt journal, describing the astonish-

*Superior figures refer to the Notes and references on pages 247–85.

ing contrast between the glittering literary and artistic life of the capital, and the grim hunger, desperation and, finally, massacre of the Communards in May 1871. Adeline Daumard's analysis of the collective psychology of the Parisian bourgeoisie and Louis Chevalier's description of its perceptions of its social inferiors bring to life again a complex social class captured by the rapier-like pencil of Daumier and, later, by the camera of Nadar and the brush of Degas. Georges Duveau's study of *La vie ouvrière* in the Second Empire contrasts with the sparkling new department stores of the capital. Beyond the shine of Proust's Paris and that of Jarry and Apollinaire during the so-called 'banquet years' of the *belle époque* lay the strikes and May Day parades and demonstrations of the working class during the same period.

Corot's painting, *The Belfry of Douai* (plate 1), could symbolize the placid stillness of nineteenth-century French provincial towns and cities, juxtaposed against the heroic Parisian revolutionary turbulence so often depicted by painters, novelists and historians. Douai, despite being the seat of the appellate court for the rapidly industrializing Nord and Pas-de-Calais departments, seemed to stir only in early July during the annual raucous festival when its five carnival 'giants' in sixteenth-century costumes stalked through the streets. The image of the soft yellow light of a Sunday morning and leisurely strollers going to the *boulangerie* for croissants seems to fit the preoccupation of historians with the urban politics of the capital and with the scanty literature of French provincial cities. But the growth of Paris was only part of the process of French urbanization during the nineteenth century. For the capital was not and is not France, and the urban experience of those who have lived in Paris is not necessarily that of most Frenchmen and women. Lyon and Marseille approached half a million inhabitants in 1900; the small towns of Tourcoing and Roubaix in the shadow of Lille and the Belgian border became large industrial cities by the end of the century, while towns like Montceau-les-Mines, Le Creusot and Decazeville seemed to have grown out of nothing. But the changes brought by even more slowly growing urban centres were just as profound (see Table 1).

It is the task of the urban historian to chronicle and analyse, but also to evoke, the urban transformation of France and to gauge and understand the impact of the process of urbanization on the political life of the nation. Three recent bibliographic essays, all written with the booming English and American 'new urban

Plate 1 Corot, *The Belfry of Douai*

Table 1 Population growth of the twelve largest cities in France at the end of the nineteenth century (in thousands, except for 1896)

Cities	1801	1811	1821	1831	1836	1841	1846	1851	1856	1861	1866	1872	1876	1881	1886	1891	1896 Total population	1896 Agglomerated population
			en 1817															
Paris	548	622	713.0	785	900	935	1053	1053	1174	1696	1825	1851	1988	2269	2344	2247	2,536,834	2,536,834
Lyon	109	106	149.0	134	150	190	221	234	256	318	323	323	342	376	401	436	466,028	398,867
Marseille	111	102	109.0	145	146	147	186	198	215	261	300	312	318	360	376	403	442,239	332,515
Bordeaux	91	93	89.0	99	99	99	125	131	140	162	194	194	215	221	240	252	256,996	239,806
Lille	54	61	64.0	69	72	71	75	75	89	131	154	158	162	178	188	201	216,276	160,723
Toulouse	50	51	52.0	60	77	76	94	94	92	113	127	124	131	140	147	149	149,963	124,187
Saint-Étienne	16	18	19.1	33	41	46	50	56	91	92	96	110	126	123	117	133	136,030	120,300
Roubaix	8	8	18.0	33	41	46	31	34	91	49	65	75	83	91	100	115	124,661	113,900
Nantes	73	82	68.0	78	76	76	94	96	101	113	112	118	122	124	127	122	123,902	107,137
Le Havre	16	17	21.1	23	25	43	31	28	62	74	75	86	92	105	112	116	119,470	117,009
Rouen	87	87	86.7	88	92	90	99	100	94	102	100	102	105	106	107	112	113,219	106,825
Reims	20	31	31.0	36	38	39	44	45	48	55	60	72	81	93	97	104	107,963	99,001
Total	1155	1175	1420.0	1550	1716	1772	2103	2144	2360	3164	3431	3425	3735	4186	4356	4590	4,793,491	4,457,104

Source: Paul Meuriot, *Des agglomérations urbaines dans l'Europe contemporaine* (Paris 1897), p. 93.

history' in mind, have made clear that the urban history of nineteenth-century France remains relatively disappointing. François Bédarida lamented that the past fifty years had produced little of interest:

[the] urban past has long remained the province of the erudite, tenacious lovers of local history who patiently collected material..... They did not really bother to connect their own town, studied with such loving attention, with the development of other towns, or the evolution of the country as a whole, and even less with the universal movements of history.

Bédarida, participating in the important conference on urban history organized in 1967 by H. J. Dyos, was concerned that the new urban history, stressing studies of class composition and social mobility using quantitative methods, seemed to lag behind in France.

By 1974 the nineteenth-century French city was emerging, in the words of Louis Bergeron and Camille Rancayolo, as 'the central character in a new generation of research', at least in part because of the new urban history.² But they cited the failings of this history, which had helped define social classes in towns and cities without really telling us how a city is organized and how it works. They faulted urban historians for largely leaving aside the political evolution of France and ignoring the social and political uses of urban space. The new urban history, then, had amounted to little more than 'social theory in an urban context', leaving the city, in the words of Jean-Claude Perrot, 'empty and seemingly indifferent to any action'.³ The new urban historians had borrowed and helped refine the techniques and methodologies of social history, but like the old human geographers, who offered excellent systematic studies of the economic functions of cities, they had entirely omitted the interaction between urban development and politics.⁴ Daniel Roche's 1980 essay also criticized the new urban history, insisting on the necessity of relating the experiences of the individual towns and cities to the large-scale economic and social processes that characterized the nineteenth century. Roche urged urban historians to consider the town and its space as a social phenomenon shaped by the 'contradictions which interact within urban space'. Indeed, recent Marxist scholarship has stressed that the growth of towns and cities accelerated the social contradictions inherent in the development of a capitalist economy. Roche left unstated the importance of identifying the relationship between urbanization and the political transformation of France, while the Marxists have emphasized the economic and social bases of political conflict in the nineteenth century. The time has come to combine the large brush-strokes of conceptual theory with the detailed analysis of the individual French town and city to begin to understand what effect urbanization had on the political development of modern France.[5] By comparing the experiences of individual towns and cities and their people over time we can understand how, and to what extent, urbanization as a historical process transformed the lives of French men and women in the nineteenth century. We must link the individual city and its people, the French national experience and the global processes of social change. Urban history is not a separate discipline that stands by itself; the study of the city cannot be divorced from the fundamental dynamics of change themselves – industrial capitalism, state-making, bureaucratization – any more than the city can be divorced from its region and its own past. The urban experience changed the lives of people who lived in the countryside as well as in the towns and cities, bringing about a political transformation of France. The historian of the nineteenth-century city has the sources available to evoke the urban experience of ordinary people, relating everyday routine – *la vie quotidienne*, as the popular series of French historical studies is called – to larger historical changes. The study of the individual city and urban traditions, neighbourhoods, faubourgs, festivals, associations and people over time with reference to the larger questions of social and political change is the task of urban history, and the subject of this collection of essays. This introduction presents a *mise en scène* which will underline some of the distinctive aspects of French urbanization and raise several themes that are as crucial to the urban historian as they were to the lives of those who lived in nineteenth-century towns and cities; it will also point to several of the most significant and distinctive features of French urbanization. Among the points that must be made are the following:

1   French urbanization proceeded at a much slower pace than that of England, the United States or Germany. While the urbanization of France was also linked to large-scale industrialization, the pattern of this industrialization did not fit the British model of heavy industry's booming coke towns and necessitates

some rethinking about French towns and cities in the nineteenth century.

2   The remarkable degree of state centralization and the domination of the capital, in contrast again with the German and English cases, greatly affected the political evolution of French towns and cities, often pitting municipalities and their inhabitants against the powerful state.

3   Although France remained to a large extent a nation of peasants, urbanization created new contenders for political power and thereby contributed to the emergence of mass political life. The organizations and conflicts of urban political life gradually became those of France. To take one significant example, the expansion in small towns and bourgs of large-scale economic activities, associated with the process of urbanization, altered peasant politics and underlines the importance of the study of relations between town and country.

4   Urban terrain became as hotly contested as the rich farmland of Beaune in Zola's *The Earth*. The growth of cities, their changing form and the increasing social division of space helped alter French political life. Patterns of residence and the way in which elites intervened in urban space have been little studied; and the use and symbolism of urban space remains a fascinating and relatively unexplored theme of research essential for understanding the process of urbanization.

Industrialization, urbanization and urban growth in nineteenth-century France

France urbanized in the nineteenth century, as its urban population doubled. It should be stressed that urbanization is not the same thing as urban growth, which is simply the increase in the number of people living in an area defined as urban. Conceivably, a country could have an increase in urban population but actually de-urbanize if, after a given period, a smaller percentage lived in urban areas than before; this may have occurred in seventeenth-century France. Urbanization is, most simply, a proportional increase in the number of people living in urban areas as opposed to rural regions.[6] To be sure, the statistical definition of what is urban is quite arbitrary. The census of 1846 first defined an urban area as one with at least 2000 people living in an agglomerated settlement. Earlier censuses in the century had adopted 1500 as the minimum figure. Two thousand people hardly seems to constitute an urban area in the Anglo-Saxon world of conurbations but, as will become clear in this volume, such urban settlements often provided large-scale economic activities usually associated with a more functional definition of urbanization. Charles Pouthas, whose study of the French population in the first half of the century remains an essential source, had feared that the arbitrary decision to classify any agglomerated settlement of 2000 as 'urban' overestimated the degree of urbanization by counting a number of small bourgs of approximately that size 'whose animation and activity only awaken on market day'.[7] But the original choice does provide a reasonably accurate and consistent point for measuring the phenomenon of urban growth and the degree of urbanization in the nineteenth century. For market day revealed the economic and political function of bourgs, an essential part of the process of urbanization. Table 2, which begins with the census of 1846, clearly shows France's absolute urban growth and urbanization.[8]

Georges Dupeux's 1974 compilation of the French censuses, adopting the definition of 3000 inhabitants living in an agglomerated settlement as urban, allows us to include results from the earlier censuses and consider the entire century. His table (Table 3)

Table 2

Year	Urban population (millions)	Per cent of total population
1846	8.6	24.4
1851	9.1	25.5
1856	9.8	27.3
1861	10.8	28.9
1866	11.6	30.5
1872	11.2	31.5
1876	12.0	32.4
1881	13.1	34.8
1886	13.8	35.9
1891	14.3	37.4
1896	15.0	39.5

Source: Paul Meuriot, *Des agglomérations urbaines dans l'Europe contemporaine* (Paris 1897).

Table 3

Census date	Number of urban communes	Total urban population
1811	422	4,201,186
1821	455	4,593,345
1831	507	5,098,920
1836	532	5,450,364
1841	503	5,281,968
1846	589	6,068,945
1851	602	6,354,845
1856	627	7,078,438
1861*	653	7,771,574
1866*	690	8,479,787
1872†	641	8,249,437
1876	674	8,867,732
1881	707	9,776,612
1886	727	10,381,513
1891	732	10,901,774
1896	724	11,282,667
1901	792	12,375,147
1906	815	12,979,404
1911	851	13,816,689

*Not including urban population of Nice and Savoie; with annexed territories, the urban population reached, in 1861 (with 661 towns), 7,851,270 inhabitants, and 8,550,728 in 1866 (with 694 towns).

†Including Nice and Savoie, but not the territories annexed by Germany.

Source: Georges Dupeux, 'La croissance urbaine en France au XIXe siècle,' *Revue d'histoire économique et sociale,* no. 52 (1974), p. 180.

presents the number of urban communes, by his definition, and the total urban population. Dupeux's statistics modify Pouthas's insistence that only with the July monarchy did France's urban population break away from the general rise in population, showing at least a moderate rise in the number of urban communes and the total urban population in the Restoration. He shows the gradual, indeed almost perfectly linear growth of the French urban population throughout the century. Both Pouthas and Dupeux agree on the importance of the periods 1831–6 and 1851–61 – the beginning years of the July monarchy and the Second Empire – in the increase in France's urban population. (For example, the population of France's district capitals – *chef-lieux* of *arrondissements* – increased by 31 per cent from 1821 to 1841, just about twice that of France as a whole.) The annual rate of increase of 2.18 per cent between 1851 and 1856 was never equalled in the century.[9] By Dupeux's statistics, the population of French urban areas increased by slightly over 300 per cent between 1811 and 1911, while the total population increase for all of France for approximately the same period was only 34.8 per cent. During the second half of the century, the urban population grew more rapidly than did the number of communes defined as urban, far faster than the total population. Impoverished rural departments, such as the Ariège, Aveyron and Pyrénées Orientales lost population to migration. Before the second world war, twenty-five of France's ninety departments had less population than they had had in 1801, and sixty-one – more than two-thirds – had less than in 1851.[10] Today in departments such as the Pyrénées Orientales, this depopulation may be seen: deserted churches, terraced hillsides long since abandoned and small villages where only old people remain. France's urbanization after 1850 seems even more impressive given the remarkable decline in the rate of natural population increase that worried Frenchmen and has offered a marked contrast with the experience of the rest of the world.

More than any other French city, Saint-Étienne seemed to replicate the British model of the nineteenth-century industrial city. The population of France's Manchester boomed from about 16,000 in 1801 to 33,000 in 1831 and to 56,000 in 1851, although it was still not even the departmental capital, that title was still retained by the small town of Montbrison. To visitors Saint-Étienne seemed to offer an awesome glimpse into the urban and industrial future. Flora Tristan, the utopian socialist, was little impressed. Saint-Étienne, she wrote,

is the sister city of Lyon, but even blacker and even more dirty ... the town hall is hideous, a large pile of rocks ... the Cathedral of St. Étienne is ignoble ... [there are] no sidewalks, except for several in the nicer quarters; a dirty little stream they call a River passes through the town, furnishing the daily needs of 60,000 bodies, not counting the animals.[11]

The town had grown so precipitously that it seemed to have no history; an army officer ordered to draw up a plan for the city's defence in case of attack (it was already an important armaments centre) could find nothing to read on Saint-Étienne's past. In one generation, the small town (which indeed did have a long history) had become a large city, with a population of 76,000, including its recent suburbs; it was a major centre for ribbon-making, metallurgy and arms manufacturing and not a single book could be found in the municipal library about agriculture. The small old city, 'badly built and chaotically organized', offered little more than the ruins of an old château now serving as a police post; the new town, many times larger, presented, in contrast with the small old town, no twisting or winding streets. One long boulevard stretched six kilometres, providing a central axis along the floor of the valley in which the city lay, met by cross streets at perpendicular angles, and paralleled by equally straight and long streets.[12]

The immediate hinterland only echoed the industry of Saint-Étienne. 'The environs of Saint-Étienne', wrote the visitor,

are generally monotonous and without charm; the countryside is furrowed with railroads. One encounters factories of various kinds almost everywhere, and especially coal mines with smoking obelisks, forges of coke that give off a thick, black smoke which can be seen from afar; it paralyses all vegetation and gives everything a black tint. At night these *fours* offer a truly astonishing spectacle, infernal to all who see the city for the first time.

In the canton of Saint-Étienne alone in 1848, almost 13,000 ribbon workers, 10,000 looms, over 3000 metallurgical workers, 3500 miners and more than 3000 building workers represented a labour force that transformed the Stéphanois.[13] The region of Saint-Étienne, subject of the David Gordon and Michael Hanagan essays in this volume, was the 'cradle of the industrial revolution' in France.

Yet Saint-Étienne was not characteristic of the French urban experience in the nineteenth century precisely *because* of its size and concentration of industry. As Hanagan notes in his essay (Chapter 9) the rate of French urbanization pales when compared to that of England during the same period, or that of Germany after its unification. France did not have, with the exception of the capital and the Lille–Tourcoing–Roubaix region, a contiguous series of urban agglomerations comparable to Lancashire or the Ruhr. France did have several relatively heavily urbanized regions: the Île-de-France, Nord, Languedoc and Provence, but the number of large cities remained few throughout the century, each serving as a regional centre. Only Paris, Lyon and Marseille had more than 100,000 inhabitants in 1841; they were joined that year by Bordeaux, in 1861 by Lille, Toulouse, Nantes and Rouen; in 1872 by Saint-Étienne, Le Havre in 1881 and in 1891 by Roubaix and Reims, for a total of twelve. France thus had twelve cities with a population of more than 100,000 in 1896, these at least one-fourth larger than Saint-Étienne. England, having had but London in 1800, claimed twenty-four. The urban population of France remained largely one of small towns and *bourgades*. More than half of that population lived in towns of less than 10,000 inhabitants. The level of urbanization, seemingly modest, none the less had great implications for the social and political transformation of France and reveals the significance of the process itself.

Nor were the large factories of Saint-Étienne characteristic of French industrialization. Hanagan's study of Le Chambon-Feugerolles, a small industrial town in its hinterland, stresses the persistence of artisanal production (the base for the development of most industries, including the ribbon manufacturing of Saint-Étienne) and rural industry. Louise Tilly's article (Chapter 7) also emphasizes the slower development of industrial capitalism in France; only gradually and with considerable variation across location and industry did small-scale service and craft production give way to large-scale development. Her comparative study of the impact of industrial capitalism in Paris, Lyon and Lille on women's work recalls the important part household and family continued to have in industrial production. In France's second city (first in gastronomy), Lyon, the manufacture of silk remained characterized by artisanal production.

Industrialization in France also retained its large rural component throughout most of the century; this, in turn, combined with the slow rate of natural population increase to limit the growth of French cities. A walk into the countryside of the textile (and champagne) centre of Reims in mid century would have convinced any British, American or German visitor of the continued importance of rural industry in France. The mechanization of the textile industry had begun during the First Empire and by 1828 there were 181 spinning factories, most powered by steam. But the mechanization of the production of merino cloth, having begun in Reims, spread into the surrounding countryside between the Suippe and Vesle rivers, employing a significant number of rural workers who produced thousands and thousands of metres of cloth each year. By 1848, there were 8000 men, women and children spinning and weaving in the canton of Reims alone, many of them not living in the city.[14] As Yves Lequin has noted in his remarkable study of the formation of the working class in the Lyon region, industry moved toward its labour force as often as peasants migrated towards urban factories.[15] Cities, then, often did not mark a sharp break with economic life in the countryside. Many migrants to urban areas arrived with considerable industrial experience obtained in rural regions, as cities concentrated industry that had previously been located in the countryside. The industrial revolution was first and foremost in France an expansion of existing forms of production, largely artisanal and rural. Even the growth of factories in towns and cities often changed little more than the locus of work for migrants; the concentration of a labour force into factories came slowly, and even then was not limited to urban areas. Ted W. Margadant's essay (Chapter 4) follows these themes. He examines the political consequences of the process of proto-urbanization, as small-scale production and marketing spread into the countryside in many rural regions during the July monarchy. Small towns, like Dieulefit in the Drôme, a centre of mobilization in the resistance to Louis Napoleon's coup d'état of 1851, were, like Le Chambon-Feugerolles in the Loire, more typical of the nineteenth-century urban experience than either Paris of Saint-Étienne.[16]

Just as French industrialization was not necessarily dependent on the growth of cities, so industrialization was not the only factor responsible for the growth of towns in France. The human geographers' classification of cities by function – agricultural, commercial, industrial, military, administrative and so on – unnecessarily simplifies the urban experience of France but reminds us that most cities had more than one economic function and that many developed without the assistance of industry. Perpignan, for example, an *agro-ville* with a large population of landless rural day labourers living within its walls, developed as a commercial and military centre with virtually no industrialization at all. The city's marketing function in the wine trade, as that of Béziers and Narbonne, had a great influence on the surrounding region, recalling the commercial functions of medieval cities. Other towns developed with the coming of the railroad: Laroches-Migennes in the Yonne; or Brive in the Corrèze, which thrived with the arrival of the railroad en route to Toulouse, while the prefecture of Tulle eighteen miles to the east has today about the same population it had in the middle of the last century. The century also brought a new kind of town: thermal or 'cure' centres, such as Amélie-les-Bains, Aix-les-Bains, Bain-les-Bains, Contrexeville and others.

In the department of the Vienne, the small town of Châtellerault developed into a major producer of arms and cutlery in the nineteenth century, its population growing from about 8400 in 1801 to over 20,000 in 1896. A faubourg developed on the other side of the Vienne from the main settlement, across from the twisting and almost impassable streets of the old town. A resident contrasted the dynamism of Châtellerault with the departmental and former provincial capital of Poitiers, traditionally a great religious centre.

The noise of its streets contrast with the silence of those of Poitiers, on which it depends. Châtellerault is still so young that it seems to grow from day to day, while Poitiers is like the cadavre of a large city. The old provincial capital has no more life. Its industry is nil, its provisioning difficult, its markets limited. It no longer exists by itself, but by the importance that it receives from its royal court, its law school, its medical school, and its administrative personnel. The town is thus political ... but its existence as the first city of the department quite forced. Its like Bourbon-Vendée, or in the Loire, like Montbrison, which is nothing in comparison with Saint Étienne or even Roanne.[17]

Yet Poitiers also grew rapidly, its population more than doubling in the course of the century – in other words, as fast as Châtellerault, which remained a sub-prefecture. The politics of the two towns varied enormously. Châtellerault, a city of workers, was always to the left of Poitiers, an ecclesiastical centre dominated during the Second Empire by Cardinal Pie, advisor to the Comte de Chambord. And both towns were active in the political struggles of the century, and not merely shaped by events in Paris to which they were to nod assent. However, the political evolution of provincial French towns, both those that were rapidly growing and those that were not, largely remains to be written.

Some of the essays presented here consider the evolution of political life in French cities from the point of view of the responses of elites and ordinary people to the two processes arguably transforming nineteenth-century France: industrial capitalism and the continued centralization of the French state.

This book asks, how did urbanization and the growth of cities and towns change political life in France? How did the special characteristics or properties of urban areas, including a greater degree of associational life, a concentration of different social groups and occupations, and the social division of space and concomitant patterns of residential differentiation, affect the political struggles of the new bourgeois elites and of the working class both at the national and the municipal level? How did the particular patterns of urban growth and social structure influence political development? What were the political consequences of the tension between the strongly centralized state and the municipalities? And how and when (or even did) urbanization and the growth of towns change the politics of the countryside and urban–rural relations in general?

State and city: Paris and its provinces

The centralization of the French government and the domination of Paris over the life of the nation greatly affected the urbanization of France and the development of its urban politics. After the women of the markets of the rue St Antoine helped initiate a march to Versailles in October 1789, to bring Louis XVI and the royal family to Paris, the government of France left Paris only twice for any length of time: during the Commune (with the people of Paris claiming power) and during the tragic years of Vichy. In some ways the capital has always remained an agglomeration of many urban villages; yet the presence of the government and its powerful and weighty bureaucracy has meant that the whole of Paris has been far greater than the sum of all its parts.

At the beginning of the nineteenth century, Paris and its immediate region comprised only slightly more than 2 per cent of the French population, far smaller a proportion, for example, than those of London in England or Glasgow in Scotland. But the capital came to dominate the rest of France – Paris and the 'French desert' in the words of J. E. Gravier in 1947. Where else but France would more than 97 per cent of the population have been condescendingly relegated to the category of 'provincials' – that is, not living in Paris? Gravier recalls for us the definition of the word 'provincial' given by the Larousse dictionary of 1900: 'provinçial, qui est gauche, dépourvu de distinction, manière: ex: avoir l'air provinçial'.[18]

De Tocqueville had insisted that this extraordinary centralization of power was well underway in the eighteenth century.[19] It was certainly accentuated by the revolution, particularly by the Jacobins and even more so by Napoleon, who, as everyone knows, like to brag that he could look at his watch and know what every school child in France was studying. Three of the most important changes that challenged traditional urban networks of influence (the kind examined by the old human geographers and their more sophisticated but often less interesting successors) – the creation of departments in 1790, the advent of the railroad in the middle decades of the nineteenth century and the creation of a banking network – all only further accentuated the centralization of power and authority in Paris and its domination, unlike England, where industrial rivals to the north of London challenged the capital for power and the political nation came to care what Manchester thought. Let us listen to Gravier's summary:

Ignorant at the same time of decentralization (that is, local liberties) and deconcentration (that is, the delegation of real authority to the prefects), the unitary French system gathered all powers in a capital that became thus the single nervous center of the national life. . . . For all professors, for all savants, the hierarchy of honors and that of salaries offered one single supreme objective: Paris.[20]

Thus traditionally arrived in the capital all of the most talented and ambitious provincials, 'all of the Rastignacs of France'. Economic planning, decision-making and resources likewise clustered in the capital, a condition well illustrated by the almost inevitable transfer of the headquarters of the most important provincial bank, the Crédit Lyonnais, to Paris in the fourth quarter of the nineteenth century. Gravier bitterly concludes:

Here it is, in every domain, France divided into two camps. On one side, Paris affirms its universal supremacy, gathers every power and refuses to delegate the smallest part. Around the 'enlightened city', its bureaucracy, its business set, and its intelligentsia, the provinces vegetate in its shadow. The supreme ambition of these citizens is to see their most gifted children 'arrive' in the capital and thus pass into the superior caste.[21]

Gravier suggested a series of reforms that would create true regional capitals with the ultimate hope of creating *l'Union française* to lead France from the impotence of the 1930s. His proposals, of course, were never implemented, any more than was

Girondin Vergniaud's federalist plan during the French revolution to reduce the influence of the department of the Seine to but one-ninety-third of the number of departments. The Seine was not and is not just another department, another licence-plate number. The much discussed recent regional proposals and indeed the revolution-*manquée* of 1968 have led to very little. And today Breton militants complain, with some justification, of the continued 'colonization' of their peninsula by the centralized state. During the spring of 1980 Breton mayors, having come to the capital to protest a lack of government action after the most recent series of catastrophic oil spills threatening fishing and tourism on their coast, encountered national military police at the Place de la Concorde. Some of the mayors were wrestled to submission by the police, who grabbed the tricolour sashes they wore as emblems of their authority in their own communes: a classic confrontation.

The centralization of the French state was a long process, often resisted during the course of the nineteenth century as peasants, provincial artisans and other ordinary people battled tax collectors, forest guards, gendarmes and grain merchants for control of local resources. The provincial 'communes' of 1871, notably in Marseille, Lyon, Saint-Étienne, Limoges and Narbonne, may be at least partially understood as the reaction of the bourgeoisie to the stranglehold of Paris on French political life, although most basically they were working-class insurrections reflecting the development of class consciousness more than the solidarity of neglected municipalities. The Nancy Manifesto of 1866 had called for a decentralization of authority and an increase in the powers of the commune, part of a movement for local liberties that challenged the imperial politics of the Second Empire.[22] Republicanism and socialism have more than simply Jacobin traditions in France. The dialectic between radicalization and repression helps explain France's three nineteenth-century revolutions, all of which began in Paris but generated social conflict and political mobilizations in the provinces before the new authorities in each case were able to consolidate their own power and repress from Paris those who had wanted to push the revolutions to the left: the government of Louis Philippe and particularly the ministry of Casimir Perier; the conservative members of the victorious coalition of 1848, who turned General Cavaignac loose on the June insurgents, and Louis Napoleon Bonaparte, who put an early end to the Second Republic; and Adolphe Thiers, who believed that the only way to make Paris pure enough to seat a strong government and protect the interests of its bourgeoisie was to slaughter 25,000 Communards. Many people in France thus became *administrés* before they ever began to think of themselves as Frenchmen. The *villes parlementaires* (such as Rennes or Dijon), proud retainers and defenders of regional liberties, gave way to towns of *fonctionnaires, cités administratives, préfectures* and *sous-préfectures*, where thousands of decrees, proclamations and laws were posted and interpreted. Bureaucracies increased so rapidly that the urban geographers casually assumed that 'administration' was an urban function as clearly observable and defined as 'agriculture', 'commerce' and 'industry'. Large numbers of *fonctionnaires* helped some cities like Caen and Besançon keep right on growing with only very limited industrial development. Towns with a 'military' function, such as Perpignan, could even be considered as 'administrative' in the French sense because their troops were usually more concerned with maintaining domestic order and repressing the *administrés* than preparing for foreign attack. For the people of Narbonne, the army was little more than a heavily armed police force; troops restored order there in 1831 and in 1907 as local citizens rebelled against the wine tax, decreed in Paris, striking their local product.

The town of La Roche-sur-Yon is sometimes cited as one of the few truly planned cities in France. Its origins in the early nineteenth century reveal at least something about the relationship between urbanization and the state in France. La Roche-sur-Yon was the kind of town Lewis Mumford would hate, a caricature of the baroque city described in his classic *The City in History*, reflecting little more than power and authority. No town in France developed less organically than La Roche-sur-Yon, or Napoléon-Vendée as it was dubbed. The town was an artificially created disaster.

La Roche-sur-Yon had been a sleepy and rather ugly *bourgade* at the foot of a château that in the eighteenth century dominated the Yon River from its hill. From the isolated hedgerow (*bocage*) country of its department of the Vendée, created in 1790 with the others, had emerged the fierce and fanatically religious rebels (*chouans*) who rose against the godless republic and its more urban, bourgeois French leaders who had come to the Vendée to force its clergy to comply with the civil constitution of the French clergy and for conscripts to defend the revolution against its enemies. The bloody civil war that resulted lasted for several years.

Early in the First Empire, a general had complained that part of the difficulty in pacifying the Vendée had lain in the original choice of Fontenay-le-Comte, to the south-east of the department, as the prefectoral capital. Napoleon therefore decided that a new town would be built upon the rubble of La Roche, burned to the ground by republican troops in 1794. Napoléon-Vendée, as the new town was to be called, could provide a military and administrative centre; new roads forged through the *bocage* country would bring French civilization to the resistant and ignorant peasants. And Napoléon-Vendée would be another memorial to the glory of Napoleon.

Napoléon-Vendée was to be a small but elegant planned town, regularly constructed, dominated by its army garrison, the prefecture and two large, perfectly regular squares, bordered by trees, containing the principal public buildings, two on each side. Streets were laid out at perfect right angles; troops could march down a large central boulevard to assemble in the main square. Masons were brought from Lyon to construct the military buildings, somehow unaware that the materials they selected would not survive the climate. Hurried preparations preceded the visit of the emperor himself to the new planned town in August 1808. Having entered his name-sake at 11 a.m., he left in disgust by 5 p.m., mumbling that cities could not be built overnight, and that even the construction of Paris was not yet completed.[23]

Built for at least 15,000 people, Bourbon-Vendée, as it became known for obvious reasons in 1815, could attract no more than 3500 inhabitants by 1836 and 6000 by the middle of the century, when it was again called Napoléon-Vendée. The town seemed to one of its military occupants 'like a newly built faubourg of Paris; they assembled everything necessary to build houses and to force the Vendéeans to travel outside their region; but they forgot to establish what alone makes possible the prosperity of cities, commerce and industry'.[24] Napoleon's dream of constructing a canal through the Vendée never could be fulfilled; and the waters of the Yon were too limpid to generate industry. Napoléon-Vendée's population consisted mostly of officials, soldiers, some merchants and *propriétaires* and a few artisans and labourers. They came from a variety of regions; but relatively few seemed to be from the Vendée. A stud farm for army horses and an asylum for mad women were the principal attractions of this nineteenth-century city, an isolated but somehow fitting example of the centralization and power of the French state. In the early 1830s, after the July revolution, the Vendée's artificial capital served a repressive function, preventing yet another insurrection on behalf of the Bourbons; the town, its politics and even its markets were resisted by the peasants of its hinterland. More often, it was simply ignored.

But ordinary French townspeople could not ignore the powerful centralized French state. The evolution of municipal socialism in the late nineteenth century reflected the conflict between the centralized state and ordinary French men and women. Joan W. Scott's article (Chapter 10) challenges the thesis that the annual May Day marches, processions and festivals of labour and munici-pal socialism served to 'integrate' workers into national political life dominated by the bourgeoisie and by Paris. Scott shows how communes with socialist majorities attempted to create within the bourgeois state an alternative model of government that was decentralized, municipal and based upon the solidarities of the extended working-class family, in opposition to the power of French capitalism and its ally, the state.

French cities and popular politics

The other prevailing image of the politics of the nineteenth-century city offers a sharp contrast to that of the sleepy provincial town, what Flora Tristan referred to the *'villes nulles'*. Many contemporary observers saw only the steady stream of migrants pouring into France's largest cities, particularly Paris, and worried about the social and political consequences. M. A. Legoyt's *Du progrès des agglomérations urbaines et de l'émigration rural en Europe et particulièrement en France* (1867) neatly summarized the principal causes of migration to towns and cities: the *mor-cellement* of the land, the lure of industrial and service work, urban charitable institutions and so on. Among the consequences, he believed, were an increase in criminality and political disruptions. 'There exists', he wrote, 'in urban agglomerations a sort of exceptional moral temperature. Thoughts and feelings are particu-larly intense there and become excited to the level of passion.'[25] He then suggested means of slowing down the movement to the cities and thus recapturing some of the lost virtues of the country-side.

By the 1890s, French cities seemed even larger and the volatile nature of urban politics even more menacing. 'The crowd' had become a fixture in the streets. Beginning in 1890, the May Day processions with red banners horrified the French bourgeoisie, reminding them of the apocalyptical Commune, and posing a threat to French society as they knew it.[26] Paul Meuriot's *Des agglomérations urbaines dans L'Europe contemporaine*, published exactly thirty years after Legoyt's book with virtually the same title, had little doubt about the political consequences of the growth of cities:

It is incontestable that political morals are more changeable in the great urban centres of population ... one can even say that in all times the urban masses have always had a more tumultuous character than anyone else. First, in any human agglomeration, passions always ferment more; furthermore, the population of great cities is renewed more quickly and tradition has less of an effect on the new elements. In reality, the general political tendency of urban and rural populations responds to the two eternal instincts of the human soul; that of desire and that of conservation.[27]

Meuriot believed that one consequence of the growth of cities had been the evolution of political equality, towards which he seems sometimes ambivalent. Yet had he considered the recent political experience of Paris, Meuriot would have noted that the bourgeoisification of the capital as a result of the rebuilding of Paris brought politics considerably more conservative than those of 1830, 1848 and 1871.

The social and political consequences of the rapid growth of cities has been the subject of much debate. Louis Chevalier's *Dangerous and Laboring Classes in Paris During the First Half of the Nineteenth Century* has offered the most articulate and sensitive presentation of the 'uprooting' hypothesis. After having earlier traced the formation of the population of the capital during the same period, Chevalier relied upon the observations of contemporaries, particularly social reformers and novelists, to describe life in Paris. Two races, biologically different and unequal before the harsh tests of disease, confronted each other. The uprooted poor, newly arrived, torn free from their rural roots, were feared by the bourgeoisie as the 'dangerous and labouring classes'. Out of the mood of anomie, unsettled desperation and criminality arose, and, by implication, the nineteenth-century revolutions and the other political disturbances in the capital. More recent work on the revolutions of 1830, 1848 and the Commune has challenged the Chevalier thesis. Those who rebelled were not the uprooted, 'dangerous' classes, nor the most poor, but rather skilled artisans defending their way of life against large-scale economic changes over which they had no control.[28] Their craft solidarities and organizations led them to the barricades, as often as not to do the bourgeoisie's fighting for it. Recently Philippe Vigier has concluded that the dangerous classes 'in the long run represented only a minority of industrial workers'.[29] But if we cannot easily accept Chevalier's identification of the 'dangerous' with the labouring classes and his linking of the climate of criminality during the first half of the century to the insurrections and revolutions in the capital, his pioneering insistence on a history of contemporary perceptions offers a convincing explanation for the savagery of the bourgeois response to the continued agitation after the revolution of 1830, the June Days, the resistance to the coup d'état of 1851 and, above all, the Commune.

For his part, Charles Tilly, attacking the 'uprooting' hypothesis, has argued that ultimately industrialization and urbanization 'transformed the struggle for power and thus transformed the character of collective violence ... in the short run rapid urbanization and industrialization alike generally depressed the level of conflict. They destroyed various contenders' means and bases of collective action more than they created new ones'.[30] In Chapter 3 Tilly describes and analyses the transformation of the forms and repertoires of collective violence in the mid nineteenth century, which once again is underlined as a crucial period of social change. Cities formed the 'leading edge' of the gradual transformation of organized political life. Tilly focuses on the colourful example of the charivari as a transitional form of protest, as ordinary people adopted familiar means to try to achieve new political goals, before the evolution of new forms of collective action, such as the routinized *manifestation* or the modern strike. In Tilly's hypothesis, urbanization entails neither a sharp break nor a complete disruption of traditions, but a combination of continuity and change. New forms of social organization developed from old, with associations ultimately replacing community as the most important basis for political mobilization and protest.

Yet community retained an important role in the evolution of French cities and the development of political life in France. Migration did provide most of the urban growth in the century, although most migrants did not travel as far as Rastignac, who came from the region of Angoulême (and very few possessed his resources, however limited he might have thought they were for the company that he intended to keep in the capital). Thus, in real life, in the 1830s and 1840s, the mason Martin Nadaud would walk almost 200 miles to Paris every spring from his native canton, Pontarion in the Creuse, to find work. He, with his fellow building workers, returned to his canton every autumn, until they finally settled in the neighbourhoods of Paris's eastern right bank, traditionally occupied by the Limousins and Auvergnats. Nadaud passed easily from a rural world into an urban one, largely because at both ends he found people very much like himself. He was not 'uprooted' from his native Creuse, but did become literate and politically aware; he helped educate and change attitudes of many people in the Creuse who had never nor would never see the lights of Paris, became a deputy from his department during the Second Republic and, after exile during the Empire, served as one of Gambetta's prefects. The urban experience changed Nadaud's life, so did urbanization transform French society, its economy and its politics in the course of the nineteenth century. Nadaud, who was more successful than all but a few migrants, was one of the very few to leave his memoirs. But many changes Nadaud witnessed in his life were part of a transformation that involved a great part of the French population. The rural community became the urban neighbourhood.[31]

Michael Hanagan's article (Chapter 9) demonstrates how patterns of neighbourhood residential geography facilitated the mobilization of industrial workers in Chambon-Feugerolles – first artisans, and then the skilled workers who came to live near them and share their organization and their militancy. Hanagan contrasts the situation of urban and rural workers, again illustrating what difference in political life the city really made. Don Reid in Chapter 8 studies a single-industry town that grew up in little more than one generation – Decazeville, a mining and company town whose famous strike served as the model for Zola's *Germinal* and helped launch the career of General Boulanger as a politician, offers an interesting contrast to Le Chambon-Feugerolles.

Decazeville had no nucleus of artisans to pass on a tradition of organization and protest. Also, without many sympathetic bourgeois allies, working-class involvement in politics could not occur until the workers of that town developed a communal identity as workers; the struggle even for identity was difficult in a town that, for most of its existence, the company controlled and supervised all aspects of life very closely. Community was important for the working class of both towns, although the political awakening of both came later in the century than for those cities and towns with an active segment of radical bourgeois to impart a tradition of first radical republicanism and then socialism. Both essays attest to the importance of identifying urban social classes and groups and placing them in space and time before attempting to understand the political evolution of nineteenth-century French towns and cities.[32]

Two of the other essays in this book consider changing urban elites and their politics, analysing the political struggles that were a consequence of large-scale industrialization. My contribution (Chapter 2) examines the urban political conflict in Limoges at the time of the revolution of 1830; young bourgeois challenged what seemed to them to be an anachronistic municipal authority that represented interests foreign if not antithetical to those of rapidly developing commerce and industry. I have tried to evoke political life in a Restoration town in the period when *le peuple* emerged as a factor in national and municipal politics. David Gordon, also considering the relationship between economic structure and political change, considers the interplay between industry and politics in the textile town of Reims and in Saint-Étienne (Chapter 5). After carefully identifying bourgeois elites in both cities, he examines the political results of different structures of economic life during the Second Empire.

The study of the impact of urbanization on French political life raises the theme of the relations between town and country, the subject of Ted Margadant's essay (Chapter 4). Historians have often stressed the antagonism between town and country, as during the French revolution, for which Charles Tilly's *The Vendée* is the classic work. Eugen Weber's more recent book argues that this antagonism was attenuated during the last third of the nineteenth century as an urban culture spread into or simply conquered the countryside and as peasants became Frenchmen. Weber's account of the place of cities in social change offers an interesting and strikingly different view to that of Louis Chevalier, a juxtaposition that recalls the title of Mumford's classic film, 'The City: Heaven or Hell?' Margadant shows how the expansion of large-scale economic activities into the countryside through bourgs and small towns – the process of proto-urbanization – transformed peasant politics. Despite differences in interpretation, Weber and Margadant both have underlined the significance of towns and cities as brokers of change; the links and differences between town and country again emerge as deserving the kind of systematic research and analysis Margadant presents here in his essay.[33]

Space, urban form and planning

The final general topic treated in this volume and deserving systematic research is the spatial organization of the nineteenth-century city and the political concomitants and significance of changes in the use of urban space. Urbanization altered the form of many cities, as newly populated quarters spread along the main roads into towns. The rapid growth of suburbs shifted the centre of many cities within a relatively short period of time, as in Grenoble. In Perpignan the destruction of the town walls at the end of the century allowed an expansion previously held in check. Villages near Paris such as Grenelle and Vaugirard, Montmartre and Passy, were integral parts of the capital by the end of the century. Everywhere it seemed that land only recently cultivated by truck farmers and gardeners, producing for the urban population while trying to protect themselves against urban chicken thieves (or grape thieves in Languedoc and Roussillon, where vine guards had to supplement the *gardes champêtres*), had been incorporated within the octroi of the city. The urban landscape changed during the nineteenth century.

Robert Herbert's essay (Chapter 6) pursues the theme of the expanding city and its extension, the suburb, in the work of the pre-Impressionists and the Impressionists. Herbert's particular focus is Claude Monet and his paintings of the bridge at Argenteuil, a village being transformed by the growth of Paris into a suburb reconciling both 'city and country, and industry and leisure' while ignoring or leaving at a safe distance the uncompromising and gritty large-scale industrialization of even one of Paris's western suburbs. Herbert follows Monet from the Gare St Lazare, to Monet's own ideal and illusion, his famous garden at

Giverny down the Seine. He captures the evolution of the perception of rapid urbanization and large-scale industrialization.

Whereas in the eighteenth century nobles and wealthy bourgeois often built houses on the exterior boulevards of French cities to escape the crowded and dirty streets of the central city, the development of the nineteenth-century faubourg was, in general, closely tied to industrialization. Large workshops and factories came to occupy the outskirts of the city, taking advantage of being outside the octroi walls, of cheaper land, easier access to rivers and greater facility of transportation of raw materials. The location of railroad stations on the edge of most cities reinforced this centrifugal tendency. Around the new units of industrial production grew up settlements of workers, also taking advantage of less expensive housing and seeking to reduce, as much as possible, the trek to work (although long trips were not rare as work and home became increasingly separated). So developed the working-class suburb. The faubourg of the eighteenth century, often no more than a crossroads, an *auberge* or two and a settlement essentially of rural *petit peuple* (artisans with rural clienteles as well as urban, such as saddle-makers, gardeners, day labourers and enterprising *commerçants*) gradually became working-class suburbs associated with large-scale industrialization. Certain exterior settlements linked to a single trade (such as those of tanners, sometimes forced away from populated zones to somewhat distant water sources by those offended by the smells of their trade, or the cabinet-makers of the faubourg St Antoine) gave way to teeming, virtually separate, suburbs of workers employed in a variety of occupations and levels of skill in France's largest cities; examples were La Guillotière, absorbed into Lyon during the Second Empire, or Belleville in Paris.

Gradually the term 'faubourg' (and today even *banlieue*) came to take on a pejorative and threatening sense for the bourgeoisie; in the nineteenth century people no longer thought of the quarter of St Germain-des-prés in Paris as an elite faubourg, but as an essential part of the city; they regarded the faubourg St Honoré, even then a well-heeled extension of the rue St Honoré, today's centre of shopping for wealthy Parisians and those tourists still able to afford the city of light, in the same way. The faubourg came to suggest the working class. Thus shortly after Louis Philippe assumed power in 1830, the prefect Chabrol warned him: 'Your prefects of police are allowing the capital to be blocked by a hundred factories. Sire, this will be the cord that will strangle it one day.'[34] St Marc Girardin, deputy from the Creuse, sounded his famous alert early in the July monarchy that the new barbarians were not to be found on the Tartary, but in the new industrial suburbs. The 'dangerous classes', once feared in the narrow passageways of Paris, now were seen as lurking in the suburbs. In 1871, after Baron Haussmann's works had chased thousands of poor workers from the crowded centre and eastern districts of the capital into the *banlieu*, the Paris Commune marked the revenge of those expelled from Paris. The Wall of the Fédérés, where some of the last Communards fell, may be found in Père Lachaise cemetery, not far from the working-class district of Belleville, where the final resistance was crushed.

The use of space and particularly, patterns of residence are important for understanding the impact of urbanization and large-scale industrialization on French political life. As Hanagan notes in his essay, the simple concentration of workers did not in itself breed militancy and organization. Over the long run, a more marked geography of social segregation emerged in nineteenth-century French cities. The vertical segregation typified by Balzac's Vauquer rooming house gradually diminished, without disappearing. The Marais, whose *hôtels particuliers* had housed the elite of Paris in the seventeenth century and well into the eighteenth century until the movement into the faubourg St Germain, had been characterized by internal courtyards, protected from *le peuple* by fortress-like walls. By the revolution, the Marais had become almost exclusively a popular quarter and its residents were prominent among those storming the Bastille in 1789. The Haussmannization of Paris accentuated the rough split between the eastern and western halves of the capital, between the Paris of 'the people' and that of the elite. Even the western suburbs were to a great extent extensions of the wealthy quarters on that side of the city (and their extensions, in time, became Deauville, Étretat, Fécamp and the other resorts of the Norman coast placed within easy reach of Paris by the railroad from the Gare St Lazare). The Bois de Boulogne and Longchamps were much more frequented by the wealthy than the Bois de Vincennes or the Buttes-Chaumont.

Obviously the population of the fastest-growing French cities increased far more rapidly than the physical resources to accommodate the waves of migrants. During the July monarchy and the

Second Empire, the central areas of many cities became saturated with those newly arrived, who found a corner of a room through a relative or someone else from their *pays natal*. Contemporaries and subsequent historians have agreed that the cramped, dirty quarters of the poor in Lille, Rouen, Paris, Rennes and other large cities were appalling. The elegant descriptions of social reformers and novelists are corroborated by the matter-of-fact and often very technical accounts of the *reconnaissances militaires* undertaken in urban as well as rural France during the first half of the century. The cholera epidemics of 1832 and 1849 thus struck the poorer quarters of Paris, largely sparing the well-to-do. There were many more poor than rich; some 80 per cent of the population towards the end of the Restoration died leaving absolutely nothing to their heirs but poverty and perhaps some knowledge of how to survive as long as possible; only a slightly smaller percentage of the Parisian dead had to be buried at public expense, the relatives and friends having absolutely no resources to assure a decent burial. Not surprisingly, the most basic stipulation of the early mutual aid associations of workers was the right to a decent burial. French cities in the first half of the nineteenth century, although some were more notorious than others, remained dirty, crowded and virtually inaccessible to all but the slowest of transport.

It was against this background that nineteenth-century French town planning developed. Napoleon, like the eighteenth-century Intendants, combined at least some interest in the practical with the primacy of the aesthetic. Yet many of Napoleon's plans for his capital were never put into effect. Years of imperial wars probably saved Paris from having even more majestic *N*s carved on virtually every new or improved public edifice. The attempts of the governments of the restoration and July monarchy to improve the urban environment of the capital were piecemeal: Rambuteau forged what was at the time one of the few reasonably efficient east–west routes through the city, the street that now bears his name. Poubelle later placed on the city streets the trash receptacles that were named after him.

The most vocal critics of contemporary urban life were the utopian socialists, whose idea of *urbanisme* corresponded to what Pierre Lavedan has called '*l'urbanisme constructeur*':[35] the city as it was, victimized by bourgeois individualism, had to be abandoned and new cities built with the aid of science. Fourier, steeped in the Saint-Simonian tradition of a belief in the power of science to advance civilization to a higher stage (to the extent that he envisioned oceans of lemonade and perfumed sweet air), planned self-contained phalansteries that would house and gratify its citizens, grouped from what he had identified as the some thirty possible types of human beings. Étienne Cabet, less interesting to read than Fourier but with a larger popular following, depicted a model urban environment in his somewhat tedious but clean Icaria; its paved streets would have stood in marked contrast to the grimy towns, such as Niort and Vienne, in which his artisan disciples lived.[36]

With the advent of Napoleon III and Baron Haussmann, town planning passed from the left critics of bourgeois individualism to the government. Armed with the power of the state to decree expropriations in the name of the public good, they undertook, with a conception of the total city in mind, Lavedan's '*l'urbanisme démolisseur*'. The intervention of Napoleon III and Baron Haussmann into the space of the capital is certainly the most well-known episode of *urbanisme* in the nineteenth century.[37] Haussmann gave Paris much of what the tourist admires today, improved the water and sewage systems, and created the wonderful market of Les Halles – savagely destroyed in total disregard for the city's history and, with the nearby quarters, replaced by a subterranean concrete shopping centre and the Beaubourg, called, curiously, the Centre National d'Art et de Culture Georges Pompidou, after the man who permitted the destruction of some of the beauty of Paris and permanent damage to its magnificent skyline.

Haussmann's work has always been the subject of much debate. The public works projects of the capital, and those of several other cities, reflected the way in which political elites could use their power to make major changes in the urban landscape by intervening in the use of space. For the wide boulevards that expedited traffic in Paris and facilitated access to the railroad stations (although sometimes maladroitly) ploughed right through a number of traditional neighbourhoods of workers, which had risen in revolt more than once within the past seventy years. The Rue Transnonain, scene of the massacre of a family by the National Guard at the beginning of the July monarchy, disappeared, leaving little more than Daumier's gripping print as a visual reminder of the brutality of class relations in the capital. The new boulevards were too wide to build barricades across, and there were no more barricades in Paris after the ill-fated resistance to the coup d'état in

1851 until the end of the second world war, and again in 1968. Haussmann's motives were neither totally aesthetic and practical, nor entirely Machiavellian. Unfortunately, we have few good studies linking urban form, planning and politics.[38] Little such work has considered cities outside the capital. The relationships between space, urban form, planning and politics remain to be examined.

The urban historian's task of analysing, understanding and describing the large-scale processes of social change must, then, include establishing how the growth of towns and cities affected the political life of France. But he or she must also *evoke* the nineteenth-century city, showing how it was organized and how it worked, bringing to life the individual and collective experiences of the people who lived there. We have much to learn from Richard Cobb, who stresses the uniqueness of each city – indeed each neighbourhood and individual. No other historian writing in French or English has so brilliantly evoked urban life. Whether writing about suicides in Paris, pregnancies or counter-revolution in Lyon, the old port of Marseille, the bus to Milly, the tenth *arrondissement* of Paris or Ixelles in Bruxelles, no other contemporary writer can better describe, relate, capture or feel the weight, the joys and the assurance of daily routine, a sense of space and of place, of death, love, hope, despair, expectation or disappointment. Cobb, like Louis Chevalier, teaches us the importance of what the former calls 'visual awareness' and, like the urban geographers of the first half of this century, to be aware of the importance of physical environment on human behaviour. The historian interested in social change must respond to Cobb's warning about imposing 'artificial collectivities' on the past by demonstrating how in the course of the nineteenth century daily life and individual routines changed, and to what extent they came to intersect with politics.[39] Urbanization created new routines, new assurances, new uses of space and new hopes, as well as new anxieties. Urbanization, in this way, altered the political life of France. Every town, city, neighbourhood and street is different, and in the nineteenth century as today the collective memory, traditions and routines of each could be as unique as the very stones used to build them. But they also shared the collective experience of social change, as urbanization helped transform society and politics in France. The historian can combine an understanding of the dynamics of social change with the rich sources available for the study of the single city over time to research, analyse, describe and again bring to life the greatly increasing number of French men and women in the nineteenth century who lived and worked in towns and cities.

2 Restoration town, bourgeois city: changing urban politics in industrializing Limoges

John M. Merriman

In April 1848 the workers of Limoges, one of France's most politically turbulent cities in the nineteenth century, met at the Champ de Juillet at the edge of the city; they then stormed through the town, disarming the bourgeois National Guard, and temporarily seized political power. The Champ de Juillet was a significant place for them to meet. The elite National Guard had drilled there during the July monarchy, ready to repress any disturbances from the lower classes. But they, the workers, had levelled and terraced the field in the months that followed the July revolution of 1830, when they were unemployed and tided over by the charity workshops established by the municipality in the hope of maintaining order.

In 1848 workers challenged for political power in France and in Limoges, as they would throughout the century in the industrializing city, sometimes violently, as in 1871. Their elected representatives would control the municipality for most of the years between the founding of the Confedération Générale du Travail (in Limoges) in 1895 and the outbreak of the first world war. But this period, when everyday life and political contention seemed to converge in the swirl of rallies, parades, manifestations, *conférences contradictoires,meetings* and strikes, lay far in the future. Yet it was the consequence of the evolution of an industrial city during the nineteenth century, reflected and at the same time accelerated by the revolutions of 1830 and 1848. These revolutions left their marks on the very stones and space of the city as well as on the collective memory of its inhabitants. Shortly after the revolution of 1830, which brought a new elite to political power in France and in Limoges, a slaughterhouse, a bridge – the Pont de la Révolution – and the Champ de Juillet were constructed in Limoges, the work of the proud bourgeois victors of the July revolution. Later changes in Limoges's urban landscape would reflect future political struggles: the Bourse du Travail, the giant Haviland factory on the Avenue Garibaldi, the co-operative L'Union, all in the predominantly working-class faubourgs, and the municipal Cirque (at least until it burned down), where socialist orators attacked the bourgeois Third Republic before cheering audiences.[1]

French politics, and particularly that of its cities, changed dramatically in the years surrounding 1830. This history can best be written in the experiences of real people in time and in space. Local history can reveal the fundamental processes of economic, social, cultural and political change when representative experience and meaningful detail are considered from the point of view of the larger experience. Limoges during the revolution of 1830 offers such a case study, because its evolution during the late restoration and early July monarchy was richly documented; it is thus possible to evoke a single city as it changed, bringing to life a number of symbolic and significant confrontations representative of the national experience – between a bishop and young anticlerical bourgeois, between a noble mayor and dissatisfied businessmen, between a dutiful prefect and his angry political charges, between two newspapers faithfully evoking contemporary perceptions – and in a number of popular disturbances that reflected, over time, the emergence of more ordinary people in French political life.[2]

Restoration Limoges had many striking vestiges of the Middle Ages. The French revolution and the empire brought war, social division, some violence and virtually no urban progress to the Limousin capital. Limoges was crowded, dark and very dirty. The *Annales de la Haute Vienne*, the town's only newspaper, admitted that restoration Limoges 'offers an image of disorder, an absence of all rules, policing and planning'. The steep inclines of its streets impeded and discouraged traffic. Sewage still ran down small ditches cut into the middle of streets. Churches occasionally gave off a deathly stench because corpses were left unattended; in 1825 the prefect complained that the smell in St Michel-les-Lions was so bad that services could no longer safely be followed. Day labourers dumped their refuse almost randomly in other neighbourhoods on the way to work. Their journeys could indeed be hazardous, leading to an official complaint that 'uncleanliness reigns everywhere in this city; at any moment one can see water and garbage being thrown from the windows'. The Abbessaille quarter, where laundresses and *flotteurs de bois* spoke a difficult patois, offered a particularly appalling scene. In the *entre deux villes* section that had grown up between the two original cities joined administratively in 1790 – the *'château'* and the *'cité'* – a filthy stream in which tanners carelessly tossed animal parts exuded an awful stench. The butchers' street in the centre of the commercial district was even worse.[3]

Several historical artefacts combined to accentuate the density and inadequate housing within the city. Limoges's physical expansion during the eighteenth century had been constrained by royal decrees and by the survival of the town walls until the time of Turgot. Rapid population growth, exclusively from migration as more people died in Limoges than were born there in almost every year, by the late 1820s compounded the serious overcrowding within the city limits, despite the rapid growth of the faubourgs. The central city reached its maximum density in the same period; only the parish of St Michel continued to expand, because of the growth of Limoges to the north, along the faubourgs Montmailler and of the route de Paris.[4]

There was little about Limoges to counteract the unfavourable impressions visitors had of an overcrowded and unhealthy city. Limoges suffered from a feeling of inferiority some outsiders found quite justified. Even at its best, Limoges was the kind of city Stendhal claimed was 'peuplés avec les âmes du sous-préfecture'.[5] Despite the city fathers' attempt to convince the king that Limoges was 'a second Rome', the town had not one single public monument, nor any imposing statue aside from numerous minor religious artefacts and cumbersome stone crosses blocking key intersections. Only one old private residence was noteworthy: the minister of justice Martignac recalled some pleasant memories of the maison Nivet, where Balzac once stayed; in a somewhat generous understatement, the great novelist termed it 'less grand and imposing than the Louvre and the Palais-Bourbon'.[6] Limoges applied to the king for the designation of *'bonne ville'* in 1821 and 1825, a title that could be affixed proudly to the town crest. The petitioners reminded Louis XVIII that the 'miraculous progress' of commerce and industry in Limoges had increased revenues by 20 per cent in the past ten years, but each time Limoges was politely and firmly informed that the country already had a sufficient number of towns of this rank. As several of these towns were smaller, the municipal council believed Limoges had been made 'an humiliating exception'.[7] Moreover, the academy had been eliminated in 1814 after a short and undistinguished existence; for a time it seemed that the royal court would be transferred elsewhere, which would have dealt an economic blow as well as a considerable loss of prestige. Limoges seemed to be a forgotten town. Even a local booster claimed that the town's elite merely imported the modes and styles of Paris, and the effect was 'similar to those light wines whose quality is diminished when they are transported'.[8]

The city fathers bristled at the idea that Limoges was a *ville perdue*, for they took pride that 'religious tradition [was] conserved with care' in 'Holy Limoges'. There were many signs of religiosity in Limoges in 1828, in addition to the large crosses of stone at some *carrefours*. A large cross stood before the church of St Michel-les-Lions. The gates of the city had once been placed under the protection of the Virgin Mary and of the saints, statues of whom had been erected when the walls were torn down. Street-corner niches sheltered about 200 pious statues and most quarters still celebrated the feast days of their respective patron saints. Religious faith seemed to have been restored along with the monarchy, even though the intense religiosity of the seventeenth century, when most of Limoges's active confraternities had been established, had long since passed. Despite the loss of its stained glass windows and the heads of most of its statues, Limoges's unfinished and rather graceless cathedral of Saint-Étienne was often full, although the wealthy were no longer able to secure their burial in its gloomy reaches because of measures taken in the interest of public health. The *Annales de la Haute Vienne* advertised brochures such as 'Six months of the lives of the Saints of the Diocese of Limoges and all of the Limousin!' and annually listed all of the ecclesiastics who had died during the year.[9]

Most associational life in the town was religiously inspired; the penitents had survived with many of the virtues and abuses that had characterized their life under the *ancien régime*. They fought to retain their traditional independence *vis-à-vis* the clergy and the municipal administration, while their pious and charitable function declined somewhat as they recruited heavily for members and sought to outdo each other in their processions and prosperity. If weakened in number, function and perhaps commitment, and sometimes mocked by a new generation who found them ana-chronistic, the penitents still attested to the role of organized religion in the society, politics and culture of Limoges. The religious calendar still dictated the significant public events, notably the Septennial Ostensions of fifty days' duration in which the butchers enjoyed a prominent role.[10] For centuries, Limoges had been a commercial centre. A new prefect, arriving in 1819, had found his administrative charges 'distinguished by the shrewdness of their judgement, their calculating and practical minds, and a great aptitude for commercial operations'. Some found this taste for speculation offensive: J. J. Juge, reflecting on almost fifty years of life in Limoges, was justly proud of the 'brilliant reputation' of the local commercial bourgeoisie, but worried that relative newcomers were tarnishing Limoges's once sterling reputation with their wild speculations and seemingly endless quest for new luxuries. Yet Limoges's commercial leaders urged stricter legal codes and regulations to discourage unscrupulous commercial practices, priding themselves on 'thrift, patience, energy and good faith'.[11]

Commerce was enriching the Limoges bourgeoisie, who used some of their profits to buy up considerable property in the communes surrounding the city. In 1828, ten merchants and two commercial transport entrepreneurs were among the leading *censitaires* (eligible to vote by virtue of taxes paid); wholesale merchants were by far the second leading occupational category behind *propriétaires* in a municipal list of voters. But if Limoges lived by commerce, much of it was retail, centred on the Place des Bancs, near the butchers' quarter. In 1819, the prefect estimated that at least 2000 of the approximately 2500 buildings in Limoges housed shops, stores or small workshops.[12]

That same year, the prefect had been struck by a marked shift in the economy of Limoges. It was not just salon conversations that convinced him that some of the capital which had been used to finance wholesale and, to a lesser extent, retail commerce, was now going into the manufacture of the city's two most noteworthy products, textiles and porcelain. One could see ever-increasing quantities of wood being hauled up from the Vienne River to fuel the porcelain kilns that had been built in Limoges during the restoration, expanding an industry that had first settled in Limoges shortly before the French revolution and had survived the turmoil of those years. The settlements across the river were also alive with domestic textile production, the leading industry in Limoges; several small factories along the Vienne were busy during the restoration and more than 1000 textile workers laboured in most quarters of the city. It was only in the late 1820s that the latter industry began to encounter the rugged competition from other areas, particularly the Nord, that spelled eventual doom for the local production of textiles. Porcelain seemed to be shaping the future of the region, employing between 800 and 900 workers in 1828 in Limoges. Limoges's other industries were considerably smaller: tanning, shoes, galoshes and *souliers de pacotile*, paper, weights and measures; in addition there was the usual range of artisans who, like those in the textile industry, produced for local consumption.[13]

Limoges's development as an industrial centre was aided by the availability of a skilled labour supply in the porcelain industry (several of the patrons had themselves begun as skilled turners and moulders) and a mass of unskilled workers from the hinterland. These workers, although they were undisciplined, never collectively challenged their employers, having no organizational resources. They evidenced no interest in politics and maintained more than a nominal religious attachment, accepting the charity of the church and the assistance of the municipality during hard times. Public order was easily maintained in Limoges. Occasionally the police dispersed a charivari: for example, a noisy crowd of 300 serenading a woman who had just been married for the third time (in this case the new groom stormed out of the house and snatched away one of the offending musical instruments); or another, of young men from 'les meilleurs maisons de Limoges' following a theatre performance in 1820.[14]

Only one major incident involving a crowd had posed a threat to public order in the restoration when, during a grain riot, *les gens du peuple* made a collective protest. In 1816, the price of grain went up sharply following a poor harvest, compounded by the consumption by troops encamped in the general vicinity. The price of rye reached 20 francs per hectolitre, twice the price it commanded in nearby St Junien. Costly white bread inevitably followed and reached 44 centimes a kilo, leaping to 70 centimes the following year. The price of potatoes, a staple of the poor, almost doubled. While the municipal administration and the prefect commissioned merchants from the city to go to Orléans to buy grain for the Limoges market, rumours of hoarding spread.

On 18 June, 1816, several wagons filled with grain – purchased at a price the poor could not afford – left Limoges for Montauban.

Some distance beyond the Pont St Martial, they were stopped by a mob of between 300 and 400 people, mostly, as usual, women. The police intervened and escorted the merchant, who lived in Limoges, to the hamlet of St Lazare, where another crowd intercepted his wagons at the cotton-spinning factory of Constantin. This time they hurled rocks and damaged the wagon with a pitchfork. One of the women arrested explained simply, 'The driver was taking the grain out of the department.' When news of the arrest of several *femmes du peuple* spread, a huge crowd gathered at the prefecture, and another woman was arrested for loudly making 'a seditious statement'. The prefect posted a warning against hoarding; the police monitored the bakers' stocks, which helped get more grain on the market, and the National Guard patrolled the streets night and day. The price of grain fell briefly, only to climb to record heights during the next year. But these events had been largely forgotten by the late 1820s. Officials and the town's leading citizens assumed that 'the people are incapable of reflecting wisely', but would not cause trouble unless 'put up to something'. Among *le peuple* there were no political plots for the police to sniff out, no political opposition to fathom.[15]

The noble mayor Pierre Hippolyte Martin de la Bastide, the bishop, and the king's officials dominated political life in Limoges, with only a handful of men wealthy enough among the 145 who could vote in the elections, to stand for the Chamber of Deputies. The top of the pyramid of wealth in Limoges often seemed more interested in staging spectacular receptions for important visitors, such as the Duchesse de Berri in 1828, than looking after the evolving interests of the city. The municipal council, appointed by the government, was strikingly free from contention and disputes, rarely meeting more than once a month to administer the budget. It consisted of like-minded social equals, including the scions of several noble families such as de Villelume, Roulhac, Pétiniaud des Mont, de la Bastide and Noualhier.[16]

Yet by 1827 political dissension was apparent in Limoges among the middle class – among precisely those whom the narrowly defined political spectrum excluded. Youthful bourgeois, like their precursors during the revolution, no longer unquestioningly accepted the traditional institutional and political role of the church. And they seldom hesitated to complain about the lack of urban progress in a commercial and industrial town even denied the title of a *'bonne ville'*. As the 1827 elections approached,

Baron Coster, the prefect, confronted the possibility that his friends, the 'true royalists' loyal to Charles X and suspicious of the Charter, would not be returned to the Chamber of Deputies. The evolution of a liberal opposition in Limoges corresponded to the organization of precisely those men who were associated with the city's increased commercial and industrial prosperity. The ministry's four seats in the department were in doubt in 1827 because the government found little or no support among those men recently enfranchised in Limoges; and the Villèle ministry lost the allegiance of many voters representing commerce and industry. Many businessmen blamed the government for insufficient attention to their welfare during the economic crisis that had begun in 1826. Liberals, active and organized in Paris and the provinces, efficiently capitalized on the business community's belief that its interests were being ignored by the government. The liberal politician Pierre Alpinien Bourdeau, a member of the Corps Législative during the empire, led a remarkably successful campaign to register eligible voters. Almost all of these were drawn from the ranks of commerce and industry.[17]

And other opposition leaders emerged: Desalles Beauregard, a wholesale merchant who had served as a National Guard officer during the Hundred Days of Napoleon's return to France; Dumont St Priest, a lawyer of some means, 'full of finesse and ambition', a liberal despite (or perhaps because of) his marriage to the daughter of the *procureur général*; and François Alluaud, the now wealthy porcelain manufacturer who had married a woman above his station known for her social graces. Of Alluaud, Coster wrote, 'his manners are gentle; having risen from a very low class – his father had originally worked as an engineer [before beginning a porcelain factory] – M. Alluaud regretted the return of the old nobility and appears to dread the influence of the court and the clergy'.[18]

François Alluaud's dread of the clergy may be traced to his childhood. Born on the commercial rue de Clocher in 1778, Alluaud later recalled that the priest who had taken responsibility for his education when he was 9 had greatly favoured the sons of the nobility, while 'the pitiless cruelties of our teachers were reserved for the children of the bourgeoisie'. During the revolution, Alluaud's enterprising father had obtained a scholarship for his bright son in the capital. There the 'study of the declaration of the rights of man and of the meaning of "men are born free and equal in rights"' replaced the ten commandments and the catechism as the young Alluaud's topics for study and reflection. Now, in 1827, Alluaud, although without political ambition and preferring to spend his time improving the production of porcelain, seemed a natural leader among liberals disenchanted with the lack of attention the government gave business.[19]

Despite Baron Coster's efforts to manage the election, the liberals won both seats in the two district *collèges*, while the government barely maintained the two departmental places, saved by the even more restricted franchise which weighted the result towards the interests of the Limousin's few landed nobility of great means. Two nights of brief disturbances followed the latter election; disappointed young merchants and clerks, for the most part disguised, 'offered' a charivari to the ministry's deputies, Mousnier-Buisson and de Montbron, who had fled his feudal château during the revolution. Some of the bourgeois carried makeshift musical instruments out of the Café Renommé, shouting, 'Down with the Jesuits! Down with the ministry!' Scandalized, the prefect noted that 'the time has come to imprint on this new generation a wise sense of direction'. He quickly added that *le peuple* took absolutely no part in the event; the guilty were 'young men whose social position should have rendered them more circumspect'. For Coster had little patience with the political pretensions of business, 'which, adopting the opinions of liberalism and peddling its lies, continues its own speculations and enterprises'. Despite constant complaining, 'they build and further augment the luxuriousness of their houses'.[20]

1828 only enchanced the mood of political opposition in Limoges. A special election saw Dumont St Priest campaign in defence of the Charter, promising, if elected, that he would appeal to the king to examine the situation of industry and commerce. The landed interests in the departmental *collège* again proved too strong, and Dumont St Priest lost by a narrow margin. The arrival of the Mission, a traditionalist religious revival organized by the conservative congregations, also broke the normal tranquillity of life in Limoges. During two days in March, the hellfire and brimstone services were interrupted by young men of commerce, who threw sulphuric acid and other smelly materials into two churches, with the now familiar shouts of 'Down with the Jesuits!' Similar disturbances followed a month later. The workers were outraged by such behaviour, having followed the Mission with fervour, and had to be restrained from taking revenge against the men of the middle class they called 'the calicots'.[21] The elections of 1827 and 1828 and the incident involving the Mission reveal the evolution of urban politics in Limoges: through the cries of protest of the young bourgeoisie excluded from electoral participation, accompanied by the 'rough music' of one of Europe's popular rituals borrowed from *le peuple*; and through the election of two deputies committed to opposing the politics of the ministry and to supporting the interests of commerce and industry, who were against the unpopular tax on drink, complained about the conditions of the royal roads on which their merchandise travelled, and proposed the election of the municipal council so that the interests of the city could be best represented. Baron Coster summed up the prevailing division in Limoges when he assessed the city's commercial and manufacturing interests: 'liberal doctrines are widely held in this class, which inevitably dreams of an equality in conditions and honours'.[22] The next two winters did little to improve morale in Limoges, bringing terrible cold and a flu epidemic. Bread prices soared but 'the people' bore their misery well; the only two thefts that month were committed by well-dressed men. Coster believed that the police, aided by undercover agents for whom he requested additional funds, could prevent any trouble from ordinary people. And as for the bourgeoisie, he planned to 'distract them from politics by occupying them' with various municipal projects that they had long awaited in vain. Free gymnastic exhibitions and fireworks on the feast day of the king also offered 'a fortunate diversion from the manoeuvres of the Paris newspapers'. Bourgeois attention was drawn to a controversial appointment of an unpopular priest in Rochechouart, a small district capital not far from Limoges, and the trial of the poet Barthelémy in Paris, a favourite of the young bourgeoisie of the Limousin. The mood of apprehension continued among the bourgeois liberals. Catcalls interrupted a play authored by a fervent Bourbon supporter. A duel pitted a young man who had insulted the king against an offended army officer. Local commerce suffered; a letter from Limoges printed in the Parisian newspaper *Le Constitutionnel* blamed the political uncertainty for the appointment of the Polignac ministry. Many bourgeois openly worried about the futures of their children.[23]

Limoges's only newspaper, *Annales de la Haute Vienne*, spoke for the prefecture in this battle. Baron Coster could proclaim that,

'Not one single line will ever be printed without my approval', because the director was an employee of the prefecture. This 'administrative, political, literary, commercial and agronomic journal' survived because of its prefectorial subsidy, administrative pressure on the department's mayors to subscribe and its status as the only available outlet for the traditional *annonces et avis divers*. The *Annales* preferred to avoid political issues, for such discussions implied 'a division of spirits'; before the 1827 election, it had 'regretted having to speak of the Ministry and of an opposition – we would prefer only one political opinion in France, as there is only a single sentiment of love and recognition for the King and for the Bourbons'. But Coster and the *Annales* faced growing political opposition from those associated with Limoges's economic development during the restoration. The paper now found itself having 'to speak the language of the time' in order to be heard. But if Limoges had a 'language of the time', it was of commerce; and that was not a language that *Annales* spoke well. After the opposition had selected its candidates for the 1827 election, the journal's editor observed that 'by its choice, the opposition has announced that it wanted to give its heart to the commerce of Limoges'. But not for two years did liberals possess a means of making themselves regularly heard.[24]

During the autumn of 1829, the appearance of a liberal newspaper was rumoured. Finally, on 15 February 1830, the young editors and directors of *Le Contribuable* published their prospectus.[25] It demonstrated how the political opposition to the Polignac ministry was rooted in the emergence of the self-conscious and organized voice of commerce and industry in Limoges. *Le Contribuable*, the journal of 'all citizens paying taxes', was to represent business. Its forceful and challenging prospectus merits quoting:

A town of 30,000 people, rich and commercial, with relations extending to every point in France, has clamoured for a newspaper to be the faithful echo of its wishes.... Limoges owes all of its importance to its commerce and its industry. Let us thus consecrate a great part of our columns to these two great causes of its prosperity. Commerce and industry live on confidence and liberty. How could they not be suffering in a region where confidence cannot exist because liberty has suffered too many trials?

The constant mood of political uncertainty and outright hostility surrounding the acts of the ministry had taken its toll on business. 'Commerce suffers because of it, public credit is affected, money remains sterile in the justly hesitant hands of capitalists, and industry awaits with anxiety outlets for its products.' What had the ministry of Polignac done to restore business confidence?

They must insult all of commerce through paid hacks, insolently and disdainfully; and, to neutralize the influence that the *patentés* [those who paid the business tax] have acquired in the elections because of their fortune and their wisdom, they threaten now to reduce this influence ... commerce scorns these insults and laughs at these threats.

The *Annales de la Haute Vienne*, drawn into a weekly polemic with its rival, railed against those 'poor misled children of the century of light', who now associate themselves with 'offensive and revolutionary writers'. Coster took action of his own, instructing *Annales* to abandon its printer because the latter had taken its rival as a client, and ordering the prosecution of the editor of *Le Contribuable* for accusing the ministry of having 'betrayed its oath'. The prefect even worried that improvements in the department's mail service might serve to expand the readership of the liberal paper. Undaunted, *Le Contribuable* began to publish twice weekly in June, demanding a revision of the electoral lists to include more voters.[26]

Three central debates formed the basis of the liberal critique of restoration politics in Limoges. First, to repeat, was the place of commerce and industry in national and local political life. The number of businessmen paying taxes had increased in the late 1820s; so had the number of taxpayers eligible to run for the Chamber of Deputies by virtue of being assessed a minimum of 1000 francs annually. In 1816 there had been but twenty, including five merchants, four *propriétaires*, one manufacturer, one transport entrepreneur, two lawyers, two magistrates and five others. Between 1828 and 1830, the number of these *éligibles* increased substantially, from thirty-six to fifty-three. Of the eighteen new men eligible for public office, no fewer than six were merchants; four were manufacturers and the others included two wholesale merchants and one transport entrepreneur.[27] If these new *éligibles* could not be counted on to vote with the government, those newly enfranchised voters seemed even less trustworthy to the prefect, accentuating a conflict already apparent in 1827:

This region, essentially commercial, furnishes a great number of modest voters by virtue of the tax on business, on which the administrative authorities have little influence; the great landed interests are little or not at all represented here.[28]

Le Contribuable accused Polignac and his loyal prefect Coster, 'enemies of commerce and industry', of attempting to 'take away the electoral right arising from the business tax of the merchants, manufacturers, incorrigible men stubborn enough to love the Charter ... [who have] the good faith to believe that it offers the protection necessary to their business and to the happiness and prosperity of France'. And yet business in Limoges seemed overtaxed and under-represented in the Chamber of Deputies, particularly as the *patente* was, with a few exceptions, insufficient to buy the right to vote. By raising the tax on business, the ministry had increased its revenue without significantly increasing the number of voters. *Le Contribuable* spoke for the majority of businesses in Limoges when it defiantly proclaimed the right of taxpayers 'to occupy ourselves with the business of government'. The group that Coster condescendingly referred to as 'a mob of petty merchants and shopkeepers' now openly discussed the possibility of tax resistance. Some businessmen signed the statutes for an 'Association Limousin', which, like the national 'Association Breton', would co-ordinate such efforts. The Chambre Consultative demanded a location more suitable than the courthouse for its business meetings, protesting when Coster tried to force them into an old convent hall.[29]

The church and its functionaries provided the second focus for the liberal critique, in particular, the controversial Bishop Prosper de Tournefort, the most powerful of Coster's political allies. Prosper lived in a palace described by Arthur Young in 1787 as 'large and handsome ... the garden of which was the finest object to be seen in Limoges, for it commands a landscape hardly to be equalled for beauty'.[30] The bishop remained a staunch traditionalist who complained about the 'profane representations' during Limoges's religious processions as he did about nude bathing in the Vienne. Upon his arrival in Limoges he had expressed the opinion that bishops had always 'signalled the dangers that threatened the alliance of altar and throne'. Like Coster, he had little use for the parvenu bourgeoisie who were sometimes remiss in fulfilling their religious duties. He refused to accept the liberals' idea that anyone could publicly discuss or question the acts of the king's government, writing to the minister of ecclesiastic affairs in

February 1830 that, 'France needs to be conquered morally, as it was physically ... she must be invested, as by the allies, with all that is required to reform minds, beginning with the young.' This nostalgia for the memory of the allied invasion could not help but offend liberals; furthermore, de Tournefort urged the ministry to withdraw the freedom of the press, the antithesis, he believed, of a properly controlled state.[31]

Le Contribuable's inaugural issue assailed the role of the church, asserting that the 'liberty' achieved during the French revolution, the beginning of an emancipation movement that had shaken all of society, was now threatened by the ministry's arbitrary actions, notably by the infamous sacrilege law of 1825. The rumours sweeping much of France concerning the re-establishment of the *dîme* contributed to the mood of fear and mistrust of the church. Shortly before the 1827 elections, a sizeable crowd turned out in Limoges to attend the funeral of a 'comedian', denied a church burial because the bishop found his humour offensive. And Prosper de Tournefort himself neither forgot nor forgave the incidents during the Missions in 1828 recalled by the large crosses standing before two churches of the city. *Le Contribuable* attacked the bishop, his budget and the seemingly exorbitant salaries of these 'gladiators in cassocks', demanding lay instruction.[32]

Even the church's charitable work during the harsh winter of 1829–30 brought complaints. The temperature plunged to record lows in December, bringing the poor further hardship following a summer drought. Bread prices rose to levels even higher than during the winter of 1827–8 and many of the poor of the countryside swarmed to Limoges seeking food and shelter. The municipal council funded charity workshops, but soon it was too cold to work. Many of the wretched, homeless beggars huddled in the doorways of churches, facing death from exposure. The municipal council allocated money for a municipal soup kitchen which would provide heat, bread, an 'economical soup' and religious instruction for the poor between the hours of 8 a.m. and 4 p.m. What happened to the poor with nowhere to go at night is not clear. Some generous families took people into their homes, but perhaps it was assumed that the others would be so fortified by whatever was in the 'economical soup' that they could survive anything.[33]

Prosper de Tournefort opposed this modest act of charity, first because the soup kitchen was to be located in the chapel of the royal *collège* where only a temporary wall would divide the shelter from the holy sanctuary. Worse, the sexes were not going to be separated. So Prosper banned all religious instruction, despite Baron Coster's promise that the poor would kneel on the cold stone floor to say their prayers before eating. Ultimately the bishop relented, approving the project and donating fifty pots of soup. The kitchen, operated by the Sisters of Charity, fed between 400 and 500 twice a day. The literary circle held a ball for the benefit of the poor and the 'dames of society' sponsored an auction, selling, among other discarded items, a 'charming armchair' owned by the bishop himself. The maternal society ventured out into the cold to bring sustenance to 177 poor mothers of suitable moral character. The prefect sponsored a musical soirée to raise money. Traditional forms of charity helped the poor survive the winter, but the episode of the soup kitchen once again put the church in an unfavourable light. The cold subsided, but not the biting and sometimes violent criticism of 'the priestly party'.[34]

The polemic between the *Annales de la Haute Vienne* and its eager and aggressive young challenger, and the tension between the prefect and the city's unsatisfied bourgeois interests had municipal implications, and also echoed national questions concerning the respective roles of commerce and industry and the church. While proclaiming their right 'to occupy themselves with the business of government' through representation in the Chamber of Deputies, Limoges's bourgeois liberals also wanted to guide the affairs of their own growing town. This was the third point of contention between Limoges's bourgeoisie and the government. The municipal council had broken with the apathetic and even more conservative departmental General Council, which had recently purchased expensive portraits of Henry IV and Louis XVI, and voted funds for the maintenance of a normal school desperately needed in the backward region. De la Bastide was often uninterested in municipal affairs and rarely left his estate and horses to come into town. He was, as *Le Contribuable* rather generously put it, 'burdened by his own numerous activities'.[35]

Some Limogeauds had, during the course of the 1820s, become concerned with improving their long-neglected urban environment, beginning with the Rue de la boucherie. The departmental General Council had allocated money for the construction of a slaughterhouse just south-west of the city on the plain of Beaupeyrat. The project was frequently discussed at municipal council meetings, but no action followed. De la Bastide, taken to task by *Le Contribuable*, did not oppose the project; but he admired the renowned religious devotion of the butchers and may have been protecting their interests. Baron Coster turned a deaf ear to complaints of the 'fetid and poisonous odours' carried by the wind from the street and the tanneries in the old *cité*, both far from his country estate. The unpaved Rue de la boucherie, made virtually impassable by the butchers' stalls, had only a ditch running down the centre for drainage. The narrow streets such as the Rue Huchette and the Rue Vigne-de-fer that radiated from the Rue de la boucherie offered only minimal space for slaughtering animals. Particularly noxious were the older houses, towards the upper end of the street, where there was no division between the shop on the ground floor and the rooms where the butchers prepared and stored meat, animal parts, and skins. The upper reaches of these houses had space for hanging meat, often right over the street. The shopkeepers of the nearby streets were not satisfied with an occasional summons given to a butcher for allowing his chickens to run wild through the streets, or for damage done by the fearful dogs of the quarter. The noble Martin de la Bastide limited himself to friendly reminders from time to time that tossing dead cows into the Vienne River was not in the best interests of the city. The only relevant municipal decree in recent years had been in 1825, when the butchers, who had complained that they could not use the fountain of Aigoulène for their purposes, were reminded that during particularly hot weather they were to slaughter only when and where authorized. The inescapable, putrid stench of their street was present in any season.[36]

Limoges's mayor seemed to have ignored the 'pitiful state' of the rapidly deteriorating eighteenth-century boulevards, while improving the route de Paris which, incidentally, led to his estate. When his municipal council decided on an absurdly impractical plan to move the Champ de Foire, which needed expansion, away from the commercial quarters of the town to a humid and muddy location down a steep hill, he failed even to respond to a petition signed by 110 of Limoges's leading citizens and to a published pamphlet in which they made their strong case. The petitioners, who waited more than two years without receiving any kind of response, included some of the leading local liberals; several of them, including Alluaud and the editors of *Le Contribuable*, offered to contribute land at no cost if the traditional Champ de Foire could be expanded by moving it a short distance away to an available site rather than to an isolated and rather foolishly chosen location. *L'urbanisme*, then, became a political issue. De la Bastide had been flattered and cajoled into accepting the position of mayor; he never felt at home listening to the complaints of the sons of commerce, even if some of the wealthiest shared his passion for land and horses. Baron Coster thus received little help from his mayor in his plan to distract the bourgeoisie from politics with long-awaited urban projects; the latter complained of the 'secret power' that seemed to paralyse the administration.[37]

The spring of 1830 carried national and political debates beyond the stage where mere distractions were enough. Baron Coster's reports to the minister of the interior and the spirited debate between the *Annales de la Haute Vienne* and *Le Contribuable* allow us to follow the last crises of the Bourbon monarchy in Limoges. The defiant vote against the king's address by 221 deputies in the Chamber of Deputies and the preparation for the election in June further polarized political opinion in Limoges, adding to the strength of the liberals, whose numbers had increased dramatically in the 1827 campaign. *Le Contribuable* thundered against entrenched privilege and urged all businessmen who had earned the right to vote to cast their ballot against 'the enemies of liberty and commerce!'.

For a long time, when we shopkeepers, lawyers, and peasants wanted to occupy ourselves with what they call politics, the men of *La Gazette* [an intransigent royalist paper] and generally all those who want absolutism sent us rudely back to our businesses.[38]

The issues at stake in the election also seemed clear to *Annales de la Haute Vienne*: 'To vote for the 221 deputies is to vote for pure democracy, that is, anarchy.' Noting the increase in the number of voters in Limoges since 1827, the voice of the prefecture again arrogantly challenged those electors risen from commerce and industry:

For any man of good faith, it is evident that holders of landed property, for whom the electoral right is granted through tax assessment, desire that the powers of the authorities be strong in order that evil be prevented and what is good conserved. Men who gamble their fortune in commercial speculations or in perilous enterprises, should be very pleased to see the extension of liberties, ready to run several more risks; their electoral right is mobile, and for that reason their vote is less reasoned'.[39]

The bishop promised to do his part to defeat the liberals, as in 1827, by counselling the wealthy faithful to vote for the candidates of the government. On the other hand, *Le Contribuable* took advantage of the opportunity afforded by its trial on a press offence to publicize the issues of the election and counter the administration's own propaganda efforts with their own. Its editors predicted that 'all of the dinners at the prefecture, all of the dinners at the Bishop's palace, all of the circulars of the administration, all of the instructions of the congregations will not deprive us of one single vote'. A liberal electoral committee prepared for victory; it was led by Alluaud's son, Victor, who had had to petition to be declared eligible to vote. *Le Contribuable* reminded its readers on 7 June that 'the town of Limoges still has not seen its commerce represented in the Chamber'.[40]

On 23 June 1830, the liberals triumphed: both Dumont St Priest, the liberal lawyer, and Bourdeau-Lajudie, a merchant, were elected in the departmental college. All four of the department's deputies were now liberal and the perfunctory cries of 'Long live the King!' were surpassed by the defiance of 'Long live the Charter!' Neither a public execution nor the news that Algiers had fallen to French troops distracted public opinion from the political crisis. On 26 July *Le Contribuable*, referring to rumours that a coup d'état was imminent, prophetically warned against any attack by the ministry against the right to vote or the freedom of the press, and against any attempt to dissolve the Chamber of Deputies or lower the *patente* so as to eliminate the most 'troublesome' voters: 'So it is thus by coups d'état that the Ministry thinks of maintaining its power. Well then, let it make such a miserable attempt. We are resigned to the consequences'.[41]

That very day, the five ordinances, a veritable coup d'état, appeared in Paris, dissolving the chamber, restricting the number of voters by increasing the franchise qualifications, and curbing the freedom of the press. On that hot Monday, Paris's artisans, among whom the printers were prominent, took matters into their own hands. Some of them had been locked out by their employers, eager to see them on the streets in protest against the government action. The raising of the revolutionary tricolour on one of Notre Dame's towers symbolized the alliance of the top hat and the frock against the Bourbon king of the nobility and the traditional church. The appointment of Marshal Marmont, who had betrayed Napoleon, as military commander roused their fury. Charles X, woefully unprepared to defend Paris and his throne, fled St Cloud with his court after abdicating.

Embraced by the republican hero Lafayette, Louis Philippe, Duc d'Orleans, became citizen-king of the French, promising a larger electoral franchise which would include the bourgeoisie of Limoges previously excluded from political life. Limoges first learned of the ordinances on 28 July. Thereafter liberals anxiously awaited news from Paris and several porcelain manufacturers seemed ready to dismiss a great number of their workers, claimed the prefect, in the hope that they would cause trouble.

Prefectoral proclamations called for calm, counteracting a wild rumour that a sentry at the château of de la Bastide north of the city had been found with his throat slit. On 29 July, the National Guard, dormant since 1826, took arms, ready to march to Paris in defence of the Charter. *Le Moniteur* later reported that 3000 workers gathered in their quarters shouting 'Long live liberty!', which, even though the report could never be substantiated, gave the impression that Limoges had risen as one man, prepared to march to the aid of the heroic Parisian population. The municipal council voted 4000 francs for the beleaguered Bureau de Bienfaisance, despite the absence of de la Bastide. Finally, on 1 August, Baron Coster received word of the abdication of Charles X. He turned his departmental administrative functions over to Alluaud, naming him mayor. The passing of the municipal reins from de la Bastide to Alluaud symbolized the passing of restoration Limoges. Henceforth, neither the *noblesse* nor the church ever had as much influence in Limoges. De la Bastide could now remain permanently on his estate, which lay, with his interests, outside the city. Dumont St Priest proclaimed himself faithful to the Orleanist cause and became the new *procureur général* of the region. Public order was only briefly troubled on 2 August, when the small army garrison and the rejuvenated National Guard crushed a rebellion in the prison. Tricolour flags and cocardes were everywhere to be seen and celebrated.[42]

While Limoges's elite debated the accomplishments of the revolution, in the weeks that followed the poor worried about the necessities of life. Many workshops had closed their doors as the revolution, following a long slump, brought the economy to a standstill. The municipal council was now forced to confront rising bread prices and widespread unemployment. On 9 August the council allocated funds for charity workshops and sent several merchants to Rochefort to purchase grain for the Limoges market to lower prices. Daily incidents occurred at the octroi as peasants and townspeople, as in much of France, refused to pay taxes; the drink tax, for example, could not be collected during the entire month of August. Several rumours of 'plots' to destroy the tax registers circulated, alarming officials. On two consecutive days workers went to the town hall to ask for official intervention to combat hoarding and prevent any further rises in the price of bread. And stories of mysterious 'gatherings' in the woods around the city followed ill-considered statements by some employers that wages in some trades would have to be lowered.[43]

At the end of August, municipal authorities announced an increase in the already high price of bread as during the previous winter, when the bakers were blamed, with justification, for the bread shortage. On 31 August, angry workers began to gather in the morning, were dispersed by the police and then reassembled at the Place Tourny in the afternoon. About 2000 marched to the gardens of the town hall, where they believed that a number of the unscrupulous bakers had taken refuge. Many in the crowd had armed themselves with sticks and pitchforks, a few even with pistols pillaged at a gunsmith's store. Finding no bakers in the gardens, they attacked two nearby *boulangeries*, whose owners, Gérald and Misset, barely escaped before their grain and bread were distributed among the crowd, furniture smashed and tools destroyed. The crowd then turned its fury on a third baker, one Samie, whose store on the Rue des petites maisons between the cathedral and the town hall turned out to be well stocked, confirming the suspicions of hoarding. The poor workers' desperate actions lasted about an hour and a half, long enough for the National Guard to assemble and carry out thirteen arrests. However, the recent transfer of power limited the effectiveness of the repression. A prosecutor had been dismissed that morning and local magistrates, 'hardly used to dealing with riots' in Limoges, released most of those arrested. Troops, gendarmes and guardsmen patrolled the streets and the night passed without further trouble; small groups of workers were dispersed the next morning in the wake of a rumoured popular assault upon the Maison Centrale to release the prisoners.

Dumont St Priest ordered an investigation, at first blaming political agitators – probably Legitimists – because he believed the workers 'sensible, honest, peaceful, professing a religious respect for persons and property'. He heard that written *convocations* had been sent to the rioters, even telling them where to assemble; but he doubted that 'rich and influential men' would actually finance such disorder, and suspected one Catherinaud, an illiterate porcelain worker who, to hide his identity, was believed to have instructed a comrade to spell out carefully the place and time the riot was to begin. Yet the only evidence for any conspiracy was a letter with mysterious 'masonic' figures and words in *argot*, as well as 'Down with the National Guard!' hastily scrawled by an unpractised hand. None of the 150 witnesses heard provided any credible testimony pointing toward Carlist or Republican troublemakers and secret pay-offs.

Who rioted? Of the sixteen suspects interrogated whose records survive (twelve men and four women, nine of whom were born in Limoges), we can identify two weavers (one apparently no longer working in that occupation), six day-labourers, one pottery worker, two bootblacks, one apprentice carrier, one wheelwright, and the wives of a carter, a porcelain worker and another day-labourer. Most could not sign their names and all existed 'without other resource than their labour'. The weaver Duraney claimed to have been working when someone he did not know brought a letter 'urging the workers to go to the Champ de Foire'. Finding nothing there, he claimed to have heard someone saying that 'everyone should go to the town hall where they are considering the bread tax'. On the way he found himself caught up in the mob at one of the bakeries. There he struck one baker's basket with a stick. Then J. B. Lafleur convinced him to go out and drink a bottle with him – a fact which explains to the historian as well as the contemporary prosecutor why this 15-year-old boy happened to be called 'Carnival'.

Other explanations seemed less likely. One Raymond insisted that he had been helplessly pushed along by the surging crowd, when some of the grain thrown from a bakery landed on him. Jacques, who believed that he had been born in the city, had heard a rumour that the mayor would distribute bread to the poor. So he took a huge hunk of bread when someone offered it to him outside a *boulangerie*, 'but I received it without any bad intentions'. When walking away, a 'bourgeois told me to put it back, and I turned it over to him without any resistance'. He told the judge that 'before this unfortunate event, no one could reproach me for anything, and the ladies in the hospice who have known me for a long time can attest to my good conduct'. Anne Auriat took a little bread with a clear conscience, having gone to the town hall 'because of the rumour that people were going there to lower the price' of bread. Léger Gauthier, a bootblack on the Place Royale who gave his age as about 16 or 17, told a similar story. Jean Brissaud, about 15 years old and a pottery worker, admitted taking four candles and some rye bread because 'inexperience and youth put me in this sad position'. He had heard a story of a man circulating a letter of *convocation*. A woman admitted haranguing the crowd at the Place Tourny, 'telling them that some people want to make the poor die and that the bakers were rascals'. She had seven children and did not want the price of bread raised. Police arrested Françoise Géry carrying a sixty-pound bag of grain to her home on the Place des Carmes; when it became too heavy, she offered a small amount of the grain to a passerby in exchange for his assistance.[44]

We may assume, with the commander of the gendarmerie, that the rioters were ordinary workers, almost certainly unskilled, 'women and workers of the lowest class of the people'. Indeed several groups of skilled workers indignantly wrote Dumont St Priest denying their participation. One letter sought to counter 'the most injurious rumours circulating about the *artistes en porcelaine*', expressing irritation that those with skills were sometimes confused with common day-labourers. The fact that all twenty-five could sign their names clearly distinguished them from the mass of the working population. Their colleagues employed by Tharaud on the Place Tourny, where the disturbances started, also insisted that they had not been involved in the 'tumultuous meetings held by day-labourers from all sorts of trades'. Another letter from porcelain workers – these were less literate, with only nine of thirty-six being able to sign – assured the public prosecutor that 'the workers of the factory of Latrille and Company' did not leave their workshops: 'a single word from our director made us return to our tasks'. They asked only some assurance from the mayor in the face of rising bread prices and the looming possibility of another miserable winter only months away.[45]

Neither the economic crisis nor the popular ferment disappeared. One month later, another crowd stormed the tax offices at the customs barrier and attempted to burn the registers. Dumont St Priest, who had earlier rejected the idea that the bourgeoisie could incite a grain riot, now expressed amazement that 'rich and influential men now desire an anarchist uprising from which they would have the most to lose'; for a petition sponsored by a wholesale liquor merchant named François Villegoureix, who owed 500 francs in taxes, had demanded the abolition of indirect taxes. Dumont St Priest, one of the architects of the revolution in Limoges, now called for absolute order; the most prominent Orleanist official in Limoges now regretted some of the 'changes in ideas and hopes given birth to by the glorious revolution of July'.[46]

Contemporaries could agree that the revolution of 1830 changed political life in Limoges. Many bourgeois entered politics for the first time. Two-thirds of the new voters eligible in Limoges by virtue of the expanded franchise were *négociants*, *commerçants*, or *industriels*, although their holdings in land still often served as the basis for their tax contribution.[47] 1830 increased not only the political participation and power of the bourgeoisie in national and local affairs but also its self-awareness as a group of men of 'capacity' as defined by their income, business activity and contribution to the reputation of their city. During the restoration, most men of commerce were lumped together in the list of voters as *'négociants'*; now they were listed with greater precision by their actual occupation. One Jean-Baptiste Reix, for example, was now listed as *'entrepreneur des bains publics'* living on the exclusive Rue Banc-Léger, the sixteenth leading taxpayer in Limoges. These men elected Philabert Chamiot-Avanturier, merchant, as deputy in 1831. Many, grateful for the new government's assistance after the revolution, became the bulwark of the new regime. They were soon dubbed *'le juste milieu'* because they found in Orleanism a secure middle way between the restoration politics of entrenched and often unearned privilege, and any claims of their own social inferiors.

Second, the revolution curtailed much of the political influence of the church in Limoges. Bishop Prosper de Tournefort no longer had the ear of the prefect and was unable to influence local politics as before, although many in Limoges claimed that the church had not suffered enough. It was no coincidence that the popularity of the religious confraternities began to wane after the revolution and that several local festivals declined. The diminished influence of the clergy contributed to the ebbing of certain traditions, such as the fires of St Jean, the burning of mannequins hung from lanterns, wearing masks during the carnival, and others.

Third, the revolution enhanced the role of the municipal council, accelerating the development of municipal politics. Henceforth men of 'capacity' would elect their own representatives who were to occupy themselves with the town's business. The victorious bourgeoisie of 1830 was determined to create a more suitable urban environment. *Le Contribuable* expressed the prevailing sentiment that the restoration's lack of a coherent and progressive policy had taken its toll on Limoges and urged those who doubted this assertion to walk the streets of the city. Alluaud's administration turned its attention to public works, at least partially because the charity workshops provided the labour, but principally out of conviction. The municipal council began to meet more than three times as frequently as it had before the revolution, enacting a series of urban projects that had been awaited in vain during the restoration.

The wishes of the majority of the population were answered when François Alluaud and the municipal administration expedited the construction of a slaughterhouse south of the city, funded by a gift from the new monarchy – eager to please its constituents – and a large loan offered by local businessmen. After considerable bitter negotiation, the butchers finally agreed to slaughter in the new facility, although many of them clandestinely carried on their old ways. The task of cleaning up their street remained. The Champ de Foire was established, as the commercial bourgeoisie had demanded, in a more spacious location just above the Place d'Aîne instead of being moved to the bottom edge of town. There a new field was levelled and terraced by the unemployed workers enrolled in the charity workshops; the Champ de Juillet soon offered a garden and a place where the bourgeois National Guard, reconstituted after the revolution, could drill. The construction of an adjacent quarter, work on streets in the town and the first plans for a new bridge, the Pont de la Révolution, demonstrated that this and subsequent municipal administrations would be more attentive to the needs of Limoges than their predecessor had been.[48]

Yet within two months of the revolution, the authority of the 'victors of July', the conservative, now Orleanist, faction of the liberal opposition of 1827–30, began to be tested. The liberals of *Le Contribuable* posed a difficult challenge even more than the

riots of *le peuple* which could be put down by troops and the
National Guard; they attacked the 'men of order' – the Orleanists
– who carried on the business of government as if very little had
changed. They complained about the lack of a complete purge of
old Bourbon supporters: 'the same men who a short time ago,
adorned with white sashes, prostrated themselves before Monsieur
de la Bastide, now, wearing tricolour sashes, crowd around M.
Alluaud.' The municipal council, at least until the municipal
elections, was still largely composed of men who 'had been
devoted to every form of despotism', claimed *Le Contribuable*,
'and to all of the congregations'.[49] The new administration found
itself in the position of defending the clergy and its unpopular
bishop against popular disturbances; and it only grudgingly, it
seemed, convinced the ecclesiastical authorities to remove the
Mission cross in front of St Michel-des-Lions, when threatened by
menacing crowds.

Dumont St Priest now symbolized the *juste milieu* of Limoges,
which, having won its political rights, sought to make peace with
the supporters of the restoration and pull up the drawbridge
behind them in the name of order. To his opponents, the new
procureur général seemed to be 'one of those cold and egotistical
men who saw the July revolution as nothing more than a mine to
be exploited for the purposes of unlimited ambition'.[50] The left
assailed the new regime for ignoring the plight of the workers; but
Dumont St Priest was more concerned with repressing popular
disturbances through the use of the army and the National Guard
now drilling on the Champs de Juillet.

'The July revolution was begun and accomplished by the
popular classes', asserted *Le Contribuable*, 'this is a fact that no
one can deny.' The artisans of Paris had fought without recom-
pense; nothing had been done to alleviate the burden of taxes that
weighed on them. At the same time, '*le parti moyen*, or of the *juste
milieu* if you insist, although acting with little cohesion, has
profited from the influence that wealth makes possible'. Now they
blocked the full development of the consequences of a revolution
made, after all, by the people. The 'social question' was thus
raised; the most liberal faction of the bourgeoisie of Limoges now
proclaimed itself faithful to *le peuple*. Who could blame the poor
of Paris or Limoges – referring to the popular disturbances that
followed the revolution – for expressing their collective irritation
with the new regime and for now asking that 'we pay some more
attention to them'?[51]

Both Dumont St Priest and his liberal critics understood that continued riots accentuated the economic crisis by contributing to a lack of confidence. But they drew different lessons. While the former demanded order, *Le Contribuable* accused the ministry of contributing to the crisis of confidence through its heavy-handed policies of repression. Instead of encouraging positive action to develop commerce and industry, such as associations, the government prevented its citizens from exercising the liberty won in 1830. Voluntary associations could provide the means by which citizens could defend themselves against any attempts to curtail the free expression of their liberties, as the '*Aide-toi*' organization had been instrumental in mobilizing opposition to the Bourbons; at the same time, the Orleanists' critics on the left urged people to form *sociétés anonymes*, 'today the only means that one can apply successfully to undertakings of great public utility', that would facilitate the growth of the economy, helping business and workers alike. The new regime's reply, of course, was the repressive law on associations of 1834, aimed at political associations, but also contributing some suspicion of voluntary associations in general, despite the 'culture of capitalism' associated with the July monarchy.[52]

Frustrated by the failure of the new depositories of power to fulfil the promises of the revolution, Limoges's left liberals easily and quickly embraced republicanism. At the same time, they were influenced by Saint-Simonism, which, encouraging the free development of associations, trumpeted the march of economic and scientific progress and heralded the reign of producers. Republicanism, dissatisfied with arbitrary definitions of political 'capacity' based on the amount of taxes paid, and Saint-Simonism, emphasizing the full development of the economy based on a republic of producers, nicely complemented each other. The radical opposition thus condemned the bourgeoisie for not sharing a greater part of its profits with the workers who helped produce the sources of their wealth.

During 1831 and 1832 republicanism won a strong nucleus of supporters in Limoges, among them a 19-year-old lawyer named Théodore Bac who was establishing a reputation for himself as a brilliant orator; Bac would dominate the political evolution of Limoges for more than thirty years. The republicans patronized the workers, serving as their political tutors. At the same time, the warm reception given Saint-Simonians in Limoges in 1831 and 1833 indicated the link between utopian socialism and the emergence of republican opposition in the early 1830s.[53] The highly paid functionaries of the July monarchy, notably Dumont St Priest, were no better than the idle nobles and high clergy of the *ancien régime* and the restoration. The *juste milieu* had, in its own interest, left untouched the most fundamental economic problems, particularly that of taxation. It was not reasonable to tax the source of progress – the producers. Indirect taxes should be reduced, or even eliminated. The existing tax structure merely served to 'consolidate the regime of riots' by weighing so heavily on the poor that they rebelled, further disrupting commerce and industry. The answer was not the blind repression by armed troops or the National Guard, but fundamental changes in line with the accomplishments of the revolution.

By 1833, republican strength in Limoges was such that Dumont St Priest referred to the republicans as a political party. When the Orleanist Philabert Chamiot Avanturier was elected to the Chamber of Deputies, his election was greeted with shouts of 'Down with the *juste milieu!*' A strong republican tradition in Limoges was born. The workers, too, had begun to manifest an interest in republican politics. As in other French cities, the revolution of 1830 served as a catalyst for the rapid evolution of political ideas that followed. Orleanism quickly demonstrated that it had nothing to offer workers; they turned to republicanism, and, in the Second Republic, to democratic socialism.[54]

Three events in 1833 combined to demonstrate how quickly Limoges had changed in the short time since the revolution of 1830: a political protest, a strike and an angry confrontation at a church. First, Jean Scipion Mourgnes was appointed prefect of Haute Vienne. His name was already associated with the hard-line policies of Casimir Perier and his *administrés* knew in advance that the new prefect did not sympathize with the struggle of the Poles against the Russians. His anticipated arrival in Limoges angered the left; about sixty people streamed out of the Café Cornelet and gathered in protest across the square in front of the prefecture. The next night about 300 people poured into the Place St Michel at the news that the new prefect's coach would soon arrive from St Junien. When police dispersed the unruly crowd, it reassembled at the Place Royale, joined by sympathetic onlookers, and began to yell 'Down with *mouchards!*' The crowd ran to greet the carriage with rocks and stones as it descended the Rue Turgot. Gendarmes escorted the new prefect and his terrified aunt and niece from the coach; armed troops with fixed bayonets scattered the protesters after three legal warnings and arrested several people.

The disturbances continued the next day when the Haute Vienne's chief administrator went to the cathedral for a mass for those killed during the July revolution. There he heard only a chorus of shouts of 'Down with the prefect! Down with the tyrant of the Poles!' Only limited numbers of National Guardsmen, mostly government employees who dared not be absent, turned out as ordered. Officers, alarmed by a decline in discipline in the Guard, called a full review the following day to restore morale and counter the republicans with a show of force.[55]

The trial records from this seemingly minor protest reveals the event's significance: workers for the first time since the French revolution joined the radical bourgeoisie in Limoges, among whom clerks were prominent, in their republican protest. Those prosecuted included a commercial clerk (whose father, embarrassingly enough, served on the municipal council), a sabotmaker, a miller, an apprentice baker, two porcelain workers and Théodore Bac, who proudly declared to the court that he was both a Saint-Simonian and a republican. The participation of the miller and apprentice baker is also noteworthy, differentiating this event from the earlier popular disturbances after the July revolution, which were directed against millers and bakers. The trial, like other such legal proceedings during the July monarchy, played into the hands of the republicans by permitting them to publicize their own case against the government.

Limoges's first recorded strike followed several months later. The decorators, but perhaps also some turners and moulders, had formed the first mutual aid society in the city in 1829. Turners and moulders formed similar organizations during the first years after the July revolution. We can only surmise about the society's impact, but the timing of such an association fits the national pattern and again underscores the significance of the revolution for workers.

The porcelain manufacturers had been struck hard by the economic crisis that accompanied the revolution of 1830. As the industry began to recover slowly in 1832, they attempted to make up for lost profits by cutting by about 20 per cent the wages paid their skilled workers. In December 1831, shortly after the Lyon insurrection of silk workers had caused a stir among the workers, an anonymous letter to two porcelain workers allegedly tried to 'excite them to demand a raise in salary'. On 12 September 1833, after two of their comrades were fired, 200 turners and moulders struck in five of Limoges's eight factories. Letters seized by the police indicated that the Limoges workers had been exchanging information about piece-rates established in Paris and Vierzon. The workers demanded a return to the wages paid at the time of the revolution of 1830. Some workers left for smaller towns in the region to find work; others returned to work with a small raise, below that which they had demanded. Finally, in mid October, the manufacturers agreed to their workers' terms, and the strike was over. Shortly thereafter, groups of tailors, spinners and café waiters gathered to demand higher wages and a number of the former struck briefly. Was the example of the skilled porcelain workers consciously followed?[56] The corporate consciousness of workers in the same trades, visible in Limoges in the years following the 1830 revolution, evolved into working-class consciousness during the July monarchy; the frustration with the results of 1830 contributed in no small way, as workers came to confront the increasingly powerful bourgeoisie of Limoges.

In October 1833 a member of the National Guard killed himself, leaving his pregnant wife behind. A priest refused to bury him, which enraged the poor man's friends. The next day a large crowd transported the body to a church and, finding it locked, placed it on a table outside. Police reports paid particular attention to the fact that some workers from the faubourg Montmailler were among those shouting insults at the *curé* and demanding that the church be opened. The priest finally complied upon receiving instructions from the town hall, another indication of the reduced authority of the church in favour of secular authorities. The crowd poured into the church, the Guardsman was blessed and then buried, and the incident was quickly forgotten. But the attitude of the workers who participated in this event contrasted with that of 1828, when some of them had rushed to defend the Missions under attack from the anti-clerical 'calicots' of Limoges.[57]

François Alluaud had already resigned as mayor in August, also announcing that he would not seek election to the Chamber of Deputies. He was more interested in expanding his industry than in politics; his aged mother had urged him to withdraw from public life after his brother and a nephew had died the previous year, probably from cholera. But there was another reason for his decision. Alluaud had been disappointed and frustrated by the behaviour of a growing number of his fellow citizens. He complained of the embarrassing reception given the new Orleanist prefect: the 'large groups running through the town that had gathered at the Place de la préfecture' had yelled 'Long live the Republic!' and sung 'songs that recalled the most disastrous period of our Revolution, accompanied by dances not the less odious'. He had personally pleaded with the rebellious young bourgeois republicans and with the workers who now expressed an interest in politics, cautioning them against 'disorders that your inexperience will prevent from seeing in advance the implications.... I entreat you as a father, as a friend...'. Several days later he resigned. Several months later the prefect applauded his 'firmness' in the 'struggle with the striking workers'.[58]

A disturbance in which workers joined the radical bourgeoisie in political protest. A strike. The refusal of a priest to bury a man and an outraged crowd forcing authorities to have the church door opened. Small events in the history of nineteenth-century France. But these three episodes in 1833 were significant and symbolic moments in the political evolution of an industrializing city. Limoges had greatly changed in the five years that had passed between 1828, when François Alluaud's son Victor had had to petition a hostile Bourbon administration, still seemingly in the hands of the nobles and the clergy, in order to be declared eligible to vote in national elections, despite his wealth; and 1833, when his father resigned as mayor. Some physical differences in the city evinced a deeper and more meaningful process than they reflected. The Sunday strolls of the bourgeoisie were now likely to take place on the new Champ de Juillet, named after the month of the revolution, which included a *'jardin de plaisance'* and an elegant place to dance. There the new Orleanist prefect reviewed the bourgeois National Guard as townspeople watched. How different must have been the attitudes of the workers towards the Champ de Juillet, which they had built. Beyond some temporary employment, the revolution of 1830 had done nothing for them. Like the minority of radical bourgeoisie, they felt betrayed. Appropriately, it was at the Champ de Juillet in April 1848 that the workers met to formulate their demands and left to disarm the predominantly bourgeois National Guard. They, at least temporarily, conquered the field some of them had constructed eighteen years earlier.

Other physical changes were also significant. The crosses in front of the churches of St Michel and St Pierre had been removed, under the threat of being torn down by angry crowds, attesting to a marked decline in the influence of the church in local affairs. The Place Dauphine, from which had begun to extend the long faubourgs that became the locus of industry in Limoges and largely housed the working class, had become the Place de la Liberté. The first stone of the Pont de la Révolution, so named to reinforce the collective memory of what had changed in the city, was laid on 27 July 1832, as the 'three glorious days' were celebrated, but not by the now republican radical bourgeoisie and the workers.[59] The butchers had been forced into a new slaughterhouse, finally completed after years of discussions and postponements. Other improvements, such as work on new streets and the levelling of the old cemetery of the grey penitents, had been considered during the restoration. But these projects were fulfilled because of the outcome of the revolution, which brought a self-conscious bourgeoisie to political power, an authority soon disputed by the radical minority of their class and the workers. The transition from the noble Martin de la Bastide to François Alluaud symbolized for all limogeauds the evolution of their town. The ascribed honour of being designated '*une bonne ville*' denied Limoges on the several occasions when the town had applied, disappeared with the revolution. The mood of the bourgeois victors of 1830 was that the city could make its own way.

3 Charivaris, repertoires and urban politics

Charles Tilly

Mardi Gras and metaphor

In the little merchant city of Cholet, south of Angers, Mardi Gras of 1826 brought the usual public skits and satires. One of the tableaux of that year contained enough liberal politics to alarm the prudent subprefect. 'A feudal lord', he reported,

> who took the name of *Prince des Ténèbres*, arrived with a large entourage. They all wore hats in the shape of candle-snuffers. They bore two signs. On the one was painted an ass bearing a torch covered with a snuffer; on the four corners were painted bats. On the other one read LONG LIVE THE GOOD OLD DAYS. Others carried nighthawks and a gallows. Finally the bust of Voltaire appeared.

The players of Cholet put on two scenes. The first was the lord's marriage, at which the crucial ceremony was the reading of a long list of his feudal rights. The second, the trial of a vassal for having killed a rabbit. The vassal hanged. The royalists of Cholet were reported 'unhappy' with this insult to their cause and to the restoration regime.[2]

Cholet's Mardi Gras tableau was quite ordinary. So far as I know, it aimed at no particular lord and brought on no prosecution. The symbols – the torch of liberty snuffed out by feudalism, and so on – were clear and commonplace. Similar skits, parades and displays of readily identifiable symbols were standard components of nineteenth-century popular festivals. Yet to eyes which have become accustomed to the concrete, disciplined protests of our own time, the play of metaphor in such nineteenth-century political statements is odd, rather *folklorique*.

As Alain Faure has recently reminded us, the folklore of Mardi Gras survived the urbanization and industrialization of the nineteenth century. In 1830 and, especially, in 1848 carnival and revolution linked arms to dance in the streets. In the case of 1848,

Faure recounts the parade through Paris streets of sixteen cadavers of citizens killed during the first street fighting of February. He narrates the antic invasion of the Tuileries, which ended with the parading of the royal throne through the streets and its burning at the foot of the July column in the Place de la Bastille. He tells us of the hanging or burning in effigy of landlords who refused to delay collection of the second quarter's rent.[3] Pageantry and metaphor were very much alive.

Nor did they die with Louis Napoleon's snuffing out of the Second Republic. Faure describes the washerwomen's colourful floats, with decorations, costumes and elected king and queen; these things thrived with the growth of Parisian washhouses after 1850 and continued to grace the Parisian carnival up to the end of the nineteenth century. Then, however, they did disappear, despite the continuation of spectacular Mardi Gras parades. What happened? In essence, Faure argues that Parisian merchants and authorities appropriated the popular festival to make it safe and profitable for themselves, while parties and unions provided new opportunities for working-class collective action. The public life of the metropolis divided increasingly along class lines. The festival, Faure concludes,

lost its feeling of being a special event, a solemn or scheduled gathering of the collectivity, an immense show without audience or actors, without staging or spectators, where each individual plays his role and social classes reveal their character.[4]

The passage is reminiscent of Émile Durkheim's analyses of religious ritual and of the passage from mechanistic to organic solidarity. It parallels Michelle Perrot's argument that during the last decades of the nineteenth century the strike surrendered its popular spontaneity and creativity to the demands of bureaucrats and organizers. Protest, they tell us, was routinized.

For all its plausibility, Alain Faure's conclusion is not the only one possible. From the perspective of a superb connoisseur of the seventeenth century, for example, Yves-Marie Bercé has treated the decline of the festival as the result of a two-sided change: on the one side, the religious and civil authorities who wanted to impose decorous uprightness on the common people; on the other, the disintegration of the solidary rural community whose shared beliefs and daily routines served as bases for fêtes, for *révoltes* and for both at once. Unlike Faure, what is more, he considers the twin processes to have been well underway during the eighteenth century. The nineteenth century, in his view, saw no more than survivals of the rich old customs – with survivals in the distant countryside alone. Despite a common belief (shared with Michel Foucault, Norbert Elias and other sages of our time) in the imposition of discipline by sour-faced authorities, then, Bercé and Faure disagree on the timing, locus and mechanisms of the popular festival's disappearance.[5]

At the risk of appearing to be an incorrigible ditherer, I suggest that both and neither are right. The nineteenth century did indeed wreak a remarkable transformation of popular collective action, a transformation which did involve a certain sort of routinization. The forms of rebellion did diverge from the forms of celebration. An important source of these changes, however, was the decline of small, loosely corporate communities which had previously provided the chief frames within which ordinary people had formulated and acted on their grievances. Faure states the first part correctly, while Bercé gives us the second part. As both agree, capitalists, officials and organizers collaborated in creating larger, more specialized, more predictable and more impersonal means of collective action. As both suggest, France's growing cities formed the leading edge of these transformations of public life.

Nevertheless, these generalizations resemble the impressions of urban street life a traveller gets from a hovering helicopter: panoramic, and correct in many respects, but missing essential details – especially those which tell us how and why the participants are getting into the action. Beyond a certain point, furthermore, the idea of increasing rationalization, routinization and control mis-states the changes that were actually occurring. For the essence of the nineteenth-century transformation was not a downward slide from spontaneity to discipline but a shift from one organizational base to another. With the growing nationalization of political power, ordinary people fashioned new means of acting together on their interests. They created a new repertoire of collective action.

The metaphor is obvious, once stated: any group of people who have a common interest in collective action also acquire a shared repertoire of routines from among which they choose when the occasion for pursuing an interest or a grievance arises. The theatrical metaphor draws attention to the limited number of performances available to any particular group at a given time, to the learned character of those performances, to the possibility of innovation and improvisation within the limits set by the existing means, to the likelihood that not only the actors but also the objects and the observers of the action are aware of the character of the drama that is unfolding and, finally, to the element of collective choice that enters into the events which outsiders call riots, disorders, disturbances and protests.

Eighteenth- and nineteenth-century repertoires

The eighteenth century had its own repertoire. The anti-tax rebellion, the movement against conscription, the food riot, the concerted invasion of fields or forests were the most distinctive forms of revolt. But a great deal of relatively peaceful collective action went on either through deliberate (although sometimes unauthorized) assemblies of corporate groups which brought forth declarations, demands, petitions or lawsuits; or via authorized festivals and ceremonies in the course of which ordinary people expressed their grievances symbolically. As compared with other repertoires, this eighteenth-century array of performances had some special characteristics worth noticing:

a tendency for aggrieved people to converge on the residences of wrongdoers and on the sites of wrongdoing rather than on the seats of power (sometimes, of course, the two coincided);

the extensive use of authorized public ceremonies and celebrations for the acting out of complaints and demands;

the rare appearance of people organized voluntarily around a special interest, as compared with whole communities and constituted corporate groups;

the recurrent use of street theatre, visual imagery, effigies, symbolic objects and other dramatic devices to state the participants' claims and complaints;

the frequent borrowing – in parody or in earnest – of the authorities' normal forms of action; the borrowing often amounted to the crowd's almost literally taking the law into its own hands.

Note the political core of such apparently 'non-political' or 'pre-political' actions as riotous festivals. Access to land, control of the food supply, precedence among corporate groups and payment of taxes were the sorts of issues about which the users of the eighteenth-century repertoire were typically contending; they *were* the politics of the day. Crowd actions, furthermore, frequently were aimed at the local or regional authorities, and usually took them somehow into account. The politicization of the revolution did not really alter these characteristics. Instead, it increased the directness of the connection between local collective action and national politics. For a time, every food riot became an occasion for stating or using affiliations with political actors on a national scale. The eighteenth-century repertoire certainly differed importantly from the repertoire that emerged during the nineteenth-century era of national electoral politics. But it was only 'pre-political' by a standard which dismisses everything but national politics as insignificant.

The nineteenth-century repertoire looks more political to twentieth-century observers for two reasons: first, because it built on the national governments, parties and special-interest associations with which we are now so familiar; second, because once formed, that repertoire survived, with relatively little alteration, into our own time. To twentieth-century eyes, it therefore appears to be a 'natural' vehicle for political action. The repertoire that emerged during the nineteenth century included the electoral meeting, the demonstration, the strike, the rally and the complex of actions we call the 'social movement'. None of these was a standard way of struggling for power in the eighteenth century. All became standard during the nineteenth, especially during the years around the revolution of 1848.

With respect to changes of repertoire, the 1848 revolution mattered more than the period after its great predecessor of 1789. Much of the earlier revolution's popular collective action borrowed from the classic eighteenth-century repertoire: the price riot, the collective rejection of the tax collector, the invasion of fields or forests where use rights were contested, the ritual punishment (in effigy or in the flesh) of a malefactor, the turning of an authorized celebration or solemn assembly into an expression of popular support or opposition all continued during the conflicts of the revolution. To be sure, the revolutionaries innovated. In terms of form, for example, the marches of various revolutionary militias against their enemies and the turbulent meetings of popular committees, societies and assemblies had few pre-revolutionary precedents. In terms of content, the parades, festivals and ceremonies of the early revolution so altered the character of their *ancien régime* counterparts as to constitute a new creation. Yet the durable contribution of the revolution to the French repertoire of collective action was slight. Perhaps the main change in the repertoire from the 1780s to the 1820s was a general increase in the directness and explicitness of the connection between national politics and previously local forms of action such as the food riot and the charivari.[6]

Charivari in transition

The charivari? Social historians of France have recently paid plenty of attention to the old custom. I need only remind you of its main elements: the assembly of a group of local young people outside the home of an accused moral offender; the whistles, catcalls, mocking songs and thumped pots and pans; the payment of some sort of penalty by the offender. The 'young people' in question were often the same company of unmarried males who took responsibility for public celebrations such as Lenten bonfires, and who exercised control over the courtship and marriage of local youths. The offences were typically violations of rules concerning proper sexual behaviour, correct husband–wife relationships and appropriate matches, although many a charivari began when newlyweds neglected to treat the local young people to a celebration. The penalties imposed normally took the form of payoffs to the assembled youths. But they could, in the case of grave moral offences, extend to being obliged to leave town.

The charivari was the twin of another widespread practice: the serenade. The serenade was, in essence, an approving charivari; the same young people assembled outside the home of the object of their attention, but now they made a joyful noise and asked no penalty. One could become the other: if the targets of a charivari made proper amends, the occasion could well transform itself into a celebratory serenade.

Do not file charivaris under 'Quaint customs' or 'Trivia'. The people involved took them seriously, authorities watched them closely, and the actions of the charivari rested on well-established rights and privileges. Like other established forms of collective action, the charivari lent itself to manoeuvre and bargaining. In February 1836 the prefect of the Somme reported an interesting case in point:

Last December some rather serious disorders took place in the commune of Mailly, arrondissement of Doullens, when M. Goubet, a local land-owner, was going to marry the tax-collector's daughter. Following a time-honoured local custom, the young folks offered the groom a bou-quet, for which he declared he would pay 200 francs. These young folks weren't satisfied with that substantial sacrifice, and claimed that they should get 600 francs. M. Goubet turned them down. Outraged by that refusal, the young people insulted the future spouses with repeated charivaris, despite the fact that M. Goubet had shown his honourable and disinterested intentions by asking the commune's mayor to give to the poor the offering which the young people had refused. In order to prevent the charivaris planned for his wedding day, M. Goubet promised 395 francs. The disorders didn't stop until he had paid that sum.[7]

The final price, 395 francs, split the difference between the two sides' initial offers. No doubt the 'young folks' of Mailly drank away a major share of the tax they had levied on the marriage; in such cases, the money often paid for a gala bachelors' party. But the payment did have some attributes of regular tax; like many French taxes, it became subject to negotiation concerning the assessed person's liability. The charivari operated within a web of mutual obligation.

Under these circumstances, as Eugen Weber remarks in his chapter on charivaris, 'It is hardly surprising that they were also connected with politics'.[8] He might have said the same thing for the serenade. Yet from an eighteenth-century point of view, the political use of the charivari comes as something of a surprise. Before the revolution, the practice remained within the limits set by domestic morality. The heyday of the political charivari, so far as I can tell, ran from the 1820s to the 1850s, from the restoration to the beginning of the Second Empire. Then the custom faded fast.

Let us look at a characteristic case or two. In April 1830 Mme Lazerme, wife of a deputy, returned to Perpignan. The previous month her husband had voted against the Chamber's address to the king; the address had stated the majority's objections concern-ing the king's veiled threat to dissolve the Chamber and arrange the election of a group of deputies more to his liking. 'Many young people of an extreme Liberal persuasion', wrote the regional prosecutor, 'imagined that Mme Lazerme had gone to see her husband, and that she was bringing him back to town.'

A charivari had been organized to punish him for voting against the

Address. A large crowd went to his house. One heard innumerable rattles, bells, cymbals and whistles; for a long time they shouted wildly: A BAS LAZERME, VIVE LA CHARTE, VIVE LA LIBERTÉ!

The local prosecutor and a royal judge who lived nearby tried to calm the crowd but, reported the regional prosecutor, 'it was necessary to use threats and armed force to stop the charivari and break up the crowd'.[9] Two supposed chiefs of the gathering were arrested and committed for trial on misdemeanor charges. Two nights later, posters appeared in Perpignan, with tones of 1793: 'MORT AU TIRAN … PAIX AU PEUPLE … LIBERTÉ ET EGALITÉ … AU NOM DU PEUPLE FRANCAIS'.[10] When the accused ringleaders were convicted on 30 April, some of their friends posted a notice in these terms:

SUBSCRIPTION. All the young people of the city of Perpignan, motivated by feelings which are both honourable and patriotic, and wanting to show their whole-hearted commitment to the cause which led to the conviction of their Comrades, have opened a subscription to pay their fines. You can contribute any amount, no matter how small; every offering placed on the fatherland's altar is of equal value. The time has come for our unjustly insulted people to make known its feelings and the honour it bestows on those who make an effort to speed the complete development of our institutions and fulfil the great destiny of our beautiful country, orphan of its glory and widow of its liberties.[11]

The local prosecutor's attempt to convict the organizers of that collection, however, disintegrated when the chief prosecution witness changed his story. The prosecutor consoled himself, and his superiors, with the soothing thought that

the prosecution must have had a good effect, Monseigneur, in the sense that the defendants and the huge audience that attended the trial saw clearly that justice is ever alert and that if its efforts did not have the most desirable results this time, they would another time, if a few demagogues should again take a mind to incite disorder, by whatever means, in contempt and hate of the royal government.[12]

The Perpignan dossier contains the standard stuff of nineteenth-century political control. Its opening event was unquestionably some sort of charivari, right down to its organization by the city's 'young people'. Yet the whole series was just as unquestionably an everyday sequence in which an opposition group states its position and shows its strength by means of a public gathering, the authorities use the crime-control apparatus to strike at the opposition group and the opponents then mobilize around and against that attack on their position. In short, the charivari had become a means of conducting politics as usual in Perpignan.

Not far away, in Toulouse, a similar transformation was occurring. In late December 1831 crowds gathered near the house of the deputy, Amilhau. 'That riotous assembly [*attroupement*]', wrote the prefect, 'was the consequence of a plan for a charivari developed a few days ago when the news began to circulate that M. Amilhau was coming here.' The prefect was confident that the 'disorder' was 'the result of incitement by radical hotheads; Amilhau was the subject of a violent article published yesterday in *Le Patriote de Juillet*. The participants came 'mainly from the faubourg St Étienne' – that is from an old, comfortable inner-city area.[13] Again the deputy stayed away. Nevertheless, the crowd stoned the troops sent to disperse them and the troops arrested three ringleaders. Later the same day the prefect was promising to prosecute any further offenders 'with inflexible severity'.[14]

Between the charivari of Perpignan (May 1830) and that of Toulouse (December 1831), nineteen months and a revolution intervened.[15] If the July revolution had no visible impact on the charivari's form, it did influence the charivari's political content. For now the opposition consisted especially of Carlists and republicans, and the language of opposition took on the vocabularies of Carlism and republicanism.

During the next few years, the authorities of Toulouse were often busy snuffing out political charivaris. Political, or politicized: some began as standard moral confrontations but rapidly became occasions for the statement of political opposition. A case in point happened in April 1833, when a widower of the Couteliers quarter remarried. He began receiving raucous visits, night after night. 'Most of the people who took too active a part', reported the police inspector

were sent to police court. But that sort of prosecution was not very intimidating, and did not produce the desired effect. The disorders continued. One noticed, in fact, that the people who got involved in the disturbances no longer came, as one might expect, from the inferior classes. Law students, students at the veterinary school and youngsters from good city families had joined in; seditious shouts had arisen in certain groups, and we learned that the new troublemakers meant to keep the charivari going until Louis Philippe's birthday, in hopes of producing another sort of disorder. It was especially on the evening of Sunday the 28th of April 1833 that the political nature of these gatherings appeared

unequivocally. All of a sudden the song La Carmagnole and shouts of
VIVE LA RÉPUBLIQUE replaced the *patois* songs that were usually sung. It
was all the clearer what was going on, because the majority of the
agitators were people whose clothing itself announced that they weren't
there for a simple charivari.[16]

The city's young bourgeois, according to the police inspector, had
taken over the plebeian form of action, and had transformed it in
the process.

It took police, National Guards and line troops to break up the
crowds that evening. The unpopular wedding took place the next
day, but on the day after (30 April), the same people gathered at
the Place du Capitole to jeer the fireworks set off to celebrate the
king's birthday. Broken up by the police, they rushed to the Place
Saint-Étienne, then sped to the prefecture to demand the freeing
of the participants who had been arrested earlier. The police got
the gates closed just in time to prevent the demonstrators from
breaking in. Arrests made that night proved, according to the
regional prosecutor, that Carlists and republicans had joined
together in the 'seditious demonstration': 'Among six prisoners,
there were three from each party'.[17]

1833, as it happens, became a vintage year for political
charivaris in Toulouse. By the end of June the police inspector was
preparing for the arrival of three deputies in the city by organizing
a 'charivari service' whose task was 'to prevent both serenades and
charivaris'.[18] On 30 June, despite these precautions, a troop of
students and workers marched through the streets of Toulouse,
accompanied by musical instruments, singing the Marseillaise, and
shouting 'Vive la République'. 'It is all the more urgent to repress
these disturbances', the police inspector advised the mayor,
'because they could link up with the charivaris and celebrations at
the end of the month.'[19] and, if fact, both the Carlists and the
republicans of Toulouse continued to promote their causes by
organizing serenades and charivaris.

The charivaris of Perpignan and Toulouse were not 'great
events'. Nevertheless they have a twofold importance. First, they
show us local people using familiar means to accomplish new ends
and transforming the means in the process; by pushing the existing
repertoire to its limits, the people of Perpignan and Toulouse were
helping to create a new repertoire of collective action. Second,
they demonstrate that the authorities themselves felt hampered by
the partial legitimacy of the old forms; within limits, we hear them

saying, people have the *right* to serenades and charivaris; the problem is to keep serenades and charivaris from becoming something else, something political. That constraint of the authorities, in its turn, became an invitation to *charivariser* instead of turning to riskier forms of action such as the full-fledged demonstration. The same sort of advantage encouraged people of the July monarchy to take advantage of funerals, festivals and public ceremonies.

The nineteenth century's middle decades saw many more such occasions. At the time of resistance to the controversial census of 1841, another variant appeared in Caen. Guizot, then both minister of foreign affairs and member of the Calvados departmental council, came to Caen to consult with his colleagues on 23 August. That night the colleagues held a reception for Guizot at the prefecture. 'For several days', reported the local prosecutor,

people had been spreading the idea of a charivari. Toward nine o'clock a number of groups crossed the square at the Prefecture, let out scattered whistles and shouted – now and then when they were under cover – À BAS L'HOMME DE GAND, GUIZOT À LA POTENCE. Then they sang the Marseillaise, Ça Ira, etc. Two persons were arrested shouting À BAS GUIZOT. They were Lecouvreur, a baker's helper, and Legout, student pharmicist in the shop of M. Decourdemanche.

They were to be tried for 'public outrage'.[20] More crowds gathered in Caen's public squares the next two evenings, but the conspicuous stationing of troops around the city kept them under control.

What happened in Caen? Another banal encounter between the political authorities and the local opposition. This time, however, the prosecutor bemuses us by his adoption of the word 'charivari'; we would be less surprised if he called the event a *manifestation*. After all, the young people gathered at a public building rather than a private house, left their rattles and pans at home, and failed to state either the offence or the penalty they had in mind. Now, it is possible that the prosecutor wrote the word 'charivari' in gentle irony. I suspect, however, that the word was deliberate and, in its way, accurate: this was, indeed, a charivari on its way to becoming a demonstration.

One more case will clarify the transformation that was going on. We move forward to 1860, and another letter to the minister of justice from a regional prosecutor based in Montpellier:

A regrettable demonstration [i.e. *manifestation*] occurred in the commune of Mayreville, arrondissement of Castelnaudry (Aude), on the 22nd of July. About twenty people, professional marauders and poachers, got together at the news of the transfer of the communal game warden, the object of their dislike, and for good reason. They went through the streets of the village and stationed themselves in the main square, especially in front of the warden's house, singing the Marseillaise and other songs of seditious character, notably an anti-national and anti-patriotic patois hymn composed during the reaction of 1815 to celebrate the fall of the First Empire. They added verses stating a desire for the return of the Republic and making threatening references to the local authorities.[21]

No mention of the charivari in this account, yet some of the lineaments of the old form of reprobation are still visible. The celebrants take their places outside their enemy's home and sing proscribed songs to make their opposition unmistakable. Whether the participants were really professional poachers or simply run-of-the-mill village hunters, however, they now put their private hostility to the game warden into the idiom of national politics. If they had carried banners, signs or symbols of their political affiliation, in fact, we would have no trouble recognizing the event as a full-fledged political demonstration.

A new repertoire

The demonstration belonged to a new nineteenth-century repertoire. Before the nineteenth century, ordinary Frenchmen had often stated grievances or demands by assembling in some public place and displaying their commitment to their cause. If that were all it took to make a demonstration, then a host of food riots, tax rebellions, invasions of fields, actions against conscription and, yes, charivaris would qualify as demonstrations. But the specific form of action known in France as the *manifestation* differed from any of these elements of the *ancien régime* repertoire in several ways: occurring in a symbolically important public place, growing from an assembly which was called in advance by the spokesmen of some special interest, explicitly identifying the affiliations of the participants, broadcasting demands and grievances by means of placards, banners, pamphlets and other written communications. *Manifestants*, in other words, rarely gathered at private residences or at the sites of protested evils, seldom acted in the course of authorized festivals and rituals, did not usually involve a whole community, and employed colourful symbols and tableaux much less regularly than their eighteenth-century predecessors. The new way of acting together showed some signs of crystallizing during the revolution, but only became a significant and regular way of doing political business under the July monarchy, and only displaced its eighteenth-century predecessors around the time of the revolution of 1848.

France's cities led the introduction of the new repertoire. By and large, rural areas retained the eighteenth-century forms of collective action much longer than did urban centres. In the case of the charivari, Eugen Weber has found traces of the old form in remote rural areas well into the twentieth century. Those charivaris, furthermore, concern local moral matters, not national politics. 'Noticeably', reports Weber, 'the political charivaris were largely restricted to towns with a political public.'[22] They disappeared, Weber tells us, with the Second Republic. My own, less thorough, survey suggests the same conclusions: urban concentration, disappearance around 1850. The charivari's replacement, the demonstration, arose and flourished in cities, and assumed much greater prominence with the revolution of 1848.

Such a correspondence strikes us, in retrospect, as neat and plausible. Yet it raises a series of interesting questions to which I do not have the answers. In village France, well-established groups of young people – youth abbeys, bachelors' companies, and the like – typically bore the right and responsibility of organizing charivaris, just as they often played central parts in the ceremonies of Lent and Mardi Gras.[23] To what extent did those groups exist, and sustain the charivari, in urban neighbourhoods? As the charivari became politicized, did the youth abbeys lose their grip on the routine, or were they politicized as well? Did the rise of the demonstration signal the displacement, not only of the eighteenth-century forms of collective action, but also of the social structures which had supported the old forms? Neither police nor journalists nor folklorists provide us with the means to answer those questions. That is a pity, because a closer understanding of the changes in social organization accompanying the transformation and demise of the charivari would provide insight into more general nineteenth-century changes in routine community life – and into the 'routinization' of protest which Alain Faure and Yves-Marie Bercé portray.

The mid-century shift toward the demonstration paralleled the rise of other characteristic nineteenth-century forms of collective action: the strike, the electoral rally, the formal meeting and others. Together, these changes constituted the creation of a new repertoire – essentially the same repertoire of collective action that prevailed in the twentieth century as well. In this repertoire, self-selected special interests and formal associations played prominent parts. The forms of action in the repertoire overlapped or mimicked the forms of electoral politics: stressing the numbers and the commitment of a cause's supporters, enunciating whole programmes for change, rarely producing violence except when another party resisted the demands or attempted to block the show of strength. The authorities, in their turn, interpreted the repertoires in the light of electoral politics: anxiously scanning a demonstration, strike or protest meeting for signs of the involvement of major political blocs, counting the number of participants with care, maintaining voluminous dossiers on militants and ringleaders, attempting to divide the potential users of the emerging forms of action into acceptable and dangerous, into legitimate and criminal, and then to use force, espionage and the threat of prosecution to eliminate the unacceptable actors from the arena.

Over France as a whole, this reorganization produced a noteable shift in the occasions on which collective violence occurred. In Anjou, for example, a partial inventory of major violent events over the century beginning in 1830 runs like this:[24]

1832   Battles between Chouans and troops, National Guard or officials in Beaupréau, St Laurent du Mottay, Montrévault, Montjean, Bois de Freigné and la Chapelle Rousselin

1839   Food riots of various forms in le May, St Rémy-en-Mauges, Beaupréau, St Pierre Maulimart, la Chapelle-du-Genêt and Jallais

1842   Food riot in Beaufort

1846   Demonstrations at the conviction of food rioters

1847   Food riots and demonstrations about food shortages in Candé, Pouancé, Cambrée, Armaillé

1848   A journeyman's fight in Bécon and railroad workers' brawls in la Poissonnière

1855   A republican demonstration in Trélazé and Angers

1897   A demonstration of striking slateworkers in Angers.

1904   Mass resistance to the expulsion of the Capucines from schools in Angers

A similar compilation for Toulouse and the rest of the Haute-

Garonne takes the following shape:

1830   At the news of the July revolution in Paris, groups in Toulouse take to the streets, threaten the prefect and fight the police

1831   At the news of Warsaw's fall to Russia, groups attack printers and shout anti-governmental slogans in Toulouse

1834   A violent charivari in Toulouse

1839   A fight between two groups of workers, and an audience's tearing up of a theatre, both in Toulouse

1840   Invasion of communal woods by inhabitants of Pointis-Inard

1841   Two violent demonstrations against the census in Toulouse

1846   Another theatre riot in Toulouse

1848   Battles of inhabitants with forest guards in la Barousse and St Béat, barricading of mayor and purchaser of the forest in Signac, invasion of public building by radicals in Toulouse, parade of Legitimists in Toulouse, attacks on tax-collectors in Boissède and St Médard

1849   Attack on troops transporting prisoners and left-wing demonstration by National Guard company, both in Toulouse

1850   Left-wing demonstrations in Toulouse and Carbonne

1851   A politicized charivari in Aspet, and a linked demonstration for the release of prisoners in St Gaudens

1861   Violent strike in Gaud

1891   Violent strike in Toulouse

1898   Fight at a public meeting in Toulouse

1904   Violent strike in Toulouse

1922   Demonstration blocking the tramway in Boulogne

The regions of Angers and Toulouse provide an instructive contrast. Before mid century, Anjou produced nothing but guerrilla attacks and food riots, while in Languedoc primitive demonstrations oriented to national politics coupled with older forms of action oriented to local issues – notably the conversion of previously communal forests into private property. After mid century, in both regions, strikes and full-fledged demonstrations became the principal occasions for collective violence. In both Anjou and Languedoc, violent events concentrated increasingly in the cities. The people of both regions were shifting towards the nineteenth-century repertoire, but Anjou lagged behind Languedoc. The

nationalization and formalization of collective action occurred
earlier in Toulouse and its region. The differences, I think,
followed directly from Toulouse's greater and earlier integration
into national electoral politics.

The experience of Paris and the Seine confirms that sense of a
shift in the forms of contention during the nineteenth century. Too
much happened in Paris for a simple catalogue of the kind I have
presented for Anjou and Languedoc. According to my best
estimate, well over 500 major violent events occurred in the Seine
from 1830 through 1929. Table 4 therefore presents a rough but
relevant breakdown of the events. It classifies the major action out
of which the violence grew: a demonstration, strike or meeting; an
insurrection or rebellion – a direct effort to displace national
powerholders from their power; all other actions. Such a classification is bound to generate controversy, if only because it requires
some judgement of the intentions of the actors and banishes
indirect efforts to make revolution from the category of insurrection and rebellion. As a rough indicator of change, nevertheless, it
deserves examination.

What does the tabulation tell us? First – as gauged by the sheer
number of violent events – violence did not fade away with the

Table 4 *Per cent distribution of chief occasions for large-scale
collective violence in the Seine, 1830–1929*

Decade	Demonstration, strike, meeting	Insurrection, rebellion	Other	Total	Estimated number of events
1830–39	47	16	37	100	32
1840–49	47	4	49	100	51
1850–59	50	17	33	100	6
1860–69	68	0	32	100	48
1870–79	25	33	42	100	48
1880–89	63	0	37	100	64
1890–99	78	0	22	100	36
1900–09	83	0	17	100	96
1910–19	73	0	27	100	60
1920–29	75	0	25	100	96

Note: Since the count from 1861 onwards comes from the reading of materials from
a randomly selected three months per year, I have multiplied the actual count by
four to estimate the total number of events for those decades.

strengthening of the state and the formalization of political organization. On the contrary: the trend runs mildly upwards. Second, insurrections and rebellions nevertheless disappeared from France's collective violence after the Commune of 1871. (To be sure, if we ran the time line forward to the 1940s and 1950s, we would see that the insurrection's death was only temporary.) Third, the proportion of large, violent events which began as demonstrations, strikes or meetings was already substantial by comparison with Languedoc or Anjou in the 1830s, and rose to become the great majority by the end of the century. The cluster of insurrectionary actions (and of attacks on troops and authorities, hidden in the 'other' category) around the Commune makes the only important break in that trend.

The third point is the one to which the earlier discussion had already led us: the emergence and conquest of a new repertoire of collective action. Concretely, the public meeting, the demonstration, the strike, the electoral rally and related forms of action became the standard means by which people gathered to make claims and voice complaints. At the start of the nineteenth century, these forms had been rare or non-existent. As in so many other things, Paris led the way to their creation and adoption. The focal point of national politics, the metropolis provided the central stage for the new repertoire.

Yet the transformation was national in scope, more complex and comprehensive than simple invention at the centre and diffusion from there. We have seen the same process working through the temporary politicization of the charivari in widely separated parts of France. The evidence concerning the charivari is precious. French contenders took a form of action which had long served the purposes of moral control, and employed it in the arena of national politics. The charivari as such did not survive as a political instrument, but gave way to the *manifestation* – more or less the demonstration we know today. The shift from the classic charivari to the classic demonstration entailed important changes: a move from the home of an offender to a symbolically significant public place, the creation of a public identity for the demonstrators, the explicit display of demands and complaints in words, songs, placards and symbols, the deliberate dramatization of the numbers and determination of the demonstrators, and so on. In its few decades of prominence, the politicized charivari had the advantages of familiarity and of a quasi-legal existence. But it gave way to a very different form, one more closely aligned with a world of special-purpose associations, electoral politics and parliamentary decision-making. It gave way to a whole new repertoire. The case of the politicized charivari and the demonstration also reminds us to take the metaphor of repertoire seriously. On the one hand, we are dealing with learned behaviour, with performances about which the performers care, with more or less self-conscious choices of means to defend or advance shared interests. While the participants may be passionate and the outcomes of their actions unanticipated, they know, in general, what they are doing. The vocabulary of 'riot' and 'protest', often applied to the sorts of collective action we have been examining, serves mainly to obscure and demean the interest of the actors in their action. On the other hand, the learning involved permits plenty of innovation and tactical manoeuvring. The rough separation of meetings from demonstrations from strikes, and so on, should not blind us to the frequent combinations and compromises among elements of the repertoire. Nor should we ignore the trial and error by which ordinary people modify a well-known form such as the charivari only to drop it later when it proves ineffective or costly. Repertoires include more than set-pieces, fixed for ever.

Does it make any difference, in the last analysis, what forms of collective action ordinary people have at their disposal? I think it does. The existing repertoire defines the room for manoeuvre people have between their own shared interests and the opportunities or threats presented by the surrounding world. The fit may be good or bad on either side – the existing repertoire may, for example, be fairly effective for those who use it, yet poorly matched to a particular group's actual interests. The range covered may be narrow or broad; some groups and eras have impoverished repertoires, others very rich ones. The shift from the eighteenth-century repertoire to its nineteenth-century counterpart may well have cost ordinary French people some of their ability to articulate their interests at a local level in a differentiated, effective way, while enhancing their ability to make themselves heard in national politics. The shift seems to have entailed their abandoning common use rights and the priority of local communities in the control of their own resources. It appears to have committed them to a world in which numbers and formal organizations count. The nineteenth-century repertoire rests on the premises of possessive individualism, of capitalism, of a strong, centralized state, of electoral politics. The change in repertoire did not, to be sure, cause these profound alterations of social life. But it was both cause and effect of people's changing ability to exert control over the basic transformations affecting the quality of their lives.

4 Proto-urban development and political mobilization during the Second Republic

Ted W. Margadant

The relationship between cities and the countryside is a fundamental theme of modern French history. Whether analysing the expansion of agricultural markets and the spread of industry, the diffusion of new mentalities and new patterns of social life, or the participation of ordinary Frenchmen in elections, revolts and revolutions, historians have compared developments in urban and rural society. Their comparisons have served either to explain conflict between cities and the countryside, or to account for the integration of urban and rural communities into a national market and a national political system. Not surprisingly, historians of the *ancien régime* have emphasized urban–rural differences, while historians of the Third Republic have called attention to the growing influence of cities over the peasantry. In the .former period, only a few cities had large numbers of inhabitants, and the vast majority of the French population resided in the countryside. The interests of these peasant producers clashed repeatedly with the claims of government tax-collectors, landlords, tithe-owners and grain speculators, who used coercive methods in order to channel rural produce into urban markets. The results were economic conflict, cultural cleavage and political antagonism between urban elites and rural populations. By contrast, cities in the latter period were increasing rapidly in size and attracting an ever larger share of the nation's population. Aided by steam-powered transport, cheap newspapers and a powerful nation-state, cities became regional centres of French society, whence urban fashions and ideas spread to rural communities. No longer were the inhabitants of the countryside impoverished, isolated and hostile to outsiders. Peasants in the villages were becoming Frenchmen in the nation.[1]

Between the stark misery of the countryside in the *ancien régime* and the increasing prosperity of the Third Republic stretches a century of economic expansion and political upheaval. At first glance, it might appear that the dynamic forces unleashed during this age of the French and industrial revolutions had only a negative impact on the peasantry: new modes of industrial production competed successfully with rural handicrafts; wider markets for foodstuffs benefited urban consumers at the expense of the rural poor; and modern political institutions strengthened the power of Paris and other cities over the countryside. Peasants often resisted these centralizing tendencies in the economy and the state, but their reactionary protests could not halt the process of urbanization. When the profits of market agriculture and industrial employment did bring rural communities into positive contact with cities, such peasant rebellions ceased. That food riots and tax revolts swept the countryside as late as the 1840s may be taken as proof, in this view, of how painfully French peasants adjusted themselves to the growth of a market economy and an urban society.

A closer examination of socio-economic change and rural politics during the first half of the nineteenth century suggests a different interpretation of the relationship between urbanization and the peasantry. The concept of urbanization generally implies a concentration of economic activities within cities as compared with small towns or villages. Yet French cities were not the only communities experiencing economic vitality in the age of the early industrial revolution. The labour force of small towns and villages could be fed more cheaply than workers in the cities, due to the high cost of transporting grain from rural producers to urban consumers. Differential labour costs encouraged French manufacturing to expand along 'proto-industrial' lines in the countryside throughout the century from 1750 to 1850. Alongside this burgeoning rural industry, cash-crop agriculture also became more important, as peasants marketed regional specialities such as wheat and sugar beets in Picardy, livestock and dairy produce in Normandy, wine in lower Languedoc and raw silk in the Cevennes. Agricultural commodities, like textile goods, entered the trading system of French cities by way of country towns and bourgs. Although miniscule in size by modern standards, these marketing centres were essential components of regional and inter-regional trade, and many of them contained growing numbers of merchants, craftsmen and shopkeepers, who mediated between the rural economy and urban commerce. Their population growth and economic specialization might be described as 'proto-urbanization', by analogy with the process of 'proto-industrialization'. Just as production expanded through dispersed rural activity, so commerce proliferated in small towns and bourgs. These 'proto-urban' communities exercised some of the secondary and tertiary functions which characterize modern cities, while retaining close ties to agriculture and peasant society. As central places in rural marketing systems, they played a strategic role in economic and social development.[2]

Small towns and bourgs were no less important in the political life of rural France between the *ancien régime* and the Third Republic. To begin with, their elites of landlords, merchants and professional men exercised administrative patronage over the peasants of nearby villages. A central location in rural marketing gave 'bourgeois' families in many country towns a claim to political leadership which they fought hard to preserve and extend once peasants acquired voting rights. Second, the craftsmen and labourers in proto-urban communities depended to some extent on the market-place for employment and foodstuffs. The greater their vulnerability to economic crises such as food shortages, the more they were inclined to lead protests against grain speculators or tax-collectors. Social conflicts which appeared to divide urban and rural populations often united the lower classes of marketing centres and surrounding villages in common defence of the local standard of living. Finally, the residents of towns and bourgs were setting an example for peasants whenever they formed organizations, competed in elections or participated in demonstrations. If they founded a religious brotherhood or a political society, they might persuade the peasants who frequented their market to do the same. If they supported a candidate for election or organized a protest demonstration, villagers could be useful recruits to their cause. By bringing peasants into a social and political system based on central places, proto-urbanization facilitated the regional diffusion of organizations and the regional mobilization of manpower. It set the stage for the political struggles of the nineteenth century, when elections, demonstrations, and revolts involved large numbers of peasants as well as townspeople.[3]

If the general process of market development encouraged peasant participation in politics, regional variations in the importance of cities, towns and bourgs had a significant impact on the scale and direction of rural mobilizations. On the one hand, large cities such as Paris and Marseilles had closer commercial relations with nearby towns than with more distant trading centres in the countryside. Small towns and bourgs often preserved considerable economic autonomy in their relationship to cities. On the other hand, country towns themselves had more active contact with nearby villages than with peripheral bourgs, which often possessed markets of their own. Entire regions differed with respect to the degree of centralization in urban commerce and the extent of dispersal in rural trade. In like manner, some political movements were relatively centralized and others very dispersed in mid nineteenth-century France. By examining in more detail the urban networks and marketing systems of France during the July monarchy, and by reviewing some evidence about regional politics during the Second Republic, it is possible to compare the structural conditions which favoured mobilizations around cities, small towns and rural marketing centres. Events such as the National Guard mobilizations against Parisian workers during the June Days, the republican insurrections against Louis Napoleon's coup d'état, and the peasant revolts against the 45 centimes tax reflected three distinct patterns of proto-urbanization and politics:

1 centralization in regions where towns mediated between conservative elites in the cities and peasants in the countryside;
2 aggregation around small towns and bourgs which embraced the cause of a democratic and social republic in alliance with nearby villages;
3 fragmentation in protest movements which peasants organized exclusively on the basis of rural marketing networks and social relationships.

Behind the political upheavals of the Second Republic were important differences in the regional interaction between cities, small towns and dispersed rural communities.

Urban networks and peasant markets

By modern standards, the French urban network during the July monarchy was underdeveloped in its scale and regional organization. Using the census of 1841, which listed all agglomerations containing at least 1500 inhabitants, it is possible to distinguish between several categories of urban and proto-urban communes: large cities (agglomerated population of at least 50,000), small cities (10,000–49,999), towns (3000–9999) and large bourgs (1500–2999). While these demographic thresholds are overly precise, they do reflect the relationship between population size and spatial influence within the hierarchical structure of cities, towns and bourgs. Cities benefited from their size and strategic location on waterways and all-weather roads to engage in long-distance commerce between regions; towns had similar advantages over bourgs with respect to the commerce of sub-regions, or *pays*; and large bourgs had better opportunities for local trade than small *bourgades* or village centres.[4] The national and regional data in Table 5 give a synoptic view of urban dispersal in the early nineteenth century: the 22 regions of the nation (grouping 86 departments) contained only 9 large cities in 1841, as compared with 92 smaller cities, 419 towns and 981 large bourgs. In most regions, towns and bourgs contained a larger share of the population than cities, and only in the Paris region did a single city dominate the entire urban and rural population. Table 5 shows that proto-urban communes, ranging in size from 1500 to 3000 agglomerated inhabitants, were especially common in the regions of Alsace, Languedoc, the Nord and Provence, where upwards of one-third of the population resided in cities, towns and large semi-rural agglomerations. By contrast, towns and bourgs were relatively rare in regions which had a low percentage of urban residents, such as Auvergne, Bretagne and Limousin. These regional variations confirm the numerical preponderance of towns and bourgs as compared with cities in the urban networks of early nineteenth-century France.

The small size of many urban centres made it difficult to construct a rational hierarchy of administrative centres during the French revolution, and the cities and towns which became departmental or *arrondissement* capitals varied greatly in their economic influence. Some departments, such as the Basses-Alpes and the Gers, did not contain a single city with over 10,000 inhabitants in 1841, and even their towns were scarcely distinguishable, with one or two exceptions, from the bourgs of more densely populated areas. More commonly, several cities and towns shared commercial influence within a department, while one of them took precedence in administrative matters. The symmetry and spatial uniformity of the administrative hierarchy should not be confused with a full-developed central place system, based on commerce and trade. Only in the densely populated plains of north-eastern

France and the Mediterranean coast were long-distance commerce, mediated through cities, and short-distance trade, mediated through towns and bourgs, sufficiently well integrated to constitute a multi-layered urban trading system. Particularly in the rugged highlands and foothills of central and southern France, cities were rare and towns differed in size and commercial importance because of local economic circumstances, such as a fertile valley, a navigable waterway, an industrial resource, or a tradition of skilled craftsmanship. Such regions had only the rudiments of a central place system, based on the intermediary role of some towns in trade between small areas. In a few departments, administrative towns had no special role to play in commercial wholesaling, and their retail trade appealed mainly to a local clientele. Elsewhere, lesser ranking towns performed the same commercial functions within their *arrondissement* as the prefectoral capital did within its immediate hinterland, and trade between these sub-regions was less important than exports to cities outside the department. Even where the prefectoral capital was a city of between 20,000 and 30,000 inhabitants, its merchants had to contend with the commercial initiative of smaller towns, whose traders might benefit from special transport facilities to other cities. Generally speaking the economic links between cities and towns were diffuse, and departmental capitals were often no more centrally located than country towns in the commercial networks of the rural economy.[5]

Just as towns often exercised some degree of economic independence in relationship to cities, so bourgs and villages frequently possessed their own marketing opportunities outside the towns. Proto-urbanization involved the multiplication of rural markets, especially in regions where peasants resided in small, dispersed settlements. Transport costs were much higher in the outlying villages and hamlets of such regions than near the larger towns, which benefited from waterways, canals or all-weather roads. It is these differential transport costs, combined with rural population growth, which explain why commercial expansion in the urban trading system stimulated peasant demand for local marketing facilities. Peasants wanted access to the urban trading system, which provided a final destination for their cash crops and handicrafts, but they also wanted to minimize their transport costs. What better method than to attract itinerant merchants to local markets and fairs, whence goods could circulate at the expense of

Table 5 *Urban population, by region (1841)**

	Totals		Cities, at least 50,000		Cities and towns, 10,000–49,999		Towns, 3000–9999		Towns and bourgs, 1500–2999	
	No. of communes	% total population	No. of communes	% total population	No. of communes	% total population	No. of communes	% total population	No. of communes	% total population
High urban										
Alsace	107	35	1	5	2	3	28	12	76	15
Languedoc	119	36	0	—	8	12	32	12	79	12
Nord	155	35	1	4	10	11	28	7	116	13
Paris region	81	60	1	44	4	4	26	7	50	5
Provence	107	38	1	9	4	7	30	10	72	12
Average urban										
Bourgogne	79	16	0	—	5	4	23	6	51	6
Centre	67	18	0	—	6	7	19	6	42	5
Champagne	62	21	0	—	6	7	18	7	40	7
Corse	11	19	0	—	1	6	4	8	6	5
Haute-Normandie	47	26	1	8	3	5	19	9	24	4
Lorraine	83	19	0	—	4	6	19	6	60	7
Picardie	95	19	0	—	4	5	15	4	76	10
Rhone-Alpes	95	21	1	6	7	6	22	4	65	5

Low urban

Aquitaine	46	13	1	5	4	2	15	3	26	3
Auvergne	42	12	0	—	4	4	14	4	24	3
Basse-Normandie	37	14	0	—	4	5	17	7	16	2
Bretagne	41	11	0	—	3	3	19	6	19	2
Franche–Comté	30	13	0	—	1	2	14	7	15	4
Limousin	23	10	0	—	1	3	8	4	14	3
Midi-Pyrénées	84	14	1	2	4	2	24	5	55	5
Pays de la Loire	49	13	1	3	4	3	16	4	28	3
Poitou–Charentes	41	12	0	—	5	5	9	3	27	4
National totals	1501	21	9	4	92	5	419	6	981	6

*These regional groupings of departments are based for convenience on the urban planning regions of the Fifth Republic.

Source: 'Tableau des Communes ayant une Population totale de trois mille âmes et au-dessus, ou une Population agglomérée de quinze cents âmes et au-dessus, annexé á l'ordonnance royale du 20 décembre 1842', *Bulletin des Lois*, 9th series (January–June 1843), pt. 1, bulletin no. 974, pp. 59–109.

middlemen instead of producers? These local markets also enabled peasants to purchase foodstuffs in times of shortage and to provide their households with cloth, hardware and other necessities. Thus, commercialization resulted in the dispersal of markets into the countryside instead of their concentration in cities and towns.[6] By the 1850s weekly markets were taking place in around 3000 different communes, and fairs were being held in around 7000 communes, at a time when fewer than 650 agglomerations would qualify as cities or towns by modern criteria of size, economic function and social structure.[7] Many large bourgs did claim the rank of towns by virtue of their weekly markets and their administrative services as cantonal seats, but a great many small bourgs also held markets, and thousands of villages held fairs, often several times a year. These markets and fairs constituted an interlocking system of weekly, monthly and seasonal gatherings for small-scale producers and traders who resided in the countryside, beyond daily contact with towns.

The system of periodic marketing existed everywhere in France, and towns often did play a vital role in its operation. Town councils financed sheltered grain markets, or *halles*, where urban consumers had first priority each market day; they sponsored open-air markets, where peasant women sold fresh vegetables and poultry to local housewives or servant girls; and they advertised the town fairground, where peasants flocked each season to spend a bit of their hard-earned cash to the delight of local innkeepers and shopowners. Most towns were growing in size and purchasing power during the first half of the nineteenth century and their leaders pressed new claims on the government for additional market days and fairs. This sometimes led to conflicts with rural communities, which wanted their own periodic markets, and town fathers could be just as concerned to defend their commercial privileges as to expand their marketing opportunities. None the less, the agricultural and proto-industrial growth of the July monarchy favoured the co-ordination of urban and rural markets, with merchants and consumers in the towns attracting the surplus produce of the bourgs and villages. Typically, rural markets were held early in the week and town markets on Friday or Saturday, so that dealers could transfer surpluses from the former to the latter.[8]

Not all towns were equally successful, however, in co-ordinating the trade of the countryside. In regions where peasants frequented a great many village fairs and where towns were rare in comparison with small bourgs, much country trade slipped out of the hands of townspeople. Livestock dealers in western France were especially willing to bypass towns in order to purchase cattle, horses, mules, sheep or pigs from peasants who resided in dispersed settlements, and rural fairs enabled these buyers and sellers to bargain publicly at a competitive price. As temporary markets, held on a seasonal basis, fairs did not require elaborate installations. A large field, located on the outskirts of a settlement near a road, was a more convenient site for a cattle or horse fair than a congested urban square, surrounded by permanent shops. The success of a livestock fair depended on the quality and quantity of the animals brought to the site, not the numbers of people who resided there. As long as dealers and herdsmen were willing to travel over mediocre roads to make a sale, villages could compete successfully with towns for the honour and profit of holding livestock fairs. Throughout the hedgerow country (*bocage*) of western France, and in the uplands of central and southern France, transport conditions did favour rural fairs, which existed in hundreds of small bourgs and villages. The seasonal rhythms of pastoral agriculture and the specialized requirements of different kinds of livestock also favoured the dispersal of fairs into the countryside, where peasants could meet frequently to balance the size of their herds against the supply of feed, the need for draft animals and the opportunity for cash. Fairs were also social events which brought pleasure and amusement to rural populations. While town fairs might offer a greater variety of entertainments than village fairs, innkeepers and beverage-dealers always did a thriving business wherever peasants gathered to buy and sell livestock. Some landlords and officials even complained that fairs had become so numerous that peasants were wasting valuable work days attending them for fun instead of profit. Indeed, by the 1850s many *arrondissements* of western France were holding over 100 fairs per year for every 50,000 inhabitants, which meant that peasants could attend several fairs each month during the spring and autumn seasons, when fairs were especially common. By multiplying the occasions for peasant sociability, fairs helped to compensate for the rarity of towns and large bourgs in regions where many people lived in hamlets or isolated farmsteads.[9]

Peasants were much more likely to frequent urban markets and fairs in the river valleys and plains of north-eastern and Mediterranean France, where densely populated villages surrounded numerous towns and large bourgs. Although many small markets also existed in regions such as Picardie and Haute-Normandie, supplying rural textile workers with grain, fairs tended to be concentrated in the towns and large bourgs. These urban fairs, which often lasted two or three days at a time, offered a variety of manufactured goods to rural consumers. By attracting traders in cloth, household goods and farm tools as well as livestock, fairs in north-eastern France reinforced the role of towns as trading centres for the peasantry. Towns and large bourgs had an even greater role to play in the marketing networks of Mediterranean France, where many peasants resided alongside artisans and landlords in 'agro-towns' or 'urbanized villages'.[10] Nearly all of the weekly grain markets of lower Languedoc and lower Provence took place in communes which had over 1500 agglomerated inhabitants in 1841, and so did many of the fairs in these regions. The mountainous interior of the south-east, with its poor roads and relatively low population densities, had more village fairs, but there, too, weekly markets tended to be concentrated in towns and large bourgs. While departments such as the Vendée and the Mayenne, in western France, had over ten times as many rural marketing centres as towns, departments such as the Drôme and the Var, in the south-east, had only two or three times as many markets in bourgs as in towns. Furthermore, many peasants in the foothills of the Alps and the Massif Central, like their counterparts in the Mediterranean plains, produced cash crops such as wine or raw silk which entered the hands of urban merchants more quickly than the livestock raised by peasants in western France. Peasants in the south-east were also more likely to purchase cloth or hardware imported by urban wholesalers and sold in retail shops. Local trade in Provence and Languedoc, like long-distance commerce, depended to a greater extent on towns and large bourgs than on periodic markets in the countryside.[11]

Regional variations in the importance of urban and rural marketing centres can be examined systematically on the basis of evidence compiled during the Second Empire, when national dictionaries and departmental *annuaires* published lists of communes which held weekly markets or fairs. For comparative purposes, it is useful to calculate the density of urban communes in each region, as well as the ratio of rural to urban markets and fairs. Table 6 presents a measure of urban density, based on the census of 1861, which defined 'urban communes' as settlements with at

Table 6 *Urban densities and the ratio of market centres and fair sites to urban communes*

	Density of urban communes in 1861* (per 10,000 km²)	Market centres/ urban communes† (ratio)	Comunes with multiple fairs/urban communes** (ratio)
Low urban densities			
Aquitaine	11	259/45 (5.8)	324/45 (7.2)
Auvergne	15	129/40 (3.2)	232/40 (5.8)
Bourgogne	16	162/49 (3.3)	331/49 (6.8)
Bretagne	14	166/38 (4.4)	242/38 (6.4)
Centre	14	199/54 (3.7)	216/54 (4.0)
Champagne	16	132/42 (3.1)	159/42 (3.8)
Franche-Comté	15	68/24 (2.8)	167/24 (7.0)
Limousin	11	66/19 (3.5)	156/19 (8.2)
Midi–Pyrénées	15	207/68 (3.1)	541/68 (8.0)
Pays de la Loire	14	320/46 (7.0)	229/46 (5.0)
Poitou–Charentes	10	137/37 (3.7)	309/37 (8.4)
Moderate urban densities			
Basse-Normandie	21	144/38 (3.8)	101/38 (2.7)
Haute-Normandie	34	131/40 (3.3)	84/40 (2.1)
Languedoc	29	96/81 (1.2)	130/81 (1.6)
Lorraine	20	112/47 (2.4)	104/47 (2.2)
Picardie	29	173/56 (3.1)	133/56 (2.4)
Provence	28	82/79 (1.0)	140/79 (1.8)
Rhone–Alpes	26	221/83 (2.7)	440/83 (5.3)
High urban densities			
Alsace	85	62/74 (0.8)	59/74 (0.8)
Nord	92	115/113 (1.0)	90/113 (0.8)
Paris region	63	98/75 (1.3)	58/75 (0.8)

*'Urban communes' are communes with an agglomerated population of at least 2000 in 1861.

†Market centres are communes which held a weekly or bi-monthly market in the 1850s.

**Communes with multiple fairs are communes which held fairs for at least three days per year in the 1850s.

Sources: The area of each region has been calculated from departmental data published in Charles A. Pouthas, *La Population française pendant la première moitié du XIXème siècle* (Paris 1956), pp. 222–3; the tabulations of market centres and fair sites are based on departmental data published in *annuaires* of the 1850s and in Adolphe Joanne, *Dictionnaire des Communes de la France* (Paris 1964); communes with at least 2000 agglomerated inhabitants in 1861 are listed in a 'Tableau' published in *Le Bulletin des lois de l'Empire française*, 11th series (first half 1862), main pt, vol. 19, pp. 190–268.

least 2000 agglomerated inhabitants. The 1156 'urban communes' of mainland France (excluding Corsica) in 1861 have been used to estimate ratios of rural to urban markets in each region. Table 5 classifies this regional data on the basis of low, medium and high urban densities, and it confirms the importance of dispersed rural markets and fairs where these densities were low. The ratio of fair sites to urban communes was very high throughout the west, and low in the Paris basin, the industrialized regions of Alsace and the Nord, and much of the south-east. Where agricultural prosperity, industrial activity, good roads and waterways, and traditional settlement patterns favoured a dense array of towns and large bourgs, peasants were never far from an urban market or fair; where economic and social conditions resulted instead in a low density of urban agglomerations, peasants were still able to exchange goods, but now they relied to a greater extent on rural markets and fairs. Market densities varied much less than urban densities in mid nineteenth-century France. While periodic markets everywhere performed similar functions for the rural populations, exchange relationships between towns, bourgs and villages differed significantly between regions and *pays*, depending on the proximity of peasant communities to specifically urban markets.

Patterns of political mobilization

The political geography of France during the Second Republic mirrored in important respects the spatial dimensions of its economy. At the national level, politicians needed to control the cities which dominated large-scale commerce and administration, beginning with Paris. The June Days marked a crucial shift of urban power from the revolutionary to the counter-revolutionary camp, due to the alliance of bourgeois leaders in Paris with National Guard units in other cities and towns. National Guard mobilizations were especially common in regions of northern and western France, where the 'Party of Order' subsequently triumphed in the elections of May 1849. Further to the south, however, many towns escaped the influence of the counter-revolution in Paris, and republicans often succeeded in maintaining their popularity after the June Days. Electoral success in departments such as the Drôme and the Gers depended less on national propaganda against urban workers than on local appeals to the interests of artisans and peasants. Here republican towns supplied nearby bourgs and villages with leadership, and 'democratic-socialists' obtained substantial rural as well as urban support in 1849. The trading areas of small cities and towns in south-eastern France became especially important when republican militants, known as Montagnards, began organizing 'secret societies' to defend universal suffrage and social democracy in 1850–1. Insurrectionary resistance to the coup d'état of Louis Napoleon often involved Montagnard networks which extended outwards from a small town or market bourg to nearby villages. Within these trading areas, peasant bands usually expected to join forces with townspeople, although troops and gendarmes sometimes put them to flight instead. By contrast, the 45 centimes tax revolts of 1848–9 were exclusively confined to peasant marketing networks and social relationships. Towns ignored or opposed these rural protests, which expressed the solidarity of village communities against government tax-collectors, magistrates and gendarmes.

Cities became the strategic centres of counter-revolution in June 1848, when over 100,000 National Guardsmen from the provinces joined government forces in Paris to crush a working-class uprising. This officially sponsored mobilization took place in an atmosphere of social as well as political crisis, and it revealed the determination of urban elites throughout northern France to defend private property and social order at all costs. Merchants and shopkeepers shared the fears of industrialists, bankers and large landowners that socialist agitators were perverting workers with slogans such as 'the right to work'. Financial panic and industrial depression, both precipitated by the February revolution, made these fears a reflection of social reality in working-class communities, such as the neighbourhoods of eastern Paris or the industrial suburbs of Rouen. Yet even in small towns and market bourgs, where most workers remained deferential to local employers, rumours of demonstrations in Paris stimulated a reactionary frame of mind among local notables. Why should unemployed artisans in the nation's capital receive special rights and privileges, such as the expensive system of outdoor relief known as the national workshops? When conservative politicians and newspaper editors, who had extensive influence in regions near Paris such as Normandy and Champagne, began exploiting these bourgeois resentments, the stage was set for a brutal confrontation with Parisian workers. In this struggle, the bourgeoisie which moved within the commercial orbit of Paris had much better communications over long distances than the working class, which possessed strong local solidarity but little capacity for regional or national action. Urban elites commanded not only the heights of the local social structure; they reached outwards to control the commercial and administrative networks which brought cities and towns together in northern France. This made them formidable opponents, once they had recovered their nerve and had resolved to halt the drift towards 'anarchy' and 'socialism' in the streets of Paris.[12]

Fighting began on Friday morning, 23 June, when workers rebelled against a government decree abolishing unemployment relief in the national workshops. The Parisian National Guard split along class and neighbourhood lines, with bourgeois units in the west joining the army while more popular battalions to the east defected to the rebel side.[13] It soon became apparent, however, that National Guardsmen from the provinces would support the cause of order without equivocation. At 5 p.m. several hundred volunteers from Rouen arrived by train at the St Lazare, determined to repeat in Paris their performance two months earlier, when they had smashed an insurrection of factory workers in their own city.[14] This was the avant-garde of a much larger force from the department of the Seine-Inférieure, organized at Le Havre as well as Rouen and including contingents from twenty towns and market bourgs, such as Yvetot and Forges-les-Eaux. Official orders from the minister of the interior to the prefects of the Seine-et-Oise, the Somme and the Loiret sparked similar mobilizations in the cities of Versailles, Amiens and Orléans, whose Guardsmen reached Paris on Saturday. That afternoon, General Cavaignac, the new head of government, issued a call to arms in the provinces: 'The National Guards of several cities have already arrived; their example must be imitated.'[15] Messages travelled swiftly by government telegraph to prefectures in the departments, and within a few days large numbers of National Guards were on the move from cities such as Besançon in Franche-Comté, Troyes in Champagne, Cherbourg in lower Normandy, Tours in the valley of the Loire, and Rennes in Brittany. Each city appealed in turn to smaller towns and market bourgs for help, and eventually National Guard detachments from over 300 urban agglomerations and proto-urban marketing centres took arms. Nearly all of these units came from regions to the north of the Massif Central and the

Rhône River valley, with especially numerous contingents from areas traversed by the new railroads and steamboats which linked Paris to its hinterland. Not every departing column actually reached Paris, and many arrived after the four-day insurrection had ended, but their enthusiasm gave aid and comfort to men of order throughout the north of France.[16]

Although urban elites led the National Guard mobilizations of June 1848, many rural notables also marched to Paris. For example, the 1500 volunteers from the department of the Manche included 'many landlords, lawyers, doctors and farmers.... Almost all the old nobility of the country had taken up arms on this occasion and formed part of the column'.[17] Workers in provincial cities were much less likely to muster ranks in the National Guard, a bourgeois institution before 1848 from which they were commonly excluded even after the February revolution. Popular participation in the mobilizations came instead from small towns and bourgs where artisans resented the competition of urban factory workers or where wealthy landowners commanded the allegiance of local communities. Even peasants from the villages joined some of the battalions which departed from country towns, and their medley of local dialects impressed Alexis de Tocqueville, who described in his memoirs the hazards of walking in the streets at night during the June Days: 'Everyone was stopped who left his house without a pass or an escort. I was constantly stopped on my way and made to show my medal. I was aimed at more than ten times by those inexperienced sentries [often National Guardsmen], who spoke every conceivable accent; for Paris was filled with provincials, who had come from every part of the country, many of them for the first time.'[18] National Guardsmen from over 100 small marketing centres and villages experienced this curious initiation to Parisian life, and many more bands of gun-toting peasants dispersed after marching to a nearby town. The tocsin rang throughout the countryside around Pontivy (Morbihan), and entire villages took arms in the plain of St-André (Eure-et-Loir), to the north of St Quentin (Aisne) and around Châlons-sur-Marne (Marne). Some of these rural mobilizations resembled the Great Fear of 1789, as rumours travelled from village to village that brigands – this time Parisian workers instead of aristocrats – were about to arrive. In the aftermath of the June Days, movements of panic spread through large areas of the Île-de-France, Normandy, Champagne and Picardy, as if to confirm that upper-class fears of social revolution were shared by rural audiences in the hinterland of Paris.[19]

The repression of the June Days foreshadowed the triumph of the Party of Order in the legislative elections of May 1849, when voters in nearly every department of northern and western France gave majority support to a coalition of Orleanists, Legitimists and Bonapartists. True, some National Guardsmen who marched to Paris had republican convictions, and many more agreed that the Constituent Assembly, whose authority rested on universal adult male suffrage, deserved conditional support. Yet the violence of the uprising reinforced the conservative backlash which had already begun in northern France, and most of the cities and towns that sent National Guardsmen to Paris in 1848 became organizational centres for anti-Republican electoral campaigns in the following year. These campaigns received support from journalists in small towns such as Château-Thierry and Soissons as well as from newspaper editors in cities such as Amiens and Rouen. Well-financed electoral committees, led by rich businessmen and landowners, sponsored politicians who had been *grands notables* during the July monarchy. These conservative spokesmen tried to associate republican reformers with socialist revolutionaries, and they played upon the social prejudices of townspeople and villages against big city workers, who seemed to threaten the jobs of local artisans and the food supply of local consumers. Some areas of western France which contributed manpower to the National Guard mobilizations had witnessed a rash of food riots in 1846–7, when craftsmen and peasants had opposed grain exports. Merchants and landowners had no reason to favour such popular protests, which threatened their own interests, but they were willing to capitalize on the social tensions which food riots revealed between Paris and the countryside. It is noteworthy that the few towns that developed left-wing sympathies after helping to repress the June Days were located in wine-producing districts of Burgundy and the Jura, or in the lumbering, metal-working or cattle-raising districts of central France. Grain-producing areas of northern France constituted a political as well as an economic region during the Second Republic, where urban elites were quick to mobilize support against republican slates of candidates in 1849, just as they had marched against Parisian insurgents during the June Days.[20]

A different pattern of political mobilization existed at the end of the Second Republic, when Louis Napoleon's coup d'état of 2 December 1851 precipitated armed revolts in the provinces, involving over 70,000 men. Now the focus of attention shifted from northern to southern France, and from cities to the countryside. At first glance, the popular uprisings which greeted news of the coup d'état resembled the *Jacqueries*, or peasant revolts, of late medieval times. Bands of villagers marched on the towns, brandishing pitchforks and staves. Angry crowds assaulted and murdered gendarmes. Bourgeois families cowered in their homes or fled in panic. Yet peasants did not rebel independently of towns in 1851, nor did they lash out blindly against the social order. They took arms in response to the appeal of republican militants in the towns and market bourgs, who had already converted them to the cause of the democratic and social republic. Many of these militants belonged to the Secret Society of the Mountain, or the Montagnards, a para-military organization which had established hundreds of branches in villages of the Midi during the preceding two years. Montagnard societies had also spread into the countryside from towns of central and south-western France during this period. Now Montagnard leaders assumed responsibility for organizing armed resistance to the coup d'état. Their movement was not centralized in cities, but it was not scattered randomly through the villages either. The peasant bands which sprang into action in 1851 were marching to the towns and bourgs that already served as organizational centres for the Montagnards. In these urban and proto-urban centres, craftsmen, shopkeepers and cultivators from as many as 20 to 30 different communes came together in large aggregations, numbering between 1000 and 2000 rebels. Even larger columns of insurgents confronted troops and gendarmes in a few departments, following the successful juncture of rebels from several towns and their respective hinterlands. Only in relationship to Paris and other large cities did the insurrection of 1851 seem dispersed in backward villages where ignorant peasants shared a violent hatred of the outside world. From the perspective of towns and bourgs, resistance to the coup d'état was a well-organized effort to join forces with nearby villages in defence of the republic.

The largest rebel town was Béziers, a subprefecture in the Hérault with around 20,000 inhabitants. Béziers ranked as a city by virtue of its size, wealth and long-distance commerce in distilled wine, or *eau de vie*, but its population included several thousand agricultural labourers and their families. Most of the landlords, merchants, shopkeepers and craftsmen who resided in town also depended on the wine industry, whose price fluctuations brought prosperity or depression to Béziers and its region, known as the Biterrois. Prices fell dramatically after the February revolution and remained low until after the coup d'état, discouraging landlords from paying high wages to agricultural labourers, and reducing local demand for goods and services. When republican militants at Béziers introduced the rituals of the Montagnards in 1850, they emphasized agricultural issues and succeeded in recruiting large numbers of peasants within a 16-kilometre radius of town. Their underground network emerged dramatically on the night of 3 December 1851, when messages from Béziers alerted Montagnard leaders in the countryside of an impending 'armed demonstration' at the subprefecture. Around 1000 peasants from twenty bourgs and villages of the Biterrois marched to the old cemetery on the outskirts of town, where they joined as many as 2000 townspeople at daybreak, 4 December. The Montagnards advanced through the streets in military formation, led by artisans and vineyard workers from one of the urban neighbourhoods, the quartier Saint-Jacques. Entering the square in front of the subprefecture, they collided with a detachment of 100 soldiers, who fired point-blank into their ranks. Eight rebels died on the spot, and the column disintegrated, as peasants cried out, 'We've been betrayed, we've been deceived.... The men from the villages only came to help.' In the momentary chaos, an angry crowd assaulted two bourgeois pedestrians back on the St Félix square, killing one of them, but soon everyone fled. It was a tragic climax to the Montagnard movement, which exposed hundreds of peasants in the Biterrois to arrest and deportation in the following months.[21]

In most of the other departments which had extensive resistance to the coup d'état, small towns played a vital role in mobilizing rural manpower. Typically, these rebel centres had several hundred men employed as independent craftsmen and shopkeepers, alongside some industrial workers, agricultural labourers or lumbermen who depended on wages for a living. Fluctuations in the export market had an immediate impact on the wage-labourers and an indirect influence on the living standards of everyone, including artisans and peasants who resided in nearby villages and traded with the townspeople.[22] At Dieulefit, for example, a textile town of 4000 inhabitants which spearheaded the insurrection in the Drôme, the justice of the peace reported in 1848: 'The importance of existing industries is such that whenever there is unemployment, for whatever reason, a general malaise is felt throughout the canton.'[23] Economic interdependency facilitated a common political awareness that low taxes, cheap credit and full employment would benefit town and countryside alike. So did the temporary depression which affected agriculture as well as industry during the Second Republic. Economic factors were less important, however, than shared political consciousness, which depended on the organizational dynamics of the underground itself. Montagnards succeeded in translating historical, cultural and social forces into a specific movement, with recognized leaders, rituals of affiliation and forms of solidarity. Once launched, their societies provoked haphazard and ineffectual police repression, which in turn stimulated popular opposition to the government. Out of these political tensions came the resolve of militant minorities in the towns to mobilize in arms against the coup d'état. Having already recruited peasants to the underground, their mobilizations naturally acquired a regional dimension. Thus, hundreds of peasants answered the call to arms which Montagnards made from small towns such as Dieulefit, Clamecy (Nièvre), Manosque (Basses-Alpes), Apt (Vaucluse), Brignoles (Var) and Vic-Fezensac (Gers).

Montagnards who resided in market bourgs and other agglomerated settlements within the countryside also took an active part in the insurrection. The populations of these proto-urban communities, which ranged in size from several hundred to a few thousand inhabitants, had direct influence over the peasants who frequented their shops, either on market days (in regions with dispersed settlements), or throughout the week (in regions with an agglomerated habitat). At cantonal seats such as Bourdeaux (Drôme) and St Sauveur (Yonne), where tradesmen and artisans were prominent leaders of the underground, crowd demonstrations against the coup d'état rapidly attracted peasant bands from nearby communes. Montagnards at Bourdeaux had already alerted villagers to take arms as soon as they heard the church bells ringing, while those at St Sauveur took advantage of a local fair to muster rural support.[24] In both cases, the political enthusiasm of artisans in the bourgs had a contagious influence on peasants in the villages. This pattern of centripital movement also existed in smaller agglomerations which functioned as communal centres for dispersed rural populations. At Roussillon, for example, a Provençal commune with a central village of 461 inhabitants and numerous farmsteads with 1023 inhabitants in 1851, artisans in the village organized the insurrection.[25] Led by a young barber named François Bourne, the Montagnards of Roussillon gathered excitedly on 7 December at a republican *cercle* (club) and sent messengers to their affiliates in the countryside. When they appeared with their weapons the following morning at the village schoolhouse, their public mobilization set an example for the peasants on the farms. Most of the able-bodied men in the commune joined the column of between 130 and 150 rebels which Bourne commanded, as he later admitted, 'in my capacity as the chief of the secret society of Roussillon'.[26] Few Montagnard leaders were so frank about their role in the insurrection, but in many areas militants in the bourgs and village centres were responsible for recruiting peasants in the hamlets and farmsteads.

Although small towns, bourgs and other 'central places' in rural society usually provided critical leadership and manpower for the insurrection, the scale of popular mobilizations also depended on *local* solidarity within peasant communities. Montagnard societies derived strength from traditional institutions of sociability, such as the village youth group, the country inn and the neighbourhood *veillée* or *chambrée*. In like manner, rebel bands developed momentum in December 1851 by appealing to the social loyalties of their recruits. By force of example, they tried to draw all the men of the community into the general current of revolt. Imitation became compulsory, as crowds demanded that everyone march, regardless of their political opinions. This pressure for unanimity reflected the economic solidarity of the peasantry in villages which claimed collective rights of usage to forests and waste lands. Communal mobilizations also expressed the collective identity of rural populations, based on shared symbols of authority and traditional forms of action. Thus, peasants gathered in front of the church at the sound of the tocsin, displayed the tricolour flag and paraded to the beat of the village drummer. Many rural crowds tried to act in the name of the commune, and some village bands sought municipal patronage or established 'revolutionary commissions' in order to legitimize their authority. The ethos of communal solidarity often enabled Montagnards to mobilize nearly unanimous support from 'the men' (*les gens*) or 'the young men' (*les jeunes gens*) who resided in rural communes. As the mayor of Cliousclat, a small village in the Drôme, reported with astonishment, 'The male population of the commune, with the exception of a few old men, the sick, and the children, all departed; the commune was left in the hands of God.'[27] By transforming the political movement of the Montagnards into a social movement of entire communities, peasants brought thousands of rebels into the field against the coup d'état.

The peasant tax revolts of 1848–9 revealed a similar pattern of communal solidarity, but these earlier protests occurred in isolation from towns and rarely involved villages which supported the republican cause. Nearly all of the 45 centimes tax riots were located in the uplands and valleys of the south-west, where peasant communities shared a long tradition of resistance to taxation. Historical analysis of these protests has focused attention on the economic misery and cultural backwardness of small-holding peasants in regions such as the Midi–Pyrénées and the Limousin.[28] Yet the most serious tax revolts did not originate in isolated villages whose 'closed economies' suffered from chronic shortages of cash. Extensive and determined resistance took place in districts where peasants customarily sold wine, attended livestock fairs or depended on seasonal migration to supplement farm incomes. Scattered protest also broke out in more isolated villages of the Massif Central, but concerted mobilizations among several neighbouring communes generally presupposed mutual involvement in periodic markets and fairs. It was the small scale and dispersed location of trading centres, not their absence, which imposed an upper limit of a few thousand demonstrators to these mobilizations. Nowhere in the turbulent areas of fiscal protest did local cities and towns draw the rural populations into urban marketing networks. Protest, like trade, coalesced around country bourgs before converging, in haphazard manner, upon small, administrative towns, where sooner or later troops arrived to rescue government officials and bourgeois citizens from crowds of angry peasants.[29]

The most obvious cause of these tax riots was popular outrage at the arbitrary fiscal policies of the new republican government. Against a background of collapsing markets for wine and other cash crops, official in Paris suddenly announced a 45 per cent increase in the land tax. Despite promises that exemptions would be granted to the destitute, administrators tried to collect the entire surtax at once, violating the customary procedure of permitting payment by instalments. Credit facilities rarely existed for small farmers in the south-west, so peasants had to borrow money at usurious interest rates or plead destitution. Not surprisingly, rural municipalities claimed that no one could pay, and even large landowners denied having any cash reserves. Faced with the ill will of entire populations, tax collectors used coercive methods in order to obtain cash from the villages: they sent bailiffs to seize the property of recalcitrant landowners, or they threatened to billet soldiers in every house. It was this policy of compulsory enforcement, applied in many districts of the south-west, which aroused general indignation and which precipitated crowd violence. At the sight of a bailiff preparing to carry away someone's valuables for public auction at a nearby town, neighbours would sound the alert, the church bells would ring, and a vociferous crowd of men, women and children would chase the intruder out of the village. For example, when a bailiff appeared on 8 November 1848 at Tillac (Gers) to expropriate the horse and the clock of a local peasant, an armed gathering of 400–500 inhabitants forced him to abandon the property and flee for his life.[30] Such was the standard form of the rural tax riot in 1848.

Alongside dozens of sporadic protests against fiscal repression, eight tax revolts achieved enough momentum to challenge the military power of the government. Located in the plains of the Charente Inférieure, the valleys of the Basses-Pyrénées, the Gers and the Haute-Garonne, and the plateaux of the Aveyron, the Creuse and the Lot, each of these uprisings began in response to the threat of arrests, each involved co-operation among neighbouring rural communities, and each resulted in armed confrontations with magistrates and gendarmes.[31] At Malabat (Gers), for example, nearby villages helped muster 3000 armed men on 6 June 1848 to prevent gendarmes from making arrests after the local inhabitants rioted against a bailiff. This mobilization had been preceded by talk of a tax strike at the market town of Miélan (the cantonal seat for Malabat), and magistrates later claimed that peasants from several villages had drawn up a 'treaty' of mutual assistance after a by-election held in town. The gendarmes retreated to Miélan with large numbers of peasants in pursuit, and they did not venture forth into the countryside again until massive troop reinforcements arrived.[32] An equally resolute crowd gathered at the bourg of St Bonnet (Charente-Inférieure) on 30 October 1848, when gendarmes tried to arrest a tax resister during a local fair. Led by their mayors, over 1000 men from several villages marched to the cantonal seat of Mirambeau, where they demonstrated against magistrates, shouting 'Down with the 45 centimes tax!' 'Down with the Republic!' and 'Long live the Emperor!'[33] More violent protest began in the canton of Gourdan (Lot) on 19 January 1849, when the tax collector brought forty troops to make arrests at the village of Nozac. Peasants were accustomed to attending fairs in the villages near Gourdan, and they rapidly mustered reinforcements to assault the soldiers, who opened fire and killed one demonstrator before retreating to town with nine prisoners. A hostile mass of between 1200 and 1500 men advanced to the rescue, and they swept into Gourdan, stoned the subprefecture, and clamoured for the release of their compatriots. Pusillanimous magistrates reached a hasty verdict of acquittal, and the peasants returned home in short-lived triumph: the following day, hundreds of troops arrived from the city of Cahors to restore order.[34]

This same cause of rural solidarity against repression brought tragedy to villagers near the small prefectoral capital of Guéret (Creuse), where gendarmes jailed four peasants on 15 June 1848, one of them for writing a placard threatening taxpayers with death, and the other three for protesting his arrest. Ironically, this was the only cause where republican political clubs linked townspeople and villagers, but club leaders played a subordinate role in the revolt, which developed spontaneously after angry women in the commune of Ajain appealed to their menfolk for help against the gendarmes. Responding to the tocsin, men from the hamlets of Ajain hurried to the village centre, while messengers sought help from neighbouring communes. A force of several hundred men assembled at Ajain, forced the priest to join them, and marched toward Guéret in disorderly fashion, parading a flag which bore the inscription, 'Our prisoners or our blood'. Arriving on the outskirts of town, they expected support from the National Guard, the firemen and the workers. Instead, they found 450 Guardsmen defending the town, along with thirty soldiers, two brigades of gendarmes and a company of firemen. A peasant deputation entered town to negotiate the release of the prisoners, but they returned empty-handed. Shortly afterwards, panicky National Guardsmen opened fire on the front ranks of the demonstrators. Twelve peasants died on the spot and another four suffered mortal wounds. The rest tried to flee, but some were captured, and a total of sixty-four suspects, most of them cultivators and artisans from hamlets near Ajain, were eventually prosecuted.[35] This violent confrontation symbolized the antagonism between town and countryside which often favoured Bonapartist politicians in areas of the south-west where peasants took arms against arbitrary tax collectors, ruthless bailiffs and implacable gendarmes.[36]

This analysis of urban networks and political movements during the Second Republic has emphasized regional variations in the role of cities, towns and bourgs in mobilizing the peasantry. Inter-regional commerce, centralized in cities, and local trade, dispersed in a multitude of country markets and fairs, were growing simultaneously in the decades preceding the outbreak of the February revolution. Where the expansion of commerce and trade brought into existence a modern urban network, as it did in the Paris basin, political movements mirrored the preponderant influence of cities. In much of France, however, conditions of transport and communication did not yet favour the close integration of small trading centres with large regional capitals. The diffusion of marketing and craft production into small towns and bourgs – the process of proto-urbanization – reduced the economic isolation of the peasantry without increasing the direct influence of cities over rural populations. In south-eastern France, where many peasants resided in large agglomerations or frequented markets in the towns, they derived ideological inspiration and organizational support from republicans in these central places. The rural populations of the south-west, where settlements and markets were often dispersed throughout the countryside, were more likely to participate in village tax riots and were less enthusiastic about the republic. Once formed during the proto-urban phase of French economic and social development, regional political cultures would persist long after armed revolts disappeared from the French countryside. Politicians in small towns and bourgs did not await the transport and communications revolutions of the twentieth century in order to mediate between the nation-state and rural society. In some regions they were already performing this task, for either counter-revolutionary or republican goals, by the mid nineteenth century.

5 Industrialization and republican politics: the bourgeois of Reims and Saint-Étienne under the Second Empire

David M. Gordon

The period of industrial growth that followed the establishment of the Second Empire profoundly changed the composition of provincial bourgeois elites, and so affected the political development of France for the rest of the century.[1] The displacement by merchant *notables* of the noble and clerical elites that had dominated many towns under the *ancien régime* in the period of the revolution and early nineteenth century was followed by a second major shift of power after mid century, caused by the development of mechanized manufacturing and heavy industry. The development of factory industry produced a new group of industrial capitalists who came to dominate the economic life of many provincial towns, while threatening the economic position of the traditional bourgeois manufacturing elites dependent upon artisan labour. As the political ambitions of the industrial bourgeoisie increased with their economic influence, members of this group came into conflict first with the older provincial elites who had occupied local offices since the revolution, and then with the imperial government, which was unable to provide a sufficient number of offices for these politically ambitious men. The political dissatisfaction of wealthy industrialists came to dominate bourgeois political life during the last years of the empire, and played an important part in rallying provincial bourgeois support for the Third Republic in 1870–1.

The political evolution of provincial France from the Second Empire to the Third Republic must take into account the economic rivalries that affected town life in this period. The most important agents in France's economic development were the wealthy bourgeois groups who controlled the nation's capital resources. This study investigates the economic and political changes that transformed the bourgeois elites in two industrializing provincial towns, Reims and Saint-Étienne. This group, which in the 1840s can be identified with the electoral lists of the *monarchie censitaire*, had dominated provincial town life under the July monarchy through the control of local capital resources as well as their monopoly of the suffrage. Having been temporarily eclipsed under the Second Republic, the provincial elites were able to regain their local influence under the Second Empire, and their position was strengthened in the 1850s and 1860s by the appearance of a new industrial leadership in their ranks. For the working class, the acceleration of industrial development and the gradual transition from artisanal to factory work marked a weakening of organized political activity in the 1850s and 1860s, a period of political transition from the traditional artisan radicalism manifested in 1789–99, and in the revolutions of 1830 and 1848, to the new labour politics of the 1870s and 1880s. But for the *notables* industrial development, which coincided with the period of European economic prosperity that E. J. Hobsbawm has aptly called 'the age of capital', allowed them to strengthen their economic and political position, while remaining the directing force behind industrialization at the provincial level, and the chief arbiters of provincial political life.[2]

The economic history of the bourgeoisie through the 1850s and 1860s has been studied here through the *mutation après décès*, the probate of wills maintained under the Second Empire, which allows a careful examination of the economic affairs of the elite by providing a detailed list of industrial investments.[3] This source, which has already been used by Adeline Daumard in her studies of the nineteenth-century French bourgeoisie, reveals the changing pattern of capital investments by this group during the crucial period of industrial transition that began under the empire.[4] While the French bourgeoisie had traditionally invested almost exclusively in small family businesses or real estate, a growing number after 1852 abandoned their traditional fear of investment in limited liability companies, and poured their funds into large stock companies. It thus became possible to mobilize national capital resources for the construction of large mechanized factories, which transformed production in many of France's traditional artisanal industries, and for the rapid development of heavy industry.[5]

One of the arguments of this essay is that the traditional economic 'balance of power' within provincial economies was seriously altered by the creation of joint stock companies, which put vast capital resources in the control of a new group of industrial entrepreneurs. The development of joint stock companies reduced the economic influence of the provincial mercantile bourgeoisie, whose limited capital resources had been sufficient for the operation of relatively small-scale businesses based upon artisan labour. With the increase of mechanized production under the Second Empire in key sectors of the French economy such as textiles and heavy industries, the differences on a provincial level between the older type of mercantile capitalists and the newer industrial elite became very important. The traditional business operations of putting-out merchants, dependent upon the work of independent artisanal craftsmen to whom they supplied raw materials and whose finished product they sold, began to be replaced by a factory labour force concentrated in more heavily capitalized manufacturing plants.

The economic struggle in the provinces between industrial capitalists and the more traditional mercantile manufacturers became a major theme of provincial economic life in this period of industrial transition. The *mutation après décès* provides important insights into the extent of this conflict by indicating the degree to which the traditional manufacturing groups became supporters of the new factory system through the purchase of industrial shares. The greater willingness of the mercantile group at Reims to invest in factory production compared with that at Saint-Étienne suggests the existence of important differences in regional investment patterns which affected the degree of economic integration between the two groups. This, in turn, suggests that similar differences might be expected to occur widely throughout provincial France, colouring the political as well as economic development of many manufacturing towns.

Economic rivalries within the bourgeois elite also affected the shape of political life under the empire, and the *mutation après décès* may be used to explore the relationship between economic rivalries and the development of provincial politics. One of the most important factors under the empire was the apparently paradoxical role that industrial capitalists played in the political opposition to the government. French governments throughout the nineteenth century had been faced with the problem of dealing with younger generations of politically ambitious men, with the last years of the restoration being a case in point. But the empire was faced by the 1860s with a uniquely powerful group of wealthy industrialists whose ambitions brought them into conflict first with

the older mercantile bourgeois elite which had traditionally mono-
polized local offices, and then with the imperial government,
which was unable to provide the new elite group with a sufficient
number of places. The degree of bourgeois opposition in different
towns was affected by local conditions, including the levels of
economic integration between the older mercantile elite which
supported the government and the newer industrial group. The
greater economic integration of the two groups at Reims helped
moderate the political opposition of that city's industrial woollen
manufacturers, while the financial autonomy of heavy industrialists in the Loire contributed to their more vigorous attacks both on
Saint-Étienne's mercantile elite and the government which supported them. The success with which the imperial government
maintained the support of the industrial group, which Theodore
Zeldin has suggested was a major problem for the empire in the
1860s, can therefore be properly explained only through an
understanding of the regional differences in economic development under the empire.[6]

Reims and Saint-Étienne have been chosen for this study of local
politics because their contrasting but typical economies underwent
considerable changes in this period of industrial expansion. Other
manufacturing centres, including Roubaix, Elbeuf, Rouen and
Mulhouse, underwent similar changes. Both cities were the sites of
important traditional artisanal industries, Reims being an ancient
centre of the French woollen trade, while Saint-Étienne was one of
the nation's most important centres for the manufacture of ribbons. Both cities experienced the progressive introduction of more
modern industrial techniques and the advent of modern capital
operations. Heavy investments in the Reims woollen industry
permitted the introduction of mechanized production in the 1860s,
which greatly strengthened the economic position of the city as a
national centre of textile production, while creating a period of
economic crisis for the city's artisan workers, who were forced to
cope with the adjustment to new conditions of more industrialized
production. At Saint-Étienne, the introduction of modern
methods of production first in the coal industry and later in the
steel industry also created a prolonged period of economic and
political crisis.

  Although both cities faced similar problems created by urban
expansion and industrial growth, the different ways in which their

two elites dealt with these problems was related to their previous development. Both were approximately the same size at the end of the July monarchy – Saint-Étienne with approximately 49,000 people and Reims with about 44,000 – but Reims was by far the wealthier of the two towns. Unlike Saint-Étienne, whose elite were hardly more than moderately wealthy bourgeois merchants, Reims's eighteenth-century elite had included both many noblemen and a wealthy church establishment, whose generous civic spirit during the previous century continued to influence the public lives of the city's nineteenth-century merchant *notables*. The city's chief source of wealth was its woollen industry. Wealthy woollen manufacturers, from whose ranks the great Colbert had come, continued to compete with royal patrons and each other to embellish the city, which in addition to being one of the best paved and lighted in France boasted an elegant Hôtel-de-Ville, and a severely classical eighteenth-century *place* reminiscent of the Place de la Concorde, and originally dedicated to Louis XV. Its magnificent cathedral, which dominated the city, had been the site of the coronation of the French kings since Clovis, while the elegant residence of its archbishop reflected the continuing wealth of its clergy. Although Reims retained its medieval walls, which were not demolished until the 1860s, it continued to benefit from the generosity of new industrial interests in the 1850s and 1860s, and was generally considered one of the most comfortable of French provincial towns.[7]

Saint-Étienne was a far different kind of place, being of little importance before the nineteenth century, when it grew rapidly as an important centre of mining and ribbon manufacturing. For centuries, the city had been a minor centre for the manufacture of *quincaillerie* (small metal utensils and tools) because of the iron deposits located in the Loire region, and for arms. But it was the transfer of the artisan ribbon-weaving trade in the late eighteenth century from Montbrison, previously the most important urban centre in the Forez and the departmental capital until the empire, to neighbouring Saint-Étienne, where innovative weavers excelled in the use of new types of looms, that encouraged the town's rapid development.

The growing wealth of the new ribbon manufacturers did not produce the generous civic spirit common in older commercial centres such as Reims. Indeed, Saint-Étienne's rapid growth resulted in a decline in the standard of living, the local authorities

making little attempt to deal with the problems of urban growth.
The new housing built to accommodate ribbon weavers along the
extremities of the city's main street (the direction of urban
expansion was governed by the narrow valley in which the city was
built) was largely without sewers, and the resulting seepage
contaminated the Furan River, Saint-Étienne's main water supply.
The wealthiest ribbon merchants constructed elegant residences
outside the town. Flora Tristan discovered this sad urban spectacle
in the 1840s, when Saint-Étienne offered not a single park or even
pavements (save for the wealthiest *quartiers*), nor even a single
monument of artistic merit.[8]

The economic profile of the mercantile elite of both cities in the
1840s may be derived from the electoral lists of the July monarchy, which contain the names of all men who were at least 25
years old and paid 200 francs in direct taxes, and were therefore
enfranchised for national elections. These lists, which thus define
the political and economic elite of provincial France, contain the
age and occupation of each voter, as well as a breakdown of their
direct tax payments into four categories: the tax on real property,
buildings and land, the poll tax and tax on personal possessions,
the tax on businesses, and the tax on doors and windows.[9] Through
these lists, it is possible to create an economic portrait of the elite
in any provincial town in France during the *monarchie censitaire*,
1815–48, and thus to assess the social background against which
political life was played. Figure 1 shows the distribution of wealth
of the *notables* of both Reims and Saint-Étienne in 1848. The
manufacturing *notables* at Reims were most heavily concentrated
in the wool and wine trades, while those at Saint-Étienne were
most prominent in ribbon manufacturing and small metallurgy
(*quincaillerie*), indications of the importance of these traditional
industries in the economic life of the towns. Analysis of the
electoral lists according to categories of wealth shows these same
established trades had a disproportionately larger representation
among the wealthier groups of *notables* than did other occupational groups.

The introduction of universal suffrage after 1848, after which
lists of persons wealthy enough to vote ceased to be made, makes
it difficult to trace the economic fortunes of these groups during
the crucial period of industrial development in the 1850s and
1860s. The *mutation après décès* is an invaluable source for tracing

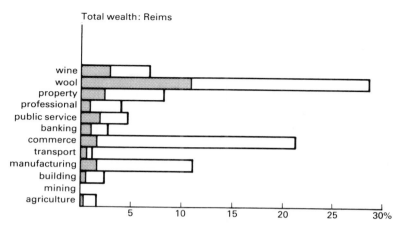

Total wealth: Reims

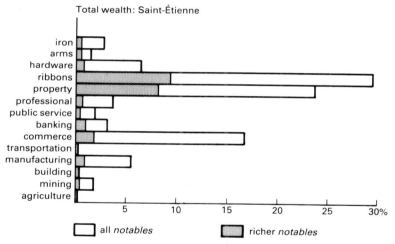

Total wealth: Saint-Étienne

☐ all *notables*　　　■ richer *notables*

Note: There were 913 voters at Reims in 1847–8, and 544 at Saint-Étienne.

Source: Printed electoral lists for Reims and Saint-Étienne, 1847–8, Departmental Archives.

Figure 1 *The distribution of wealth among the richer* notables *in 1848*

changes of wealth in this period. However, it does not show exactly which individuals in the register had sufficient wealth to have been classed as voters under the July monarchy, and thus makes difficult any long-term study of the elite. The group that corresponded in wealth to the *notables* of the 1840s has been traced after 1848, therefore, by estimating the size of minimum fortunes recorded in the *mutation* that would have carried a tax assessment of 200 francs or more before 1848. This estimate was made first by noting the fortunes of individuals in the electoral lists who died and appeared in the *mutation* during the 1850s and 1860s, so as to discover the size of the fortunes left by known electors at the time of their deaths.[10] The linkages between the electoral lists and the *mutation* were then further checked by comparing the wealth of all adult males at Reims and Saint-Étienne who died in 1852 with the proportion of voters within the adult male population in 1848. Since the voting population of Saint-Étienne in 1847–8 represented 3 per cent of the total adult male population, the level of wealth of the richest 3 per cent of the adult males who died in 1852 was assumed to represent the minimum amount of fortune necessary to be considered a *notable* according to the procedures of the July monarchy. At both Reims and Saint-Étienne this test yielded minimum fortunes of approximately 20,000 francs. The minimum fortunes of known *notables* in 1848 at death was also about 20,000 francs. Thus men aged 25 or older with estates recorded in the *mutation après décès* worth at least 20,000 francs between 1852 and 1869 (765 men at Reims and 581 at Saint-Étienne) were chosen as representatatives of the group under the Second Empire that would have been considered 'notables' by the standards of the July monarchy, and thus the elite of the 1850s and 1860s.[11]

At Reims the *mutation* makes it possible to trace the level of investment in mechanized spinning and weaving mills that began to transform the woollen industry in the 1860s. Despite the introduction of mechanized wool-combing (the process of preparing raw wool for spinning) in the early 1850s, the other sectors of the woollen industry remained dependent on artisan labour through the 1850s.[12] This was due in part to the sluggishness of the woollen market, and the belief of most manufacturers that mechanization would create high factory overhead costs that would make firms less able to adjust business expenses to inevitable fluctuations of the market, and thus make them more liable than artisanal firms to bankruptcy in periods of low product demand. Small producers were also encouraged to keep capital investments low by the relatively inexpensive spinning bobbins and looms used in cottage industry and small urban shops, with the result that the industry was divided among several hundred relatively small enterprises, many with limited capital resources. The essentially familial character of the French textile industry also discouraged the development of large firms. Entrepreneurs preferred to maintain smaller family businesses within which they could preserve business secrecy. Suspicious of new and untried manufacturing processes, and unwilling to seek outside investments that would open their businesses to strangers, most of the Reims woollen firms in the first decade of the empire remained unwilling to undertake larger, anonymous associations of capital.[13]

This attitude was entirely transformed between 1860 and 1865, a period which Tihomir Markovich has called the great watershed in French economic development, and which witnessed a revolutionary change in Reims's business practices. Encouraged by the rising demand for woollen produced by the cotton famine created by the American civil war, the woollen industry began the intensive mechanization of production.[14] Enormous profits allowed manufacturers to acquire new machines, as the total value of Reims's woollen production rose from 75 million francs in 1862, when the first effects of the cotton famine began to be felt, to over 105 million in 1867.[15] Encouraged by this rising market, the introduction of an increased number of mechanized wool-combers made wool-combing more efficient, while mechanized spinning also greatly expanded. By 1866 over 76,000 mechanized spinning bobbins operated in Reims, with another 58,000 in firms owned by Reims merchants throughout the department of the Marne. The number of mechanized looms also rose dramatically, from 577 in 1860 to over 4000 in 1870.[16] Factories became increasingly concentrated on the periphery of the city; contemporaries were struck by the rapid and dramatic decline of rural industry in the face of competition from the new weaving mills established after 1860. The process furthered the displacement of traditional handloom weavers, who, like the artisan wool-spinners, were forced increasingly to move to the factories by the reduction of wages for handloom work.[17]

The rapid development of joint stock companies to help finance mechanization emerged as one of the most important aspects of this economic revolution.[18] Before the 1860s there had been few joint stock companies in France, but in 1863 the government simplified the procedures for establishing these *sociétés anonymes*, with the result that joint stock companies greatly increased in number in all major sectors of industry.[19] This facilitated the accumulation of capital for industrialization and also helped the integration of the older manufacturing interests with the new industrial entrepreneurs.

One of the most important of the new joint stock companies, the Wagner–Marsan company, financed through the sale of 1000 franc shares and operating 7000 mechanized spinning bobbins and 200 mechanized looms, was selected by Turgan's *Grandes usines* (a nineteenth-century compendium of the world's most important industrial companies) as symbolic of the changes taking place in the city. Turgan praised Reims 'as one of the very few industrial centres where the creation of a giant new establishment such as Wagner–Marsan, equipped with the most recent innovations, was not thought a threat to the interests of the other establishments, and where the organization of the new firm was not stopped at all costs by the more or less well founded fears of the manufacturers of the same product'. Rather, the more established firms had not hesitated to supply advice and capital to the new firm. 'Even those manufacturers who because of age or habits were hostile to the new methods, also willingly invested their capital, finding the creation of such establishments an honour for the city.'[20] While perhaps too lavish in its praise of the investors, Turgan does accurately portray the enthusiasm with which the *notables* of Reims invested their enlarged profits in the new mechanized industry.

While the pooling of capital resources by traditional and innovative manufacturers was begun at Reims through the introduction of *sociétés anonymes*, no similar developments took place at Saint-Étienne, which thus provides an even clearer example than Reims of the tensions that developed under the Second Empire between more traditional manufacturing interests and the newer industrial interests that challenged them. While in the 1850s and 1860s both traditional manufacturers and industrial innovators co-existed within the woollen industry at Reims, at Saint-Étienne the older and newer groups were divided between separate industries; ribbon and arms manufacturing remained under the control of the older established manufacturing group, while coal-mining and steel came increasingly under the control of the newer industrial interests. Economic and political rivalries between the two groups at Reims were reduced by investments of the old elite in the enterprises of the industrial innovators, a fusion that was facilitated by the relatively gradual pace of change in the textile industry. In contrast, the economic spheres of the steel and coal industries in the Loire remained separate from the economic sphere of the established ribbon merchants, both because of insignificant local investments in these rapidly growing new industries, and because the need for large capital investments in the new industries forced the steel manufacturers to seek funds outside of the region. This diversity of interests, and the economic conservatism of the older bourgeois group at Saint-Étienne, prevented the development of business ties between the newer manufacturing group and the established elite to which the imperial government looked for support, and therefore created a more vigorous political opposition at Saint-Étienne than at Reims. Deprived of the hope of all but very limited government political patronage, several of the wealthy steel manufacturers began to seek political office by encouraging a local political opposition. The conditions under which heavy industry in the Loire developed helps explain why Saint-Étienne became one of the most important centres of opposition to the imperial government in the last years of the empire.

Although ribbon manufacturing remained Saint-Étienne's most important industry throughout the period of the Second Empire, by the 1860s its most brilliant period had already passed.[21] Faced with increasing competition from mechanized Swiss ribbon manufacturers at Basle, and the loss after 1861 of the American market, the number of ribbon manufacturers declined in the 1860s (Figure 2). Small metallurgy also suffered in the same period. Unlike the other manufacturers, *quincaillerie* in addition faced very strong competition from French as well as foreign manufacturers, and local manufacturers were fearful of risking new investments to improve production methods. Instead, they sought to maintain their position in the market through a constant and immoderate lowering of labour costs. Reduced to desperate conditions, the artisan *quincailleurs* were scarcely able to improve methods on their own. The constant pressure to lower their prices resulted in the inevitable decline in the quality of their product, and this further reduced the market for Saint-Étienne's goods.[22]

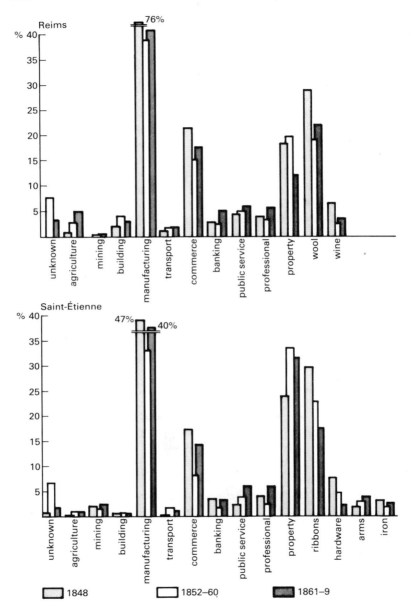

Figure 2   *Changing occupations of the elite under the empire*

The conservative attitude of Saint-Étienne's traditional manufacturers and the sad results which this had for small metallurgy may be contrasted with the changes introduced by the region's rapidly growing heavy industries. The innovative leadership that had characterized the development of the coal industry in the 1840s and 1850s had passed by the 1860s to the steel industry. The initial fusion of smaller companies in the early 1850s, when the weak steel market necessitated more productive uses of capital, was followed by further concentration at the end of the decade, encouraged by the establishment of free trade with England, which required further economies of scale. The development of the railroad network in the late 1850s, followed by the growing number of French military orders in the 1860s, made the large companies that now emerged highly profitable. Thus the Petin and Gaudet company, whose most important parent company had been founded earlier in the century by the English Jackson brothers, came by 1860 to employ over 8000 workers on an annual payroll of 6 million to 7 million francs; it produced an annual product worth over 30 million francs, and paid a 10 per cent dividend to its shareholders.[23] Through the early 1860s the company continued to receive large orders from the navy as well as from the railroads, and by 1865 it had produced the armour plating for twelve French frigates and three floating batteries, as well as for two Spanish frigates and three Italian corvettes. The company's forges, now a major employer of the Loire's skilled *quincailleurs*, made the cannon for the armoured frigates *Solferino* and *Magenta*.[24] In 1866, when the company employed over 9000 workers and produced an annual product valued between 40 million and 50 million francs, it received the further privilege of exclusively manufacturing the barrels of the new *chassepot* rifles, which it maintained until 1869.[25] The giant rival of Petin and Gaudet, the Compagnie des fonderies et forges de Terrenoire, le Voulte et Bessages, had also grown through a series of mergers, until by the late 1860s it surpassed Petin and Gaudet in the production of Bessemer steel, the industry's most important product.[26]

A number of smaller companies engaged in the manufacturing of steel and machine parts also benefitted from the prosperity of the 1860s. These included the Jacob Holtzer company, founded early in the century by Alsatian immigrants, whose directors were to be among the most important leaders of the bourgeois republican opposition, and the Aciéries de Firminy.[27] The Compagnie des fonderies, forges et aciéries de Saint-Étienne, founded in 1865, also attempted to compete with the larger companies, and received some government orders, despite the fact that military orders did not usually go to smaller firms until 1869, when arms contracts were awarded among others to the Firminy and Holtzer companies.[28]

Despite the capital needs of the rapidly growing industry, the *maîtres des forges* were mostly unable to tap the capital resources of the older mercantile elite, and so remained outside the closed circle of ribbon manufacturers. Dependent upon capital resources from outside the region, and from capital investments provided by excess profits (a practice common in the French steel industry), they remained unattached by the financial and familial ties that created common political interests within the elite at Reims.[29] Throughout the period of the Second Empire investments by the elite in industrial enterprises at Saint-Étienne were well below those of Reims, especially during the 1860s. The proportion of investors in French industries and railroads was respectively 8 per cent at Saint-Étienne as compared with 22 per cent at Reims, and 7 per cent as compared with 28 per cent (Figure 3). Investments in the new industrial sectors were made by only 9 per cent of the elite at Saint-Étienne between 1852 and 1860, and 13 per cent in the 1860s, despite the very rapid growth of heavy industry in the Loire in this period; in the same period almost one quarter of Reims's elite (24 per cent) invested in local industrial development.[30]

While investments in local industry appeared during the 1860s to be one of the major financial interests of Reims's woollen merchants, most of the ribbon merchants of Saint-Étienne concentrated their limited investments in a few major railroad companies, or in such non-speculative issues as municipal utility companies. The reticence of the more established bourgeoisie at Saint-Étienne to invest in the new heavy industries may be explained in part by the fact that the most dramatic industrial growth in the Loire took place outside of ribbon-making, which was the main business concern of Saint-Étienne's merchants; at Reims the woollen manufacturers were investing in an industry in which they had traditionally been the leaders. But the cautious attitudes of the ribbon manufacturers may be contrasted with those of another group, the liberal professions, who were similarly divorced from direct participation in the steel and coal industries, but provided a higher percentage of investors in these businesses. The fact that

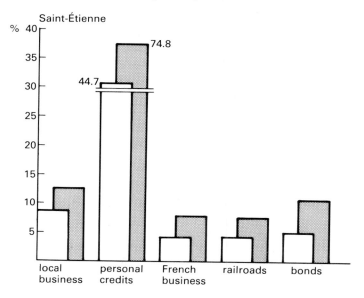

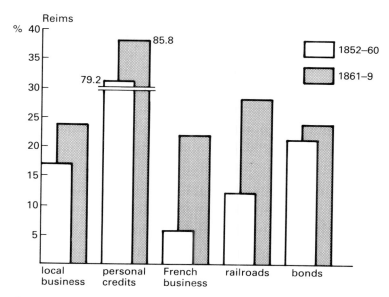

Source: *Mutation après décès*, 1852–69, for Reims and Saint-Étienne, Departmental Archives, series Q.

Figure 3 *Investments under the Second Empire*

many of these men were also newcomers to the city may help explain why this group was more receptive to the new sector. Coming from outside the city, they may have been freer from the exaggerated suspicion of joint stock companies that characterized the highly provincial attitudes of Saint-Étienne's merchants.

The pronounced separation of industrial and mercantile capitalists was to have profound consequences for bourgeois political life in the 1860s. The development of a new industrial elite helped strengthen the growing bourgeois opposition to the empire, and at both Reims and Saint-Étienne several of the most enterprising of the newer manufacturers emerged as leaders of opposition groups. Even with the relative integration of the newer and older manufacturing groups at Reims, many manufacturers were resentful of not exercising a political influence equal to their economic standing in the city, and were angered by the prefectorial administration's inability to find political offices for them. Among the most volatile members of this group were younger manufacturers, who were among the most enthusiastic proponents of the new industrial processes. 'Knowing past revolutions only as history,' the *procureur* reported, 'they are encouraged by youthful ardour and inexperience to use political agitation to further their ends.'[31] At Reims this group included many of the city's most important pioneering industrialists such as Villeminot-Huard (who had made a fortune manufacturing machinery for the woollen industry) and Warnier; both were leaders of the highly influential Société Industrielle, which, having started in 1857 as an organization to promote technical innovations in industry, began increasingly to concern itself with political questions.[32]

Liberal influence in the Société increased in 1866 with the succession of Jules Warnier to the presidency of the organization. Warnier typified the younger industrial group, being both politically ambitious as well as a supporter of free trade and industrial modernization with which the Société Industrielle was closely identified. 'An aristocrat by instinct, but a democrat through ambition', wrote the subprefect, 'Warnier has already won a considerable reputation among the bourgeoisie because of his intelligence and ability, and is preparing himself for future political struggles through his courting of the working class.'[33] Combining support for free trade with demands for broader civil and political liberties, Warnier worked in the last years of the empire to create a political following with which he could displace the political interests of the traditional manufacturing group. The vice president of the Société, Victor Rogelet, a wealthy woollen manufacturer, supported Warnier, as did Isaac Holden, another member of the board and founder of the city's first large wool-combing factory, while both of the secretaries of the Société were considered dangerous democrats by the local administration.[34]

Political rivalries were even more in evidence at Saint-Étienne, where the members of the liberal opposition, divorced from the city's ribbon industry, were more willing to make radical political appeals to the ribbon workers; at Reims, working-class unrest would have adversely affected the liberals as much as their conservative opponents.[35] Frederic Dorian, a partner in the Jacob Holtzer company, had first run as the opposition candidate in the 1863 Corps Législatif election against one of the government's official candidates.[36] Francisque Balay, one of the wealthiest ribbon manufacturers, had on the other hand no difficulty in securing the government's support for his candidacy in the election.[37] Dorian, whose reputation for paternalistic treatment of his workers and his support for liberal reforms had already won him a political following among the city's workers and petty bourgeoisie, was only the most conspicuous of the new generation of heavy industrialists, excluded from participation in political life since 1852, to challenge the older group.[38] In a region where even the most successful heavy industrialists provided important financial backing for the local opposition press in the late 1860s, it was not surprising that smaller manufacturers, such as Dorian and Jules Holtzer, whose companies had not been equally favoured with government patronage, should also find their way into the leadership of the opposition.

While Balay received little electoral support from Saint-Étienne, Dorian carried the city easily. The opposition benefited from the unpopularity of the ribbon manufacturers, for whom, the *procureur général* wrote, the workers reserved their greatest hostility, and from the support of the petty bourgeois elements who also resented the political rule of the mercantile elite.[39] Although the *procureur* at first hoped that Dorian, being allied to one of the region's most influential families (he was related by marriage to the Holtzers), would draw away from the artisanal and petit-bourgeois elements that had made his electoral success possible, the bourgeois opposition continued to court these groups with increasing success through the rest of the decade.[40] The municipal council elections of 1865, which displaced many of the mercantile elite with less wealthy members of the bourgeoisie, increased the number of Dorian's political allies in rebellion against the old economic order.

The industrial elite controlled popular and petit-bourgeois political unrest through lavish expenditures of money, and the vast sums that industrial development put at the disposal of the liberal opposition of the late 1860s distinguishes this political group from the liberal leaders in 1848–9.[41] One of the most important ways in which these funds were used was to finance a local opposition press. The development of the opposition press throughout France had been made possible by the liberalized laws of 1868, and in that year two important opposition papers began to appear in the Loire, both considerably subsidized by heavy industrialists. Since the official provincial press depended upon government subsidies provided through fees for the publication of legal notices, the opposition press, deprived of this source of income, relied heavily on the support of wealthy members of the opposition. *L'Éclaireur*, Saint-Étienne's new liberal paper, received generous financial contributions from Frederic Dorian; the new legitimist paper, *La Loire*, received support from Jullien and Carrete, both directors of Terrenoire.[42] Previously, the company had consistently supported the government, but by the late 1860s it had grown large enough to cease being as heavily dependent on government orders. The management now began to work to establish an independent political following. The paper also received funds from wealthy legitimist landowners, and soon began a vociferous campaign against the government that resulted in its editor being tried twice in the early months of 1869.[43]

At Reims the bourgeois opposition also started a new liberal paper, *L'Indépendent rémois*, which demanded an end to government interference in workers' organizations. In 1869 it supported Warnier's friend Jules Simon for the Corps Législatif against Edouard Werlé, the imperial government's most important political agent and long-time mayor of the city.[44] Although the paper could not ensure Simon's victory, it did help sway working-class opinion in support of the bourgeois republic proclaimed in 1870. By announcing their own support of the republic following the fall of the empire, the members of the liberal opposition further consolidated their own local control and also stole the thunder of working-class republicanism expressed by radical organizations that had emerged in the late 1860s. Far from producing a social revolution, the establishment of the republic marked the triumphant culmination of the liberal political revolution begun at Reims in the last years of the empire.[45] Working-class organizations, already weakened by the division of the work-force between artisan and factory workers, were further inhibited by the Prussian occupation of the city, which had begun early in September. While bourgeois property remained inviolate, the power of the old conservative group now gave way steadily before the political onslaught of the industrial manufacturing elite. The liberal-republicans easily defeated the conservatives in the municipal elections of 1871 and Warnier, spokesman for the new industrial interests, was soon elected to the National Assembly.[46]

The decline of the imperial government's influence on local elections proceeded even more rapidly at Saint-Étienne. By 1869 the government was unable to find a suitable candidate for the city in the legislative election of that year, and was thus forced to abandon Saint-Étienne to the opposition forces. These included not only the liberal Comité de l'Union démocratique of smaller manufacturers and heavy industrialists led by Dorian, but also the legitimist opposition, led by landed aristocrats and some heavy industrialists, which like the liberal group had been able to gain control of many working-class votes. While the more moderate opposition at Reims had only hinted at more general reforms during the electoral campaign of 1869, the liberals at Saint-Étienne spoke more boldly of the need for a republic. The liberals depended upon the support of artisan and industrial workers, while the Legitimists depended on the support of the rural population and urban recipients of church charities. Only the mercantile ribbon interests, having relied on the backing of the imperial government in past elections, possessed no influence within the working-class mutual aid societies or church based organizations through which mass political support was organized. The main threat to the bourgeois opposition groups came not from the government, but from more radical workers organizations that had developed in the late 1860s. Made up largely of the more radical ribbon weavers, these groups found spokesmen in figures such as Antide Martin. A leader of the republican movement in 1848–9, he warned the workers against well-to-do liberals who constituted themselves *grands électeurs* through organizations like the Union démocratique, and who hoped to impose their own candidates on the voters. Martin proposed that the electoral committees be kept as widely representative as possible of the general population.[47] Suggestions such as these, despite being voiced in radical, poorly financed (and therefore short-lived) newspapers like *La Sentinelle populaire*, posed a real threat to the attempts of the liberal opposition to guide working-class radicalism along lines favourable to bourgeois interests; the radicals therefore found themselves as much a target of the liberal *L'Éclaireur* as the imperial government or the legitimist opposition. The radical threat appeared grave enough to the Union démocratique that Dorian, who had originally not planned to run again in 1869, decided to represent liberal interests in the election.

The more extensive organization of the liberal opposition, the greater prestige of its leaders and the influence of the Union démocratique on public opinion exercised through *L'Éclaireur* allowed the liberals to elect Dorian in 1869, and to continue to control local political life through the 1870s.[48] Even the short-lived 'commune' at Saint-Étienne in 1871 did little to weaken the political power of the new alliance of smaller manufacturers and modern industrialists, who, despite certain radical elements among artisanal ribbon weavers, could depend on the support of other working-class elements, especially the region's steel workers.[49] Dorian had been the first to attempt to achieve national political office in 1863 in defiance both of the imperial government and the older mercantile interests. Now within several years other industrial leaders also came to support the overthrow of the empire in favour of a political system more responsive to their ambitions; these included leaders of the republican opposition such as Hutter and Holtzer, but also more conservative industrialists such as Jullien and Arbel, a director of the forges of Rive-de-Gier.[50]

At Saint-Étienne and Reims the new *notables*, after first coming to dominate more traditional mercantile manufacturers through their greater financial resources, had begun by the last years of the empire to acquire other traits of a local aristocracy as well: in particular, a local political clientele created through a new type of industrial paternalism. The provision by industrialists of subsidized housing, free education and pensions, known to other manufacturing centres as well, was especially evident in the steel industry. The inability of the imperial government to accommodate this newer industrial group within the system of the empire, and its persistent reliance after the 1851 coup d'état on the more traditional mercantile leaders of local politics, forced the new industrialists into political opposition.

The policies of the imperial government had favoured rapid industrial growth. But its fatal political attachment to more traditional mercantile manufacturing groups, which were losing their economic pre-eminence at a local level and which were no longer able to dominate the rest of the bourgeoisie politically as they had done earlier under the July monarchy, forced many new men into the republican ranks. Clearly large-scale industrialization helped both to create political dissidents among the bourgeoisie and shape the conditions that protected the bourgeois republicans against the threat of independent radical working-class political action. The introduction of factory industry, which helped to disrupt the unity of old artisan communities, combined with the repressive policies of the imperial government, weakened the ability of the working class to organize politically in the old manner of artisans during the period of the Second Republic. Thus, despite the new mass of urban voters who seemed ready to enter and perhaps radicalize the political arena, local elites continued to predominate, recapturing the position they had briefly lost under the Second Republic. The paternalistic programmes of industrial employers, combined with the new divisions within the working class, allowed bourgeois liberals to believe that they could depend upon the political loyalty of their employees in their struggle with the imperial government. They thus confidently renounced the repression of the empire in favour of greater popular political liberties. Republicanism seemed the means through which they could win political power.

The lengths to which dissident industrialists were willing to go in their appeal for popular action was determined, of course, by local conditions. The financial integration of the older mercantile and newer industrial interests in the Reims woollen trade, ties solidified through joint stock companies, created a community of interests among rival groups with regard to the future of the woollen industry and the state of labour relations. This inclined the liberals to be more cautious in their treatment of strikes and in the encouragement of the radical demands of workers. But at Saint-Étienne, development of new heavy industries independent of the traditional ribbon manufacturing interests of the elite produced internal dissension. Republican industrialists at Saint-Étienne encouraged the radical demands of the city's artisan weavers against their employers; the republican elite was also willing to provoke working-class agitation both among the town's artisan weavers and among proletarian miners against the town's traditional conservative leadership. In the 1880s, of course, further development of industry and the emergence of trade unions created new challenges to the *notables*, but during the Second Empire this development lay in the future. The late 1860s was an important period of transition in French urban economic and political life. New industrial interests emerged within France's bourgeois elite and successfully consolidated their opposition to the imperial system and, at the same time, their control of provincial politics. They spoke for the popular republican movement and by doing so helped to establish a socially moderate Third Republic.

6 Industry in the changing landscape from Daubigny to Monet

Robert L. Herbert

In communicating with his colleagues outside his own specialty the art historian is often guilty of mystification. By stressing the several components of pictorial structure (line, colour, shape, arrangement) he protects his profession by identifying it with a set of arcane mysteries that are hidden from the uninitiated. Historians not principally concerned with the visual arts are tempted to conclude that art really consists of these mysteries and either they exclude art from the evidence they use in their own work, or else, despairing of their role as outsiders, they merely use art as an embellishment. It is true that most art historians believe that they deal with history. They demonstrate that artist Y has borrowed a portion of his composition from the earlier artist X, and usually they deduce from this a causal relationship. However, this is often a false teleology. Simply by stating that one pattern has preceded another, the art historian feels that he has been engaged in 'history', when all he has done is to name a chronological sequence. Real historical analysis, which would tell us how Y's painting fits into his culture, is set aside in favour of the conviction that forms of art have their own teleology, independent of the cultures that gave them birth.

Two related assumptions support the false teleology that dominates art history, and both come from the hegemony of abstract art, apparent successor to the nineteenth century's art-for-art's-sake.[1] One is the belief that art springs only from the subjectivity of the artist and therefore that the historian is free to ignore socio-cultural history. The other, already mentioned, is that the forms of art, to the extent that they are not purely subjective and idiosyncratic, are related principally to one another, as distinct from the society in which they have found existence.

These assumptions are often strengthened when the art historian sees others use art merely to illustrate historical events.

Such use, confined to the subject matter of art rather than to its complicated inner workings, convinces the art historian that he is right to separate art from social history. This is all the more true when the user is that kind of historian who begins with a critical event, say a revolution, and then goes out to find art that 'illustrates' it. Such art frequently is not that which itself is revolutionary, not that which is the real bearer of a new pictorial language, but art which only represents socio-political events. An example would be the historian of late nineteenth-century France who shows us pictures of factories, strikes and political leaders rather than the landscapes of Monet or the café scenes of Manet and Degas.

The historian who uses art for its subject matter alone is just as remote from the history of art as the specialist who talks only of colour and composition. The historian who wishes to deal meaningfully with art must explain why its subject cannot be understood properly unless its structure is analysed. Pictorial structure interprets subject. Each is proper evidence for the cultural historian, but his work is incomplete unless he demonstrates their interdependence.

The first examples of paintings that I give offer a good introduction to the general theme of this essay. Corot's painting (plate 2) and Sisley's (plate 3) show the same road south-west of Paris. Corot (1796–1875) was a long generation older than Sisley (1839–99), and his view of the road, a fresh and new vision for his day, speaks for the values of the mid century. Although artfully contrived, it appears natural. Two rural persons are moving slowly along the road at a pre-industrial pace. The dirt road has slightly irregular edges, grass and foliage on both sides are abundant, and the view towards the outskirts of Paris is a deep one that contributes to a sense of expansiveness, in this serene meeting of countryside with city.

Sisley could have chosen a similar view, but instead takes us further down the same road, nearer to Paris. The increased traffic along such routes has led to the use of urban modes of road building. Along the edge of the road a cobblestone drain has been placed, and a curb erected. Relatively young trees, spaced with military precision and regularly trimmed, mark one side of the road in contrast to the more countrified aspect of Corot's roadside. In moving from one picture to the other, we have gone from country to suburb or, rather, from a relatively unmodernized

Plate 2   Corot, *The Road to Sèvres*

Plate 3   Sisley, *The Sèvres Road*

suburb to an urbanized one. We have entered the world of modern France, and we sense the presence here in Louveciennes of Baron Haussmann's and Louis Napoleon's imperial order. From Paris have been exported the canalized edges of the road and the implacable regularity of the trees, visible signs of the growing *mainmise* of Paris upon the nearby suburbs, and of the suburbs upon the countryside.

To this partial analysis both the historian and the art historian might object that the images Sisley painted were really there, and therefore that I have only identified subject matter. The first reply to such an objection is an obvious one. Sisley chose that view, and merely by doing so, he draws attention to the modernization of Louveciennes in preference to a more untouched rural road which he could easily have found in that vicinity. That his choice of view is an intentional one is indicated by the fact that the building whose wall shows to the right is none other than the famous château of Madame Du Barry. A conventional representation of this site by an earlier artist would have disclosed more of the château in order to evoke history more overtly. Sisley was an adherent of naturalism which in turn was the style of progressive bourgeois culture. Naturalism meant a facing towards the present, a turning of the back upon history, a rooting out of values, both pictorial and social, that attached to monarchy and theocracy. Into this banal view Sisley has introduced Madame Du Barry's château in a matter-of-fact way that assimilates it by giving it a new modesty, a plainness that puts history in its place.

The second reply to the objection that I am dealing only with subject matter is to point to the intimate connection of Sisley's pictorial structure to his subject. Considered simply as a piece of abstract organization, Sisley's painting, compared to Corot's, is a taut network of geometric forms. The road makes a truncated triangle whose abrupt termination emphasizes its rather flat shape. The ground to the right is a five-sided polyhedron, and to the left the regularity of the trees is reinforced by the block-like patches of sunlight along the road. Compared to the Corot, Sisley's sharp perspective and the sudden plunge over the brow of the hill have an almost automotive speed. He seems to have absorbed the spirit of the imposition of order and regularity over nature which is more than a metaphor for the Second Empire's alteration of the environs of Paris: it is its very embodiment. The forms of his art are in inextricable harmony with his subject, not because he consciously made them so, but because experience and instinct led him to a point of view and a pictorial organization that suited his endeavour.

Most artists of Corot's generation had sought out relatively unaltered roadways and villages, despite the encroachments of the growing urban-industrial revolution, and they favoured a correspondingly softer, more irregular set of forms. It is no accident that the Barbizon artist Théodore Rousseau, painter of the villages on the fringe of Fontainebleau forest as well as of the forest's exuberant growth, consistently fought the government's piercing the forest with new macadamized highways. His love of the intertwined branches of forest and the thatched cottages of villages was also the love of a matching set of lines, colours and shapes. They would prevent him from seeing Sisley's site as anything other than ugly.

Such comparisons of Impressionist and pre-Impressionist paintings are therefore instructive because they show us how to deal with the formal language of paintings as well as with their subjects. In providing the context for the study of forms, they deal with the two generations which witnessed the rapid suburbanization of the environs of Paris. Reactions of artists to these changes were not always predictable – far from it – and in the remainder of this essay I want to explore other comparisons of the two generations. I will take Monet as the exemplar of Impressionism, and for the preceding generation, an artist he knew well, Charles Daubigny (1817–78). The choice is not arbitrary, for Monet learned a great deal from Daubigny and he painted along the same riverbanks and the Norman coastline the older artist favoured.

Daubigny, known today principally as a painter, was also a prolific printmaker and illustrator.[2] In both media he stands as one of the principal artists devoted to the suburbs and the countryside near Paris. As is true of many artists, his oils and prints display two different ranges of subject matter, and the contrast between them is illuminating. In making prints, whether or not illustrations to specific texts, Daubigny represented a relatively large number of topical subjects. Prints often embodied present concerns and, since they were serially reproduced and cheap, they shared in an active circulation of artistic and social ideas. When working in oils, however, Daubigny's instinct was to choose more 'permanent' subjects suitable to the more disinterested mood that he and most others associated with painting. This contrast of the typical and the

Plate 4   Daubigny, *La Vapeur*

reflective was also the contrast of city activity and country solitude. Printmaking was more commonly a social enterprise than painting, which was a rather private activity associated with release from the city. Daubigny's friend Frédéric Henriet praised his paintings in 1857 because 'nous procurent-elles abondamment de ces illusions de repos, de liberté, de solitude, qui sont presque du bonheur'.[3]

Daubigny's prints and illustrations include a number that deal with the industrialization of the countryside. Among them are those he provided for the 1851 edition of the *Fables* of Pierre Lachambeaudie (1807–72).[4] Although commissioned works, the illustrations probably reflect Daubigny's sympathies with the author's Saint-Simonism. Daubigny was an ardent republican, and apparently friendly to the utopian ideals of the Fourierists and Saint-Simonists which appealed to so many artists who matured in the 1840s. Lachambeaudie's constant message is the need to accept industrialization and to overturn the royalists and landowners who oppose progress. Once radical, by 1851 this view was the spearpoint of entrepreneurial capitalism in France, and erstwhile Saint-Simonists began to enter the government of Louis Napoleon in increasing numbers.[5]

In *La Vapeur* (plate 4), Daubigny shows an old man and his son looking out over a broad landscape (Daubigny seems to have based it upon Le Havre). Two trains pass over a viaduct, and in the distance, maritime commerce is indicated in the plumes of smoke from two steam vessels. In his fable, Lachambeaudie has the father, fearful of the train, ask his son what it is that he sees, the child of Providence or of the Devil. The son replies that steam conquers natural obstacles by harnessing nature's own force for its purposes. By bridging chasms and rivers, and defeating time, it will bring products to remote places and join peoples heretofore separated. Myths of old will become reality:

Au nouvel Amphion, qu'à ta voix enchantée
Naissent des monuments utiles, glorieux;
Poëte, à la douleur que ton luth fasse trève;
La vérité bientôt remplacera le rêve,
Et la réalité sera le merveilleux.

[To the new Amphion, at the sound of your enchanted voice
Monuments are brought forth, both useful and glorious;
Poet, may your lute call truce to pain;
Truth will soon supplant the dream,
And reality will be marvelled at.]

Lachambeaudie recognizes that industry transforms the countryside, and he is sensitive to the loss that nature (and the poet) must bear. In *Les Deux Rivages* (plate 5), Daubigny interprets the poet's most autobiographical and most bittersweet fable. Lachambeaudie writes that in his childhood in the country, both banks of the river were equally verdant. At age 16, when he was leaving home to seek his fortune, one riverbank was taken over by industry and new construction replaced the trees. Now old, the poet hopes that progress will not have removed the last plants of his ideal domain. The course of life has two banks. In youth, both are flowered, but later, need takes over one half of our illusions. The fable ends:

Heureux, quand la vieillesse arrive,
Si quelques fleurs encor restent sur l'autre Rive!

[There is happiness, when old age arrives,
If a few flowers remain still on the other Shore!]

Daubigny interprets the fable quite directly. Construction has taken over one bank while opposite, four washerwomen symbolize the traditional use of the river, whose banks they leave untouched.

Plate 5   Daubigny, *Les Deux Rivages*

The tree overhead divides the two worlds with its dead limbs to the left, a vine and live limbs to the right. The boy poet on the near bank leaves both worlds behind, but in Daubigny's spirit, if not Lachambeaudie's, he puts his back to industry and walks toward the world of nature and illusion.

For the two sides of *Les Deux Rivages* are the two realms of Daubigny's artistic activity. His prints frequently show the transformation of the countryside, but his oils represent instead the unsullied villages, meadows and riverbanks of France. Typical of his paintings is *The Bridge between Persan and Beaumont-sur-Oise* (plate 6). Avoiding the rail line along the bank to the left, and the small industrial centre of Persan, he painted the old road bridge and the village of Beaumont, precisely because they were unaltered. The women and the geese in the foreground are witnesses to the unchanging life he sought out, and the absence of any steam traffic on the river permits the water to reflect the illusions of timelessness. Daubigny hardly ever painted the steamboats along the Seine and the Oise, although we know that they were so common as to inspire the hatred of riverside innkeepers, ferrymen and towpath workers, rapidly being done out of their livelihood. In several etchings in his autobiographical album of 1861, Daubigny represents both steamboat and train. *Le Départ* (plate 7) shows the train which often took him back and forth to Paris, and the steam tugs which plied the rivers. The world of oil painting was a different, and an ideal realm. For Daubigny, as well as for Théodore Rousseau, Camille Corot and J. F. Millet, nature and the traditional village formed an ideal world in which they actually lived, but one that was carefully nurtured in their paintings, protected from the incursion of insistent modernity.

Daubigny's paintings are the chief witnesses to this retention of a pastoral ideal, but occasionally his letters are especially revealing. In September 1854, returning to Avallon to seek out a favoured site, he found it so changed by progress that he fled it immediately. To his friend Geoffroy Dechaume he wrote:

Mon vieux, décidément, j'ai du malheur. Tout ce que je voulais faire est rasé: arbres coupés, plus d'eau dans la rivière, maisons abattues! Aussi, en désespoir de cause, je me sauve et vais voir si le Père Eternel n'a pas dérangé les montagnes du Dauphiné. J'espère que non.

[Decidedly, old chap, I am unfortunate. Everything I wanted to paint has been torn down: trees cut, no more water in the river, houses knocked

Plate 6   Daubigny, *The Bridge between Persan and Beaumont-sur-Oise (detail)*

Plate 7   Daubigny, *Le Départ*

down. Therefore as a last resort I am clearing out and will see if the Eternal Father has not rearranged the mountains of the Dauphiné. I hope not.][6]

A few days later, settled in the countryside not far from Lyon, he opposed the calm of nature to the international preoccupation over the Crimea. His anti-war republicanism shows in his references to Barbès, to the 'ratapoils' (Daumier's invented right-wing figure) and to Dupont, Lachambeaudie's friend and fellow *poète populaire*:

Ce pauvre Barbès est donc sorti de prison? As-tu lu ce qu'il a dit sur la guerre? Ils sont ici plus ou moins ratapoils, et les mots guerre et victoire ne sont pas épargnés. Quand on observe le grand calme de la nature, 'les querelles vaines des cabinets européens', comme dit Pierre Dupont, vous apparaissent bien davantage, et on se demande à quoi ça sert de tuer des gens qui ne sont pas las d'être vivants.

[So poor Barbès is really out of prison? Have you read what he has said about the war? Here they are more or less *ratapoils*, and the words 'war' and 'victory' are not spared. When one observes the great calmness of nature, 'the vain quarrels of European governments,' as Pierre Dupont says, appear the vainer, and one asks oneself what it serves to kill people who are not tired of being alive.][7]

The contrast that Daubigny felt between the repose of nature and the cares of contemporary life continues the age-old yearning for release and tranquillity that is a constant theme in western art and literature from Pliny to Van Gogh.[8] It is none the less essential, when dealing with the cultural history of France in the third quarter of the century, to point to the awareness of both worlds, city and country, because neither was independent of the other. The rapid industrialization of France lay behind the rise of landscape, which is nothing other than its counter-image. The fact that Impressionism eventually replaced Renaissance art as the dominant world style is proof enough of the need to look into its origins.

Claude Monet (1840–1926), the greatest of Impressionist landscape painters, reveals the dichotomy of city and country in many aspects of his rich and varied work. His subjects range more widely than those of Daubigny, and they include many paintings of Paris as well as of a number of villages along the Seine and the Norman coast. Especially revealing and especially wonderful are his paintings at Argenteuil, where he lived from 1872 to 1878. Argenteuil was a suburban village that bore the evidence of a wholesale transformation under the impact of the urban-industrial revolution.[9] It is an especially good site for study because it was neither city nor country. Monet's paintings there give witness to the complicated pattern of change in a region that was indeed 'nature' and which lent itself to 'landscape,' but one which was neither Paris itself nor the relatively untouched villages favoured by Daubigny.

In his *Railroad Bridge at Argenteuil* (plate 8), Monet reveals his unstated ambition to be the painter of modern landscape. The contrast with Daubigny's bridge at Beaumont (plate 6) is striking in several regards. Because formal structure interprets subject, we might begin by noting the abruptness, bordering on harshness, with which Monet presents the bridge. Daubigny's bridge is woven into his composition by its environing foliage and by the shapes of nearby buildings which echo its arches. We see both ends of the bridge, where one comes from and where one goes, and we sense the firm anchor it has on both banks. Not so Monet. His bridge hurtles in from the left edge, unmediated by foliage, and it cuts sharply across the canvas.[10] This harsh presentation suits the bridge, for it carries trains, not foot passengers, and this particular rail line was relatively new, cutting across the eastern side of Argenteuil to a new station on the edge of the older section of the village. The bridge is of new design, for the comforting arches still used in metal bridges of the 1850s have given way to a compound structure that is put together in units, then hoisted atop the piers.

In the foreground of Monet's picture, instead of Daubigny's restful grass, flowers and reeds, there is a homely pathway showing signs of the recent construction. Along its edge is a low barrier that retains the new embankment. It is of utilitarian design that makes no concession to traditional railings (to a modern eye it looks like a highway divider). It helps speed the eye along the near shore (we linger in the Daubigny), and makes all the more striking the rightward leap of the bridge. The spanning of the river is made the more dramatic by the way it dwarfs the figures below. That we are below the huge bridge is evident from the way Monet constructed the events on the ground plane. From the two men our eye passes to the near sailboat, then on to the other sailboat in an oblique line that reinforces, but does not parallel, the diagonal of bridge and piers. The alternating light and dark of the piers is repeated in the two sailboats and in the men's clothing, aiding the march of

Plate 8 Monet, *The Railroad Bridge at Argenteuil*

Plate 9 Monet, *Railroad Bridge*

our eye off to the right, and providing a rhythmic contrast and support for the straight thrust of the bridge above.

The two men are at a key spot in the whole network of crossing diagonals. They stand along the axis of the shore, an angle which their own shadows accentuate. The tops of their heads just touch the line of the opposite shore, another instance of Monet's artful organization. That shore is another of the slanting lines of this composition. The two men look out along the receding diagonal formed by the boats. Like the engineers or onlookers pictured in nineteenth-century books devoted to the marvels of modern construction, they are witnesses to the promethean triumphs of new industry. As though there were invisible strings in their hands, they stand within Monet's network of geometric forces, his organizing lines whose unflinching straightness is the very embodiment of modernity. This is because they record man's ability to surmount nature, to span her waterways and chasms, to defy her with the unyielding patterns that man imposes upon her for his own purposes. Their modernity, both in Monet's painting and in actuality, resides in their very unnaturalness.

The starkness of the bridge is somewhat relieved by the merging of the train's windblown smoke with the clouds above. They form a canopy of blues and whites that symbolizes the peaceful blending of man-made and natural vapours. The wind that blows the smoke also propels the sailboats below and they, too, soften the impact of the bridge, thanks to their association with natural pleasures. The near boat beats upwind as the other runs in front of the strong breeze. Although they move in opposite directions, their paths cross under the span, caught there along Monet's organizing diagonal.

Another picture of pleasure boating at Argenteuil (plate 9) shows the same bridge, this time from upstream. Its composition is not at all the same, and the differences are revealing. To the art historian, these differences are of vital importance even though, superficially, the subject is the same in both pictures. In this second painting, done about a year after the first, Monet has moved upstream along the same bank of the Seine, going under the bridge to arrive on the other side. This places the viewer perhaps 200 yards from the vantage point of the other painting. To our right is the talus of foliage-covered earth which supports the railroad tracks above. This artificial mound and its growth form a pictorial cushion for the bridge, giving it a different feeling from the abrupt geometry of the other canvas. In fact, the more we compare the two, the more we realize how unlike they are. It is true that in the fiction of the later picture, the bridge darts dramatically back into space to give us a sense of the movement of the train, but it is also true that the foliage at the right softens the juncture with the picture's edge. Our imaginary position is on this verdant bank, no longer on the scruffy embankment of the earlier painting, and so our associations are with the colourful natural growth here and on the shore opposite. This integrates the bridge with its setting at Argenteuil, as distinct from the stark separation it exhibited in the earlier painting (plate 8).

Nature, in other words, is arranged by the artist so as to enframe his dynamic bridge and train. The strong afternoon sun which comes from our right is seconded by the wind which pushes the train's smoke to the left. The sailboat is tacking against the wind, which must be fairly strong because it pushes the train's smoke sideways. By stressing that sun, wind and sailboat are all going along the axis of the river, at right angles to the bridge, Monet reinforces the symbolic confrontation of the boat, symbol of leisure, with the train. Together the boat and the railroad stand for the new Argenteuil: the modern suburb which has given up its agricultural role to the pressures of urban leisure and industry. Both boat and railroad represent the new forces that were radically altering Argenteuil, forces that disrupted traditional life in this village, creating wholesale changes in the use of the river and its shore, in land ownership and land use, in the types and numbers of local residents and in the work that they did.

A special word needs to be said about boating at Argenteuil, for the risk is that we do not recognize Monet's sailboats for what they really were: principal agents in the transformation of Argenteuil from country village to suburb.[11] Before 1840 Argenteuil's economy depended upon several kinds of agricultural produce and scattered local industry, including the plaster called 'plaster of Paris'. A few people made their living taking care of towpath horses, maintaining riverside inns and the local ferry. All this changed with astonishing rapidity in response to the expanding population of Paris and its need for leisure. The Seine widens at Argenteuil and this makes it one of the best spots near Paris for sailing. Boating clubs were established there,[12] and thanks to the railroad, the village was only fifteen minutes (nine kilometres) from the Gare St Lazare. Boat rental agencies took over some of the shoreline, and renting villas to vacationers loomed ever larger in the local economy.

Monet's willingness to address himself to these alterations of riverside life did not, however, mean a wholesale adoption of the industry which was rapidly expanding at Argenteuil. It is true that artists of the preceding generation, such as Corot and Daubigny, could not bring themselves to paint pleasure boats nor new railroad bridges, which embodied changes they could not tolerate. By comparison with them, Monet seems more of a spokesman for the changes affecting the once-rural villages along the Seine. None the less, there is abundant evidence that at Argenteuil he screened out much of the rapidly growing local industry, showing factories only at a considerable distance, with few exceptions, or else avoiding them entirely. In the second of his bridge pictures discussed here, the whole truth about the site will reveal why his reconciliation of nature and railroad is a surprisingly complicated issue.

Were we able to stand where Monet places us in the Philadelphia picture (plate 9), we would realize how artful his choice of view was. Immediately behind us and to our left were several large factories, and along the shore just to our left were industrial warehouses and loading docks.[13] The industrial uses of the river, which Monet uniformly avoids at Argenteuil, and the factories, which show only in a few pictures, are hardly hinted at in his painting of the bridge. Instead he literally put that all behind him, and shows us the sailboat, and the train as it leaves Argenteuil headed towards Paris. The excitement of the train, as it hurtled over his head, and the opposed movement of the sailboat, were the images that distilled his sense of modern Argenteuil and its relationship to Paris. In this distillation they stood for the reconciliation of city and country, of industry and leisure, of railroad and river, of metal bridge and green foliage, of industrial steam and natural wind. Steam and wind are forces which move things, and motion is the very essence of change.

The factories and docks which surrounded Monet as he painted this picture were embodiments of industry and therefore of change, but they were not easily reconciled with the river and with natural light and movement. Monet's break with Barbizon art was not a complete one, in other words. The natural light and wind, and the riverbank foliage which Daubigny and Corot had so loved, are still present in Monet's painting, even if accompanied by suburban boat and train. Strong effects of outdoors nature were Monet's link with the preceding generation, and permitted him to blend old and new. It is symptomatic that in the only painting at Argenteuil which shows factories in relatively large scale,[14] Monet put them in mid distance rather than in the foreground, and represented them under the softening effects of snow.

In most cases, when Monet showed factories at Argenteuil, they were far off in the distance of his pictures, as in *Sailboats on the Seine at Argenteuil* (plate 10).[15] In this view we are across the river from Argenteuil, looking over a group of moored sailboats toward the easternmost extension of the village, marked by two smoking factory chimneys. Monet probably painted this picture from his studio boat, a device he had borrowed from Daubigny. It permitted him a variety of views that would otherwise be difficult, as well as the convenience of a modestly equipped floating studio. In this painting we feel the intimacy that resulted from being on the water, so close to other boats that the nearest ones are cut off by the edge of the frame. The undulating reflections, like so many eels, seem to work their way right under our feet. In mid distance two sailboats are getting underway, their favourable wind made clear by the smoke from the distant chimneys. Once again industry and leisure are juxtaposed, and once again industry is peacefully absorbed, this time by integrating it with the river view. We see part of industrial Argenteuil across a broad reach of luminous water, as though it were some suburban Venice, purified by its exposure to brilliant light and air.

Other subjects that Monet painted at Argenteuil also reveal his conception of suburban life, even those which seem innocent of any contemporary references. *Gladiolas* (plate 11), for example, is one of a large number of paintings that show his wife in their richly flowered garden. Properly understood, it becomes a 'modern' picture that shows how Argenteuil reflected the impact of Paris. In fact, this painting reeks of the city dweller.

Thanks to the work of Rodolphe Walter, and Daniel Wildenstein's collaborators,[16] we know a good deal about Monet's life at Argenteuil. From 1872 to 1874 he rented a house from a notable local landowner, Mme Aubry-Vitet. He transformed its garden into a flowery wonder and often painted his wife and child, in proper middle-class dress, surrounded by blossoming plants. From the first rented garden he could see a new house being built next door, on a portion of Mme Aubry-Vitet's land that had recently

Plate 10   Monet, *Sailboats on the Seine at Argenteuil (detail)*

Plate 11   Monet, *Gladiolas*

Plate 12   Millet, *In the Garden*

been sold and subjected to *lotissement*. Its owner and builder was one Alexandre Flament, an enterprising local carpenter and furniture maker. In 1874 Monet moved his family into Flament's pavillion, becoming its first tenant. Once again he turned his passion for gardening to good account and filled his rented yard with all manner of flowering plants. *Gladiolas* shows his wife Camille in this second garden, one of a great many in which she appears, sometimes with their son or a friend.

In the preceding generation, most notably in paintings and drawings by J. F. Millet at Barbizon (plate 12), a village garden was presented as such: it had Brussels sprouts or cabbages, and chickens pecked among them. The most common flower was that of the fruit tree, whose produce is edible. Millet had rented his village house, as Monet did later, but through his paintings he associated himself and his family with traditional villagers. Monet, by contrast, identifies himself with the transplanted city dweller who gets rid of the cabbages and chickens, and instead plants the flowers which transform the rented yard into a miniature estate. Despite his enormous debts – or perhaps because of them – Monet was living high off the hog (to use an anachronistic, small-town phrase), and he shows his wife as though she were the mistress of a château. The situation is a distillation of the suburbanization of Argenteuil. The local carpenter's land grows more valuable as Argenteuil expands, so he builds upon it a villa whose rental income is greater than he could obtain from the land itself. The city artist to whom he rents comes to Argenteuil to find suitable subjects to paint, not far from Paris where his market is located: dealers, exhibition galleries and clients.

The contrast between Millet's vegetable garden and Monet's flowers is that between a pre-modern village and a suburb. Millet's ideal was the rural community untainted by the modernization of urban life, which he had deliberately fled. Monet's ideal was that of the middle-class city dweller who thinks of the village as a place to build his domain, a garden of colour and beauty which will be a compensation for the need to work – and from which vegetables, those symbols of need and of work, will be excluded.

Some contemporaries lamented the conversion of such villages as Argenteuil to suburban extensions of Paris. Adolphe Joanne, the relatively sober author of guide books to the environs of Paris, could not hold back his opinion of the new suburban villas:

These habitations, more pretentious than picturesque, affect all forms and styles of architecture. Here is a garden of a few square metres, possessing a jet of water in a tiny basin, some statues, a gazebo and a greenhouse; it is called an English garden. There, the façades of houses are erected, some on the model of the Alhambra, others on that of Herculaneum or Pompeii.[17]

Fortunately Monet's taste was not that which Joanne deplored, but the flowers that he cultivated none the less stood for the bourgeois who surrounded himself with a garden of his own devising that contrasted with the traditional use of the land. Even an enclosed village garden of former days, managed by a typical resident, would have had vegetables and a few chickens. Élisée Reclus, the great geographer, in an essay of 1866, lamented the loss of these traditional village gardens with their farmyard aspect. 'For strollers walking down the muddy lanes of this make-believe countryside, nature is only represented by well-trimmed bushes and masses of flowers seen through the bars of fences.'[18]

We need not, in consequence, attack Monet for debasing village traditions. I have wanted instead to make evident the particular truth of his real, and his painted gardens. They represent the creation of an ideal environment, away from the city, released from immediate urban pressures, an environment shaped to his own liking as the recipient of natural light and air which, then, his artificial pigments could reconstruct.

Monet's rented villa was on the eastern side of Argenteuil, a district that had been undergoing drastic alteration since the Franco-Prussian war. The railroad used to end across the river, on the Paris side, but now it was brought across the new bridge – the one Monet painted (plates 8 and 9) – into the edge of the village, where a new station was erected. Monet's villa was diagonally across the street from the station.[19] He often had to leave his flowered garden and take the train to Paris, in search of the money he constantly needed. His frequent use of the Gare St Lazare led him, in 1877, to paint his famous group of twelve pictures of the great train shed and its outlying tracks. To complete this review of industrial images in Impressionist painting, we should look at one of these paintings of the Gare St Lazare, and we should juxtapose it to the contemporary painting of his garden at Argenteuil. The truth of Impressionism is found in the juxtaposition, not in either picture alone. Like Daubigny's and Lachambeaudie's *Les Deux Rivages* (plate 5), there are still two sides to Monet's pathway in 1877, one flowered and the other industrialized.

In order to paint the Gare St Lazare, Monet rented rooms nearby and frequently stayed there, although his wife and child remained in Argenteuil. His choice of subject was a daring one in 1877. Some courageous critics had called for paintings of modern buildings, but generally they were considered suitable only for commemorative pictures. A few artists however, including Édouard Manet and Gustave Caillebotte, had made paintings of the tracks and bridges near Gare St Lazare. Like these two artists, who were among his friends and supporters, Monet was committed to a form of naturalism which sought the characteristic truths of a scene or activity. For that reason he did not portray the façade of the station nor the great waiting hall which contemporary chroniclers made so much of. Instead he took the viewer out in the shed (plate 13), and even there, it is not just the train but the structure

Plate 13   Monet, *La Gare St Lazare*

and the whole activity of the station which is his subject. The locomotive is relatively small and, because it is seen frontally, it lacks the mass and power often associated with it. The puffs of steam on the ground at either side hide its wheels and further diminish its threatening power, making it float in an atmosphere of light, steam and smoke. We can see by the placing above of its clouds of blue smoke that it has just entered the shed. Nearer to us on the left is a stationary caboose, also seen from one end so that movement is denied. To the right are a trainman in the foreground and passengers further back on the quai. It is a classically balanced picture, given a great control by its overall symmetry. Not only is the overhead vault centrally placed, but also its vertical supports are the same distance from the left and right edges.

Monet has drawn our attention to these spindly iron columns on either edge. In doing that he has caught the spirit of Eugène

Flachat, the engineer who had made of this shed one of the most daring of contemporary structures. Clever use of iron supports and overhead braces let Flachat construct a very wide span, which he pierced with those huge skylights. Monet lets the sunlight flood down from those skylights on to the tracks in the foreground, and he gives as much prominence to the geometric shadows of the overhead network as to the tracks. In fact, we come to understand this picture as a celebration of the moist outdoors sunlight which occupies the whole centre of the composition, the sunlight which penetrates the station. The smoke and steam which join outside with inside also join man's vapours with nature's atmosphere.

The whole picture is therefore an homage to modern engineering, and more particularly to Flachat's having overcome solid mass in favour of light and air. Is this not the very ambition of this gifted landscapist in his own art? When we think of the Impressionists, do we not think first of their denial of traditional sculptural mass and darkness in favour of light and air? And can we not recall that Louis Napoleon and Baron Haussmann had brought light and air into Paris by widening streets and creating new parks and squares? To carry these analogies one step further, we need only remember that one of the demands of progressive social forces in France, as in England, was for ridding cities of dark, fetid courtyards and streets, of dark, windowless factories and slums.

Lachambeaudie's enthusiasm for modern engineering in the preceding generation, was precisely because it could bring about more vital and healthier conditions of travel and work. Flachat himself had been a prominent Saint-Simonian – he was one of Enfantin's original group of disciples – and his rebuilding of the Gare St Lazare was the fruition of what had once been a utopian ideal. By Monet's day, progressive capitalists had adopted many of the Saint-Simonists' ideas. The railroad trains and bridges that Corot, Millet and Daubigny were unable to countenance, could now be assimilated into the poetics of painting. In the most profound sense, the light and air of Monet's railroad station were interwoven with social issues.

If the history of Monet's painting ended with the Gare St Lazare, the historian would have an easy job of it. His art had ranged sufficiently over city, suburb and country to encompass train station, railroad bridge, factories seen at a distance, seaports, pleasure boating, private gardens, village streets, meadows and riverbanks. Industry had its place in this broad adoption of the contemporary landscape, and there was little reason to assume that it would not continue to figure in his pictures.

Yet after the series of paintings of the Gare St Lazare in 1877, Monet never again painted any subject that could be construed as an industrial one. No more railroad bridges, no more factories appeared in his paintings. Furthermore, he never again painted the buildings and streets of Paris, with the exception of a few pictures of parks and gardens, and even these disappear entirely after 1878. In that year he moved to Vétheuil, on the Seine beyond Mantes, and remained there after his wife's death the following year. By then he was living with Alice Hoschedé, and their combined children numbered six. He began painting often on the Channel coast, and at the end of 1881 established residence at Poissy (which he detested, and refused to paint save for two or three pictures). Then in 1883 Monet settled his expanded family in Giverny, on the Seine half-way to Rouen, and there he spent the rest of his life. Giverny was beyond the reach of immediate Parisian influence and had nothing of the suburb about it. Besides Giverny, his subjects were the cliffs and small ports of Normandy (with evidence of tourism expunged), the rocky coast of Brittany, the Mediterranean coast, the meadows, villages and riverbanks of Normandy, the cathedral of Rouen and his own estate and water gardens. These gardens were the fulfilment of the dreams first sketched out in his rented gardens at Argenteuil.

Art historians will offer Monet's own subjectivity as the explanation for the abrupt termination of his interest in both city and suburb and in the transport that linked them. His wife's lingering death in 1879, followed by his combining families with Alice Hoschedé (whose bankrupt husband gradually took his distance), were emotional events of the first order. Forsaking Paris and its suburbs can be seen as a search for the tranquillity of unspoiled village and rural subjects, that release from city cares which Daubigny and Millet had sought in the preceding generation.

And yet the historian of culture concerned with its social meaning cannot rest content with explanations rooted in the subjectivity of one artist. Of course it would be foolish to ignore such evidence. The richness of psychological inquiry is especially apparent when dealing with the poetics of art. Such inquiry, however, should supplement and not usurp the role of social history.

In the work of Monet's younger contemporary, Vincent van Gogh, there are instructive parallels. Van Gogh's social mission and his art were interwoven in the early 1880s, when he drew and painted the peasants and townspeople of the Borinage. During his two years in Paris he learned the new palette of the Impressionists and painted a number of subjects similar to theirs. The tensions of living in the French capital were too great for him, and when he went to the south of France in 1888 it was in search of an ideal world in which cultivated fields and valleys were in sight of the small towns he preferred. The community of artists he hoped to establish in Arles would have re-established a society whose loss he regretted, a society devoted to the pre-industrial truths of town work and field labour, and to their celebration in art. His Japan, he called it, out of conviction that Japanese artists lived in co-operative communities; he also thought of it as a revival of seventeenth-century Holland, knit together by common beliefs.

Van Gogh's utopian dream could not survive its abortive test in the presence of that egocentric bully Gauguin, and eventually Vincent was driven north to Auvers, where he could seek the help of Dr Gachet, artist, collector, friend of the Impressionists and specialist in mental disturbance. In Auvers Van Gogh tried to achieve balance, painting those magnificent last pictures of thatched cottages of Auvers, of its wheat fields and gently rolling countryside. He committed suicide out of awareness of the distance there was between reality and illusion.

When we are reminded of Van Gogh's poignant odyssey, we are so drawn to its familiar, purely personal events that we are apt to forget how much it speaks for modern man. For in a larger sense, Van Gogh and Monet are alike. Industry and the suburbs enter prominently into their art, but tensions inherent in creating an ideal world in painting drove them away from images of railroad bridges and large cities. In flowering trees and haystacks, wheat-fields and Norman villages, they chose images that would cleanse man of the effects of industrialization.

If the art of either painter had been entirely isolated from that of his fellows, we might be entitled to interpret it as purely subjective and purely idiosyncratic. This is not true, however, for Monet and Van Gogh shared a number of aspirations, and the effect of their art on subsequent generations is owing to their having touched a chord that vibrates deep within modern man. Moreover, in the paintings of Paul Cézanne and of Camille Pissarro, of Winslow

Homer and of Giovanni Segantini, early 'modern' art came to us peopled by peasants, fishermen and villagers. It was still possible in the late nineteenth century to hold up such images to the face of industrialization as a world towards which to aspire. Despite the vitality of the rural communes of our day, and despite the attractions of living the winter in Vermont by a wood stove, we no longer believe that we can return to a pre-industrial condition. It is unlikely that Monet believed he could, either. In the last decades of his life, dominated by his paintings of water gardens, he had to be aware of the degree to which his art was an illusion. In order to get from his house to the water gardens he had built (detouring a local stream for the purpose), he had to cross over the branch railway that bisected his estate. Although he never showed this rail line in his paintings of waterlilies, we must take it into account if we are to comprehend the inner meaning of his art.

Le cours de notre vie a toujours deux Rivages;
Tous deux, dans notre enfance, et fleuris et joyeux,
Sont pleins de doux pensers, de chants insoucieux.
Plus tard, sur une Rive étendant leurs ravages,
L'intéret, les besoins et les prévisions
Emportent la moitié de nos illusions.
   Heureux, quand la vieillesse arrive,
Si quelques fleurs encor restent sur l'autre Rive!

[The course of our life has always two Shores;
Both, in our childhood, are enflowered and joyous,
Full of gentle thoughts, of uncaring songs.
Later, over one Shore, ravages are spread by
Interest and need, and anticipated wants
Take away half of our illusions.
   There is happiness, when old age arrives,
If a few flowers remain still on the other Shore!][20]

7 Three faces of capitalism: women and work in French cities[1]

Louise A. Tilly

French industrial capitalism developed later than that of England. We recognize both as species of capitalism because of their central confrontation: between holders of capital who increasingly made the binding decisions concerning the disposition of all factors of production, including labour, and workers who increasingly laboured for wages at means of production over which they exercised little or no control. The common features of the industrial phase of capitalism in both countries were increased division of labour, growth of large-scale production and distribution, supervised and disciplined work, the concept that E. P. Thompson calls 'time-thrift and ... a clear demarcation between "work" and "life"'.[2] Those powerful features of industrial capitalism created a common ground of experience in France and England, for workers in manufacturing and non-manufacturing industries alike, for skilled and unskilled workers, for young and old, for men and women.

Yet there were differences, which matter because the context from which people came strongly affected the character of their encounter with industrial capitalism. The differences also matter because the differing experiences of industrial capitalism became the sources of contrasting responses to its demands, hardships and opportunities. For those reasons, it will not do to take the experiences of English, male, manufacturing workers as prototypes, and to imagine other encounters with industrial capitalism as incomplete replicas of the prototypical experience. This paper takes a deliberately contrary tack: it examines the varying experiences of women in three French cities – Paris, Lyon and Lille – in the strong hope of identifying features of those experiences that were specific to women's lives, but also with the aim of singling out the particularities of France's capitalism. The paper asks what factors shaped women's labour-force participation and what role migration played in those patterns. It asks how capitalism evolved in the three cities, and how women's work changed as a consequence. It follows a standard important nineteenth-century genre in comparing cities and their hinterlands. For the development of industrial capitalism in France, despite some distinctive features, was associated with the growth of cities, accentuating and at the same time drawing upon the process of urbanization. First we have Paris, capital of France, metropolitan city of consumer industry, commerce and administration; second, Lyon, the southern silk-manufacturing centre; and finally, Lille, in the north, a centre of textile production.

Paris, Lyon and Lille form a rough continuum from industrial diversity to industrial uniformity, from the enormous range of Parisian production to Lyon's combination of manufacturing with commerce to Lille's heavy – although not exclusive – concentration in textiles. Yet the three cities shared a common sequence of economic development. Small-scale service and craft production gave way to large-scale industry and commerce. Male workers experienced a dramatic series of changes: shops became larger and more mechanized; new occupations appeared; wage-labour became the rule; for a time, old skills became more valuable before losing their power in the face of the mechanization and fragmentation of production; individual and group control over work declined. Both the urban economic changes and the transformations of male occupations are well known. Here we focus on female workers to see which experiences they shared with men and which were specific to their sex. What did industrial capitalism mean to women in French cities?

Let us define *work* as production for exchange or labour for wages; we shall examine the work of both single and married women. Work for single women was sometimes a life-cycle stage, sometimes a permanent condition. Married women's work was very common in the nineteenth century, but it was often fragmented – sometimes as a part-time combination with household work, sometimes as an intermittent episode in household experience.[3] Since very few women outside the popular classes produced for exchange or worked for wages, working-class women are the primary focus of the analysis.

In France, nineteenth-century bourgeois observers noticed, and generally deplored, the rise of women's wage work. Villermé, a medical doctor who wrote in the 1830s, was outraged by the hygiene and health problems of urban concentration and early industrial work.[4] Jules Simon (echoing Michelet, whose facts were less firm but whose strictures no less fierce) worried about the moral problem of women's work. In the preface to his *L'Ouvrière* (1860), he declared that 'The book before you is a book about morals.' He then noted that he had spent about a year travelling to visit various industrial centres for his study of women workers '... and I confess with regret that my most serious fears were all exceeded. There are memories that will not leave me.... What is the evil? It is that woman, become a worker, is no longer a woman.'[5]

Writing some fifteen years after Simon, Leroy-Beaulieu remarked that before the nineteenth century, 'no woman, except one from the highest classes, was leisured or devoted herself exclusively to the care of her home and family. Women would have been greatly astonished to learn that their husband's wages alone could provide their food and support, or that the words "woman worker" were "ugly and obscene" [as Michelet put it].' Leroy-Beaulieu insisted that the situation be examined without prejudice, questioning unfavourable circumstances and seeking ways to overcome them. He objected to the idea of the family, not the individual, as the fundamental unit of society. He argued against a rigid sexual division of labour. He insisted that all individuals have the right to dispose of their own labour, and that work was a poor person's property.[6] By contrast with Villermé, Michelet and Simon, in short, Leroy-Beaulieu argued the classic liberal interpretation of women's work.

Villermé, Michelet and Simon saw capitalism through the prism of paternalistic moralism. They feared the consequences for women and the family. Leroy-Beaulieu countered by emphasizing the increased productivity brought by industrial capitalism, and comparing it favourably with a less productive past. He welcomed capitalist notions of the freedom of women, as well as men, to sell their labour power. Elsewhere, it is true, he noted the dual roles of married women as workers and mothers, expressing a typical late nineteenth-century concern: how was the labour force to reproduce if women were both mothers and workers? For Leroy-Beaulieu, however, morality was not the central issue. Practical problems were paramount: women workers were needed. Ideally, young, unmarried women would work while mothers cared for their families. If this were not possible, ways should be found to help working mothers.[7]

Both the conservative and the liberal position misrepresented the changing character of women's work. Conservatives imagined the involvement of women in paid production as a dangerous novelty, while liberals saw the rise of wage-labour as a liberating opportunity. With the advantage of distance – and the recent proliferation of historical research on the subject – we notice the flaws in both opinions. On the one hand, we see women's work becoming increasingly subject to the logic of industrial capitalism, increasingly subordinate and supplementary to men's work. On the other, we see relations to household and family playing a powerful part in the availability of women for different kinds of production. The combination of the two circumstances meant that women's work experiences, on average, were quite distinct from those of men. It meant that women had to adopt different (and, on balance, probably more difficult) strategies for coping with the need to earn money. It meant, in sum, that women had their own encounter with industrial capitalism, one which was not merely a shadow of men's experience. In order to sense the varieties of female involvement in industrial capitalism, let us look closely at the women of Paris, Lyon and Lille.

Paris

This beautiful city, boasting ancient urban, royal and religious monuments, was the political, economic and intellectual capital of France in the *ancien régime*. By the second half of the eighteenth century, it had reclaimed the royal government and its administrators from Versailles. In 1789 and in the ensuing years of revolution, Paris was the locus of dramatic events and day-to-day struggle. The city was relatively small physically, huddled around the Seine and the Île de la Cité, the island on which the royal administrative buildings were built; the Seine was also an active port for water-borne commerce. On the right bank, to the east, lay the city hall, to the west the royal palaces. Beyond the Marais the faubourg St Antoine was a thriving artisanal centre where craftsmen produced for the inhabitants of the city. Rousseau described another face of the city; entering the faubourg Saint Marceau, he saw 'only small, dirty and stinking streets, ugly black houses, an air of filth, poverty, beggars, carters, sewing women, women hawking herbals and old hats'.[8] Productive work in Paris, then, tended to be consumer- and distribution-oriented, whether the customers were the rich who bought the elegant furniture or carriages produced by the artisans of St Antoine, or the poor who bought the old clothes and herbs sold in St Marceau.[9] A report written in 1789 noted that 'considered as a *fabrique* city, there is no comparison of Paris with Lyons ... : the high cost of labour means that in Paris, one can't afford to set up manufacturing except that for which the raw materials are very costly, or in which the process is very complex and refined and based on fine art'.[10]

How did women fit into this consumer-oriented economy of perhaps 600,000 persons, an economy based on the presence of wealthy clients as well as the poor who served their needs and were themselves, in turn, customers for the cruder products of their peers? Briefly, women formed a substantial proportion of all workers, but they did relatively few types of work.

They numbered about half the domestic servants, a massive group in such an economy. Servants, especially those serving bourgeois rather than aristocratic masters, were most often migrants from rural areas. By virtue of their occupations, servants were dependent, yet the whims of their masters could leave them independent, though penniless and vulnerable, if they were dismissed. Because they lived with their masters, to some extent they were physically separated from the neighbourhoods where the popular classes lived.

Women were less likely than men to be found in the productive sector. The few female trades organized in guilds were primarily selling trades. Restif de la Bretonne, a cranky but perceptive observer of pre-revolutionary Paris, in fact believed that selling was women's only trade: 'the women of the populace were uniquely employed in peddling useless things like flowers'.[11] Seamstresses were the major exception. Apprenticeship to a seamstress meant that the mistress would

show her the trade of seamstress and all other things she does, without hiding anything from her, ... treat her humanely, ... give her food, lodgings, heat, and light, ... pay for her laundry; in particular ... teach her religion and ... send her to religious instruction so that she may be able to take first communion.[12]

Women, Jeffrey Kaplow concludes:

... were thus limited to activities outside the guild structures. Some of the jobs that had traditionally been theirs now no longer existed, casualties of the great metropolis. If they still functioned as midwives and nurses, they were no longer very often called on to act as professional mourners. . . . In the main, they had to work as domestics and as retailers of food, clothing and other assorted items.[13]

Women were common figures in the thriving commerce of the city, much of it carried on in the streets. The *poissardes*, or market women, a contemporary German account noted, were 'linked by blood or clientage relationships to all the respectable men of Paris who shine shoes, carry coals, clean out sewers, build or tear down walls'.[14] During the revolution the street-market women took part in many of the demonstrations or protests in the capital, initiating the march to Versailles in October 1789.

By 1851 Paris had grown to over one million inhabitants, but the range of women's occupations had not notably broadened. Paris remained a city of consumer industry and women were still active in garment-making, domestic service and marketing. Zola's gritty realistic novel *L'Assommoir* offers a series of sketches of women's occupations in the chief female characters, all residents of the urban slum called the Goutte d'or. Gervaise, the heroine, was a laundress who by hard work finally acceded to the ownership of a small hand laundry but, owing to back luck and drink, lost her business. Her daughter Nana was apprenticed as a flower-maker but became a prostitute. Madame Lorilleux, Gervaise's sister-in-law, assisted her husband as a gold chain-maker, heating gold wire, pulling it through a metal plate to make it even and fine, tempering it and forming it into links.[15] Another view of a married woman's work life around mid century is offered by Victorine B, a worker militant in the First International who was a boot sewer when her husband, a master shoemaker, was out of work or unable to work; her wage earning was frequently interrupted by her child's illness and other family concerns. She lamented the necessity which forced married women to work '12 or 14 hours for pitiful wages, forced to leave their children or aged parents untended . . . women . . . shut up for long hours in unhealthy shops with inadequate air and light'.[16] The wife of the Paris carpenter described by Frédéric Le Play in one of his family monographs in 1856 took in sewing for tiny money wages and some payment in kind. (Le Play was one of the early French sociologists who collected worker's life histories in 1855 and after.) She had quit her more taxing work in the central markets because of health.[17] Le Play and his followers always carefully considered the earnings of married women, whether in wages or in kind, even though they were often very small, for they were serious contributions to family welfare. These contemporary accounts bear accurate witness to the kind of work done by women in the mid century. A young woman of the popular classes was certain to work for wages, most often in domestic service or the garment industry, in jobs that were limited in scope and poorly paid. A married woman was likely to continue working in the same kinds of occupations, although as she had children she might well have had to reduce the number of hours she worked or go through periods when she did not at all. Family claims were powerful and sometimes contradictory, for they assigned heavy home responsibilities to married women and at the same time often required them to earn a wage.

By 1900, Paris was a city of 2,700,000. A British government report on *Cost of Living in French Towns* (reporting data for 1905 and 1907) noted that there was a large resident urban working class, but many workers were by then housed in surrounding suburbs. In the city, a 'position of special importance is occupied by the motorcar, electrical, brass and bronze, furniture, clothing, sugar refining and leather industries'. The 1901 census classification of the labour force by industry (the most recent available to the inquiry) shows that the clothing industry, the metal industry, and commerce were by far the largest employers in the city.[18] Of these 'big three', the garment industry and commerce were the primary employers of women. They also were an even larger majority of servants than in earlier periods. Servants were still most often rural migrants. Thus Juliette Sauget and her sisters were sent (from rural Picardy) by their parents into service. Sauget went directly to Paris and only later returned to the regional capital of Amiens.[19] A more common progression would have been from countryside to provincial city to Paris. Although servants in Paris often came from areas relatively close by, there were well-established networks by 1900 through which young women from more distant areas, such as Britanny, travelled to Paris for domestic service. Daughters were sent by poor families to save their wages for marriage. Servants remained dependent and vulnerable. Their wages, hours and working conditions were not regulated by law and their lodgings were not subject to laws on housing. Thus hours were long, housing unhealthy and cramped, wages often uncertain.[20] In times of prosperity a servant could find other jobs easily, and servant turnover often represented an unspoken rejection of poor conditions. By 1900 reform efforts, and the law of supply and demand, had begun to regularize wages and improve conditions. There were proportionately fewer live-in servants than fifty years earlier. The role of service as an entry position for young women to the urban economy had declined.[21]

Rural to urban migration brought other workers to Paris also. Jeanne Bouvier, born in 1865 in the south of France, had worked first in a silk spinning mill, then as a domestic servant on a farm, responsible also for some farm tasks. After another period in a silk mill, she emigrated with her mother to Paris to work for a small brush manufacturer. Dismissed from that job, she was helped by cousins to find a place as a servant. Then they found her a job as a hat trimmer. When that trade floundered, she did piecework sewing. Finally, she entered a ship as a seamstress and she gradually worked her way up to skilled status.[22] Her experience resembled that of many others. In addition to women in garment shops, which employed a permanent skilled work-force of young unmarried women primarily, there were some 80,000 seamstresses working at home in Paris in 1904. The invention of the sewing machine and its dissemination after 1860 had made the rapid expansion of home work possible. Jobbers in the 'sweated' trades were delighted to put out sewing to women who provided their own machines, tables, light and heat, and worked long hours for low wages. Such women were a flexible and exploitable work-force. Women who worked in shops before marriage could continue at home when they had children.

There were many continuities with older patterns of women's employment in Paris at the turn of the century. There had been a considerable change, however, which heralded the future. This was the development of large stores and offices which hired clerical workers. The department store was a French innovation, a consequence of a differentiating and specializing organization of work. Bon Marché, the first department store, was founded in 1852; by the end of the century there were six department stores in Paris with large work-forces, ranging from 1200 at the Bazar de L'Hôtel de Ville to 4500 at Bon Marché. In 1910, 20 to 25 per cent of the workers in these stores were women.[23]

Such work was attractive – despite its very real problems, as discussed below – partly because of the excitement and glamour of the department store as an institution. One contemporary critic noted that among saleswomen, 'misplaced *amour propre* prevents many of them from taking work [which would pay better] and leads them to choose this job, where they are not workers but *demoiselles, demoiselles de magasin*'.[24] An advertisement for the department store Printemps burbled that it was a 'palace for women, enchanted, full of caprice, where the woman reigns supreme'.[25] Behind the glittering decor, poor working conditions persisted. Women worked long hours, often on their feet most of the day. A law requiring that employers provide chairs or stools for all women employees was passed in 1900, but the women were often forbidden to sit when shoppers were present. Only in 1906 were French salespeople guaranteed a weekly day off by law. Contemporary reports remarked on the frequency of tuberculosis among store employees who worked in the stuffy, dusty stores. Zola called them 'machines that eat women'.[26]

Women also worked in government offices, such as the postal and telephone services. In 1891 about 45 per cent of post office workers were women; in 1894 the service moved to increase the proportion of women workers and 'feminize' the service. Male unionists were quick to point out this was a move to save money, for the women's wages were about 60 per cent of those of men. Critics decried the working conditions of women telephone operators, working on their feet in over-heated rooms, mouths and ears pressed to their instruments, conditions it was feared would cause 'genital disorders'.[27] Women nevertheless flocked to these jobs and became an important proportion of workers in the service sector.

Women in Paris were never primarily engaged in production work in the nineteenth century except in the garment industry. Throughout the period, service and commerce were the most important employers of women. What changed was the scale of work and the role of discipline and supervision. The street market woman of pre-revolutionary Paris gave way to the department store clerk of 1900. Independent wage-earning in the new areas of office clerical work took the place of domestic service. Service and commerce became capitalistic. The garment industry and luxury production although also rationalized and capitalistic, remained partly small scale, including home work, and, at the same time, partly larger scale. Women were still strictly limited in job options, and the kinds of jobs they held were few in number.

Lyon

'Lyon', the Abbé Expilly wrote enthusiastically in the 1760s, 'rich, beautiful, ancient, populous, commercially vigorous, the most important city in the realm after Paris...'.[28] By the end of the eighteenth century, on the eve of the revolution of 1789, Lyon no longer possessed the political and economic autonomy characteristic of its earlier history. Finance capital had moved to Paris, and the main streams of trade had shifted north. Nevertheless, the city had a vitality and vigour based on the manufacture and commerce of the *grande fabrique* of the silk industry.

The old walls of the city were tumbling into ruin, and the worker suburbs of La Guillotière and Croix Rousse, though outside the walls and not in the city proper, were none the less part of a continuously built-up urban area. The city and its suburbs numbered about 143,000 inhabitants, while the population of the city proper at the time of the first national census (1801) had been 109,500.

Since the revolutionary and Napoleonic periods saw important changes in the organization of work and technology of the silk industry, the picture of 'old' Lyon presented here dates from before 1789. It was drawn by Jean-Claude Déglize, an official of the Napoleonic empire, who used documents in local archives to trace the occupational structure of city on the eve of the revolution.

Lyon had the usual component of workers in consumer industries: bakers, butchers, tailors, seamstresses, all of whom worked most often in household units with perhaps an apprentice or two. The wives of craftsmen worked in the shop as helpers. The four most prominent Lyonnais industries were the manufacture of silk cloth, silk stockings, elaborate woven braid and hats. In silk textiles, almost two-thirds of the workers (20,000) were wives, daughters and minor sons of masters, or young girls who came to Lyon to do various tasks preparatory to weaving (such as silk reeling and spinning), or to work as auxiliaries in weaving proper. These girls, the *dévideuses, tireuses* and other specialized workers, were often part servant, part production worker, living in the household/shop of their masters. In the hat industry, similarly, about one-fifth of the workers (1114) were women or girls who did the preparatory tasks and the hat trimming.[29] The social and geographic origins of these women can be traced in their contracts of marriage, which also spelled out the value of their dowries, slowly saved from years of arduous work.

There were two chief categories of women silk workers. Unskilled young women or girls, most frequently migrants, did the reeling, spinning and drawing, or pulled the cords of the loom to advance the brocaded pattern. (The latter were called *tireuses*, or drawgirls.) Skilled workers such as the *tordeuses*, who looped the cords which would produce the pattern around the warp, or the *liseuses*, who programmed the patterns for the looms, were more likely to be Lyonnais-born, daughters or wives of masters. If they worked in the shop of a master who was not kin, they were better paid than the migrant workers. Women were seldom guild members; craftsmen opposed their entry for they feared that women would 'crowd' the craft and drive men's wages down.[30] Silk-spinning and weaving were urban industries in the eighteenth century. Only the cultivation of silkworms and the first steps of pulling and reeling were done in the countryside.

All the workers in this luxury trade were at the mercy of 'deliveries of raw silk, on the whims of fashion, and on foreign competition'.[31] Later, when the drawgirls were allowed to become weavers, the number of *tireuses* declined.[32] The period from about 1778 through to the revolution brought hard times to Lyon; the revolution caused a decline in demand for elaborate brocade. Pressure on the workers' standard of living ensued, followed by unemployment or under-employment and, finally, a strike in 1786 for better wages. In all these changes, migrant girl workers fared poorly because of their tenuous and often dependent position. Employers sometimes felt no obligation to pay their wages in difficult times, as in the case of a master who died leaving his widow assets of 56 livres and wages owed to his *tordeuse* and *dévideuse* of 200 livres.[33]

Located at the confluence of two major rivers, Lyon attracted migrants from a large area, mostly from the eastern, relatively close provinces of Bresse, Dauphiné and Vivarais, or to the west, the Auvergne, and to the north, the Bourbonnais. But migrants came from farther east as well, from Savoy and Piedmont in the Italian kingdom of Sardinia. The girls who travelled from their native villages to work in Lyon did so because migration presented a chance to save a dowry, a prerequisite for marriage. Their families could not provide them with this essential start to life, so it was up to the young women to work and save for themselves.

Lyonnais wage-earning men needed a contribution from their future wife if they were to set up housekeeping and equip a weaver's shop. Marie Meunier, an orphaned silk worker, for example, contracted marriage in 1787 with a master silk weaver, naming a legal guardian for herself since she was a minor. She wished to marry before her majority because of the 'great expecta-tions' which she had been promised, a dowry of 100 livres for herself and 100 livres for her husband. This was an advantageous contract for the weaver, who had no capital, but as Maurice Garden points out in his history of eighteenth-century Lyon, such a fortune was on the threshold between poverty and getting-by. He demonstrates, by other examples, that a couple could set up a household and shop with 200 livres, but if they had many children, the daughters would have to work without wages for their parents and would not be likely to receive as much at their own marriage as did Marie Meunier.[24] Her case is somewhat unusual also in that she received her dowry at a young age and married while still a minor; the age of marriage of female silk workers was likely to be closer to 30, because of the time needed to amass a dowry.

Although the wife of a weaver had a more secure economic situation than did a young migrant working for wages in a shop, the master's wife also faced uncertainty because of the tenuous economic base of these households. Years of cyclical downturn or the illness or death of the master weaver could spell disaster. Jeanne Michon, a former *dévideuse* who had brought a 300-livre dowry to her silk-weaver husband, inherited on his death only 'an old wooden bed ... a Catalonian spread, a blanket, a canopy, a feather puff, the whole greatly worn and worth only 12 livres'.[35] The wives worked in the shop beside their husbands, and at the same time had many children, despite late marriages. This was partly a consequence of the custom of busy mothers sending their infants to wet-nurses in the countryside. Silk weavers' wives then became pregnant again very quickly, for they did not benefit from the contraceptive effect of prolonged nursing. Thus many of these women had annual childbirths and their completed families were very large. The custom of wet-nursing was linked also to an exceptionally high level of infant mortality (67 per cent of the wet-nursed babies died in their first year), and silk-weaving families seemed to be having many children to ensure that some would grow to majority.[36]

At the end of the eighteenth century the city of Lyon, then, had an economy in which women were important productive workers. This economy was in crisis, and families were plunged into poverty by such crises as the death of a wage-earner or declining business demand. The city was not just a 'devourer of men' but a devourer of men, women and children.

By the middle of the nineteenth century, textile production had industrialized for cotton and linen. The silk industry of Lyon had changed less, and in different ways. There the definition of 'worker' given by Le Play still held true. For Le Play, workers were 'persons performing manual labour (other than a personal service for a master), sometimes part proprietors, or owners of a small business, for whom the primary source of income was wages'.[37] It was the ownership of his tools, in the case of the Lyonnais silk weaver, as well as the glove and hatmakers, metal turners and other workers, which differentiated them from pure proletarians. Lyonnais workers, writes Yves Lequin, the historian of the nineteenth-century city, were 'vulnerable to the play of international markets, business cycles and their bosses' decisions, yet they owned, to a small degree, the means of production'.[37]

Armand Audiganne, an economic journalist writing in 1873, suggested much continuity when he wrote, 'One fact is striking, right off; that is family life. The stable workers, owners of one or more looms, are almost all married. Since the assistance of a wife is indispensable for the multitude of tasks auxilliary to weaving, they marry young. By the nature of his work, the weaver stays in his home....'[39]

Gradual modification of household workshops had begun, as we shall see also in the case of cotton, at the spinning stage rather than with the final weaving of cloth. The processes of pulling and reeling silk moved into large shops in towns and villages near Lyon, and country women primarily were hired to do the work. The mills often were run by steam engines or water wheels, and their workers did highly differentiated tasks, supervised by foremen who imposed strict discipline. Reeling and spinning mills with attached dormitories, specific to silk manufacturing, developed about this time. These mills, in which girls and women formed the majority of workers, were located primarily in the region to the south and east of Lyon. The first of these *internats*, as they were called, that at Jujurieux, was founded in 1835. Here nuns sometimes supervised the personal lives of the girls. The factory dormitory appeared first for spinning mills, but as weaving factories began to replace urban master weavers and their family-based business, they, too, frequently built dormitories for their workers. In 1859, Reybaud estimated there were 40,000 girls in such mills in the south-east of France.[40] Leroy-Beaulieu, interested as he was in changing patterns of women's work and eager to promote ways for wives to be able to focus on family life instead of wage work, welcomed the *internats*. He noted that it might seem a strange means of promoting domesticity – snatching adolescents out of their family's home and shutting them up in factory dormitories. Yet, he argued, 'the *internat* is one of the most appropriate institutions for promoting ... the strengthening of the family'. The silk entepreneurs, in their choice of young women and adolescents as workers, made it possible for these women's wages to help their mothers stay home; their savings could also help them, after marriage, to be full-time wives and mothers. However, Leroy-Beaulieu ignored the low wages, the contracts which gave these wages directly to the girls' parents and the conditions of life and work in the *internats* in his enthusiastic endorsement.[41]

In Lyon proper, women and girls handled other preparatory processes, such as preparing warps and winding woofs, sometimes in specialized small shops, sometimes in the weaver's shop, as had long been the custom. Silk weaving was still done by both men and women, but women were most often weavers of non-figured cloth, while men specialized in brocades and other types of silk with woven designs. Fine elaborate weaves of the most elegant types continued to be produced on the unwieldly draw looms (*grande tire*). New figured weaves were produced by mid nineteenth century on jacquard looms. These new looms had proliferated through the city, especially in the suburb of the Croix Rousse, after their invention in 1804. They were looms with programmed cards which controlled the feed of thread to produce the design, thus eliminating the arduous task formerly done by the drawgirls.[42] In the early nineteenth century these looms were also installed in small artisanal shops in the countryside.

The weaver's wives and daughters provided some of his labour force, but the role of migrant girls was also significant in the industry. The autobiography of Norbert Truquin, a wandering worker who settled in Lyon as a weaver in the 1850s, quotes his boss's description of how the girls were recruited:

the bosses go to recruit apprentices in the Dauphiné, the Bugey and Savoy; they are provided with character witnesses by the parish priests of Lyon. They then present these documents to the country priests who tell them which families have daughters the right age. Introducing themselves, with the priest's backing, they are natually welcomed.... They explain how their workers save hundreds of francs, what good marriages they have made if they're economical, and the country girls quickly sign up to go to Lyon. Their parents sign contracts for them as apprentices for a four year period, although four months is an adequate apprenticeship.

It's mostly 15 year old girls who are hired.... Working seventeen hours a day in unhealthy workshops, where there's never a ray of sunshine, half of the girls get chest illnesses before the end of their contract. Meanwhile, they are accused of whining if they complain, while the most able and rapid workers are flattered with praise to work faster; when they can no longer work they're accused of imprudence. They are sent back to their parents in the country, but it's often too late....

[Truquin notes] my boss swore that most of those who left the shops took the road, not to their homes, but to the cemetery.[43]

Writers of the early nineteenth century were fond of noting the relative wealth of the Lyonnais *canuts* (the male weavers) for, compared with the factory spinners of Lille (described below), shod in clogs and living in cellars, the *canuts* wore boots and lived in well-furnished rooms. [44] The numerous migrant women workers, however, were less likely than the *canuts* to enjoy even relative superiority. Unlike the men, proletarianized women workers were very unlikely to be owners of the means of production, even such a small investment as a loom; consequently their wages were lower and their vulnerability to the market even greater than that of the men, who were still part artisan as well as part proletarian.

Lyon's women workers, like the men, must be seen in the broader context of the city and its region where, as Lequin put it, 'changing one's sector of work did not always mean geographic displacement, and industry moved toward its labour force at least as often as the peasant to the factory; the industrial development of the urban centres themselves was rooted in the countryside'.[45]

During the last quarter of the nineteenth century, Lyon's productive base changed, as did its relationship to the countryside. 'Industrialization rediscovered its rural vocation.'[46] Agricultural crisis undercut the viability of peasant production, and rural folk sought work nearby in the decentralizing silk industry, while others migrated to the city. There the old silk trades were declining in importance. A 'crumbling' of the old concentration in silk and a diversification of economic activity occurred in Lyon.[47] The *canuts* died out and their sons went into new trades. Their wives and daughters sometimes continued to work in silk specialities, such as tulle embroidery or other fancy-work. In 1903, the parliamentary commission on the textile industry could find no *young* silk weavers. They wrote in their report, 'it is ... the complete and definitive ruin of Lyonnais silk weaving'.[48] Men worked instead in metallurgy, the expanding machine industry, construction and in business. The economic activity of the centre became services and commerce, as the city literally deindustrialized. The number of industrial production jobs in the city for women, as for men, declined. Lequin's study of marriage in 1911 shows that proportionately fewer of the brides and grooms were industrial workers than at mid century. Young urban women worked instead in services and commerce. The silk industry with its large female labour force was to be found in the suburbs and nearby small towns.[49]

By 1906, there were said to be 100,000 girls in the still flourishing *internats* and numerous women who worked on a daily basis in the same mills. Lucie Baud, a woman who later became a union militant, described her first jobs:

I began my apprenticeship at the Durand factory, Vizille, at the beginning of 1883. I was 12 years old. There were about 800 women weavers in the factory then. We usually worked 12 hours a day, occasionally 13–14; the shuttles of the looms crossed at the rate of 80 times a minute; very few girls could run two looms at a time, but sometimes they managed to oversee three looms with two workers. One could earn 130 to 150 francs a month; that is, if you worked really hard, and the fibres were good quality....

Several years later, at the beginning of 1888, I went to work at Duplan's mill. There one could earn a bit more because the equipment was better. The looms moved faster, and the silk bosses made the women run two looms at a time. Nevertheless, work was again speeded up when silk gauze came into fashion. It meant lower salaries but no one dared protest, as we had no organization. Each year, there were new modifications, new looms, new processes, and yet, with each improvement, there was a new salary reduction.[50]

The 1906 conference of the silk workers' union declared that 'the silk spinning mills have become female prison camps'.[51]

Women's work had industrialized and ruralized at the same time in the Lyonnais region. The former artisanal heart of a regional industrial system was now a regional commercial and distributive centre. Women workers in the city were more likely to work in offices or commerce than in production, just as in Paris. The *internats* in the region hired women into a system that exaggerated some characteristics of capitalism: descipline and supervision, large-scale production units, finely differentiated work, attempts to increase productivity. The women who lived in the dormitories, however, did not experience a separation of work and life, but a merging of the two in an expansion of supervision from work into 'life'. The system was thus paternalistic and moralizing and, at the same time, a particularly oppressive form of capitalism.

Lille

Lille is situated in the flat northern plains of French Flanders, near the Belgian border. Until the mid nineteenth century, the city was dominated by its towered citadel and was contained within ancient stone walls. When Napoleon requested reports on economic and social conditions from his prefects (heads of the department administration) in the Year Ten (1804), few supplied as exhaustive and thorough accounts as the prefect Christophe Dieudonné of the Nord. His text provides the basis for an overview of women's work and the economy of Lille at the beginning of the nineteenth century. Dieudonné noted the industrious reputation of the department, its lack of devotion to science and *belles-lettres*, in these words: 'the genius of its inhabitants is directed toward commerce and industry. One remarks that they have astonishing talent in these pursuits. Although they are slaves to routine and tradition in matters that don't affect their pocketbooks, they know very well how to innovate when they find it in their interest'.[52] Capitalism found fertile soil in the Nord.

Lille then had a population of 55,000, already very crowded within the walls. The city had long been a centre of trade and manufacturing, primarily of textiles, lace, thread and industrial chemicals such as oil.

Dieudonné's tabular summary of workers in all occupations in the department gives us some idea of female occupations. The table is not divided by sex, but occupations are designated male or female by the gender ending of the word designating them. Here is the entire range of women's occupations: midwife, seamstress, dressmaker, lacemaker, spinner, florist, gardener, fine lingerie sewer.[53] There was not much variety among women's occupations; most were connected to the production of cloth and clothing. But this very sparse list poses some problems. Surely there were female servants and, even more surely, women who aided their husbands as artisans, keepers of cabarets or small shops. Dieudonné's list is not helpful unless we recognize the principle on which it was constructed. It notes only independent workers for wages, not those who received room and board for their work, such as servants or aides in a family economy.[54]

Linen was produced by hand processes in the more rural communes of the province. A study of the countryside before the revolution remarks on the dispersal of textile production as supplemental work for peasants, who were able to combine industry and agriculture and resist migration into the city.[55] Lille itself was the centre of the cotton industry, of lacemaking and production of consumer products. In this period, mechanical spinning of cotton in factories had already put women spinning at wheels out of business. Young women and children worked at the auxiliary tasks in the spinning mills while men ran the spinning-jennies and mules. Bolts of rough wool cloth called *camelots* were woven in the city also, by male hand-weavers and female *redoubleuses* who lived and worked in the grim workers' neighbourhood of Saint Saveur.[56] Both this wool cloth production and that of knitted goods, formerly done by women, had declined during the revolution and ensuring wars.[57]

The other female occupation discussed at length by Dieudonné was that of lacemaker. The Lille *dentellière* did not do as fine work as the Valenciennes lacemaker, who took ten months to complete a pair of lace cuffs for a man's coat; Lille lace was less fine and detailed. Fashions had changed during the revolution and the simpler lace of Lille was more in demand than the elaborate Valenciennes lace, associated with the aristocrats of the *ancien régime*. The lace industry, Dieudonné concluded, 'provides unmarried women and wives in this populous city a means to subsist at this period'.[58]

Most women in the popular classes did some kind of income-producing work during most of their lives in this period. In addition to the occupations discussed above, women commonly sold food, drink or other small items in street markets or small shops. On the whole most women in Lille at the beginning of the nineteenth century were more likely to be engaged in this type of informal work, or independent work as a servant when young and single, or as part of the household production unit when they married, than in independent wage work.

By mid century Lille had industrialized and increased in population. Its experience offers a classic case of capitalist concentration and growth of the cotton textile industry. In 1851, there were almost 76,000 persons crammed within the old walls, an increase of óver one-third in less than fifty years. Visitors remarked on the growth of the city, 'all out of proportion to its space', and described it as the 'epitome of ugliness'.[59] It was not until 1858 that the walls of Lille were levelled and five industrial suburbs annexed, adding 40,000 inhabitants. The expectation that healthier, less crowded housing conditions would then be possible was not fulfilled, however. The reason was the continuing in-migration that resulted from the growth of the cotton industry. In 1832 Lille had 50 spinning mills with 180,000 spindles; in 1848 it had only 34, but with 400,000 spindles; by 1853 it had 525,670 spindles in action, with 635,790 at the end of 1859. Between 1849 and 1859, the value of the means of production in Lille had increased by 18 million francs.[60]

About 10,000 workers, male and female, worked in the spinning industry. In the 1850s mechanical linen-spinning also grew rapidly, and by 1856 it employed over 10,000 workers.[61] A third branch of textiles, the production of sewing threads of varying fineness, continued as an artisanal trade, whose workers considered themselves the aristocrats of textile workers. The masters who worked in this trade were most often natives of Lille, residents of Saint Saveur, husbands of skilled lacemakers. Thus a core of the old skilled workers remained at their craft in the heart of the old city while, at the same time large steam-powered mills attracted migrant workers; during the 1850s thread-making was also gradually moved into mills.[62]

It was primarily the spinning of cotton and linen that employed women in simple, differentiated tasks transforming the raw fibre into progressively finer and more tightly wound thread. Pierre Pierrard has reconstructed the work life of 'Maria Verkindère', a prototypical Lillois linen mill worker, one of the 12,792 women (there were 12,939 men) in the spinning mills, according to the 1856 census:

Maria Verkindère had never gone to school; at age 8 she started work as a doffer in a cotton mill. She could neither read nor write nor sew. Married at 18 to a fellow worker, a thread-maker, she had a daughter whom she left each day with an elderly neighbour who cared for the child along with a half a dozen other children.[63] She rose at 4 in the morning; within a half hour, the bell of the mill called her to work.

From 5 a.m. to 8 p.m., Monday morning to Saturday night, 300 days a year, Marie stood at her work in the damp linen mill, in an immense hall heated to 90 degrees, tending a spinning machine – for 1 franc 50 per day. The tough linen fibre was hard to twist without being soaked in hot water, so jets of almost-boiling water were extruded along the machine, bathing the batts of linen and filling the room with moist heat. The spinsters, their feet in standing water ... dressed in a minimum of clothing.... Maria tended three hundred twirling bobbins, unable to take a moment off except when the boy and girl assistants stepped in quickly to remove the filled bobbins. Maria took her brief respite to examine her poor feet, swollen by the constant dampness, covered with sores.

The midday whistle signalled the sudden halt of the machines. Like most of the workers exahusted from so many hours on their feet, Maria sat against the shop wall to eat her buttered bread and stewed fruit for lunch....

[When] Maria, worn out, running with sweat, dirty, left the steamy box in which she had been working since early morning ... [she dressed warmly to go home] because in the winter the sudden change in temperature on leaving the mill could freeze the moisture on the workers' clothes.[64]

The visual image of workers covered with ice particles is complemented by another, that of Ardouin-Dumazet, who described the linen workers of Wazemmes as 'emaciated, their blonde hair (many are Flemish) full of linen thread and whitened with the dust of the mill'.[65]

Most women with children did not work in mills, but they needed to earn a wage. One of these women was Sophie Ternyck, whose life history was found in the records of the charity society of St Vincent de Paul, to which she had to apply for assistance in 1858. She was 39 that year, native born, a resident of a tiny third-floor room in one of the suburbs annexed in that year. She had very few belongings, but was the mother of a 7-year-old son whose father, a locksmith, had disappeared despite his promise to marry her. Sophie was a shirt-maker, one of 800 Lille women who reported that occupation in the census of 1856. She had worked since age 13 for the same company, in the shop at first, now in her own room. Her task was to pull a thread every centimetre of the width of a man's shirt front, then pleat the linen into tiny half centimetre pleats between the pulled threads and secure them with a fine seam. Sophie was paid 3 francs 50 per 100 pleats, and by working ten hours a day, she could earn 1 franc 65. This meant working constantly; she was unable to do her own shopping or errands and her son had to do them for her. Ill and unable to work, she had pawned her good clothes by the time she applied for aid and possessed only the dress and clogs that she wore. In the best of times, her meagre wages barely covered housing and food for herself and her son; every additional expense meant taking out a loan. The social worker inquired about kin who could help her. Her brothers and sisters were all workers too. Her aunt, a 50-year-old unmarried lacemaker, skilled in producing bobbin lace, was finding her wages pressed downwards as the trade declined under competition from machine-made lace.[66] These women, poorly paid and concentrated in textile and clothing trades, were typical Lillois workers.

Although many workers, especially those practising the fine skilled trades, were natives of the city, Lille also attracted many migrants, particularly from Belgian Flanders where cottage textile production collapsed in the first half of the nineteenth century. The growth of Lille and its region's industrialized textile production required many workers, and manufacturers went so far as to pay premiums to migrants who entered their employ. Whole families tended to migrate in order to find jobs – for the children and adolescents, as well as the adults. Belgians met with ethnic hostility – a popular chant went 'do-re-mi-fa-sol-la-ti-do, all Belgians have got to go!' – and criticism of their alleged willingness to accept scab wages, their incomprehensible Flemish tongue, and so on.[67]

Few women could live independently on the low wages they received; most were part of a household economy in which wages were pooled. Men's wages were higher than women's, but an adult man's wage was often unpredictable, for he was liable to arbitrary short weeks or layoffs, seasonal or otherwise. As he grew older, his wage-earning powers declined. Consequently, as daughters, working-class women were obliged to contribute to their family's budget; as wives they more often ran the household and contributed by saving and scrimping, but over the years wives, too, were often called on to add to the family wage pot.

A study of wealth in Lille, based on the compulsory registration of movable property at death, shows that 82 per cent of the Lillois workers who died in the 1850s (91 per cent of workers in large-scale industry) had no possessions to pass on to their heirs. The gap between the average value of a worker's wealth in that period and that of a factory owner was 1 to 10,000.[68] Under such conditions, women's work was a necessity, not a choice.

By 1900, Lille had decentralized. As a result of this centrifugal process, the consequence at least partially of the disappearance of space within the city limits for either factories or workers' housing, large industrial suburbs became the sites of the more modern and productive factories. Inside the city proper were business head-quarters, and large-scale commerce flourished. A study of registrations at death in 1908–10 shows a very different social composition of the population compared with that of mid century. Aside from the intermediate group – small shopkeepers and artisans, already in decline in the 1850s – the proportion of workers among the population as a whole was greatly reduced, with the proportion of workers in large-scale industry down to 40 per cent. There were relatively few textile workers, some of whom still performed pre-industrial work, for example hand-weaving or embroidery on tulle, rather than the factory work of the mid-century industrial boom. There were many more mechanics, railroad workers and metal workers.[69] A new world of work had opened up: the world of offices, in which clerks were employed by large businesses or government. And workers were clearly in a better economic position than they had been; relatively few died with no property to report. The value of the average deceased worker's property had tripled since the 1850s. However, so had that of the industrialist; the wealth ratio of workers and businessmen was still 1 to 10,000.

What did these changes mean for women workers? Since several sectors in which women workers were especially represented – textiles and domestic service – became less important sources of employment in Lille, there were proportionately and absolutely fewer women in these occupations. Very few women worked in the new heavy industry – railroads, metallurgy, machine building. On the other hand, women were very likely to be employed in commerce and offices, whether for private business or the government. Single women flocked into the new white-collar jobs; they were likely to have the schooling required for such work since state-sponsored schooling had become compulsory in the 1880s. In the industrial suburbs, working-class wives were more likely to be textile workers than they had been at mid century, while the children of workers' families spent more time in school. Although working-class families had more material possessions, they also evidenced higher expectations, both for their own standard of living and for the future of their children. Worker families still expected their daughters and sons to contribute to the household economy for many years; this was one of the sources of higher living standards among workers in the period around 1900.[70]

Nevertheless, the old modes of work lingered around Lille, as elsewhere in France. The elderly tulle embroiderers and weavers who died in the city in the early twentieth century are one example. Not far from Lille, in smaller cities such as Halluin or Avesnes-les-Aubert, whole communities lived and worked to older rhythms, the women in them caught up still in household production. The testimony of an 85-year-old woman in 1976 evokes the life of these workers:

... the men didn't like to have their wives away from home. They were needed in the cellar.... It was a big half-dark room, lit only by several high windows. In it were the looms. Everyone in the village wove during the winter months for eighteen hours each day. Once I had finished my schooling, I too had 'my' loom..... I was still so tiny when I first wove that I had to have wooden 'skates' attached to my feet so I could reach. My legs were too short to reach them!

We got up at 4 in the morning each day. We washed with water that came from the court 50 metres away, where a well served all the families in our *coron*, and dressed. Hop! we went down the ladder to the cellar with the two coal oil lamps. In the meantime, my mother lit the round stove that heated the main room of the cottage. The stove had niches in its main section, where we could warm our frozen feet when she called us, at around 10, to come upstairs and get our coffee [chicory] ....

While we were weaving, Mama cleaned house, scoured the floor, scraped the table with a shard of glass, threw fresh sawdust on the tiles and boiled potatoes. At the same time, she wound the lengths of thread we would weave the next day on to bobbins. My sisters and I made handkerchiefs that we wove into big linen rolls. My father, who was stronger and more skillful, made wider pieces of linen. These wide bolts of cloth were more difficult to manage but they were much sought-after at that time.

Come Saturday, we would run, one at a time, to the merchant's agent, a neighbour in the *coron*. We tried to waste as little time as possible. He

would collect our completed work and pay us for it. My earliest memory is earning two francs a week. When my handkerchiefs were perfect, as I learned to make them, the boss gave me a tip of 5 sous. Later, I earned up to five francs a week. I always ran home and gave the money to my mother....
We couldn't make ends meet with these pitiful earnings. All winter long, we lived on credit. We could pay our bills only when we came back from the season in the country. Each year we worked for 6 months on a farm in the Seine-Inférieure, far from home.[71]

This hand-weaving industry continued in the region of Cambrai until the first world war; in spite of its restoration after the war, there were few active weavers. Thus lingering remnants of hand production involving women, whether daughters or wives, co-existed with the growing modern service sector and commercial occupations, as well as the older factory textile industry, well into the twentieth century in France.

Lille offers a classic example of a city and its region whose manufacturing was transformed by industrial capitalism in the nineteenth century. Women workers in household textile production were largely replaced by female mill workers and urban household garment workers, both characteristically low paid, by about mid century. Yet change continued in the occupational structure of the city, as heavy industry became more prominent and women's jobs in manufacturing were relocated to peripheral cities or suburbs. In the cities proper, young single women were more likely to be employed in commerce or business, and married women likely to not work at all if they were mothers.[72]

What jobs women held were very closely dictated by conditions in the urban economy, the result of business decisions made by the capitalists of the region. Yet it was perfectly possible for such manufacturers to take advantage at the same time of relatively isolated specialized workers, including women, such as those in the weaving villages. For workers like the handloom weavers, industrial growth did not tempt them to work in urban centres, but to resort instead to temporary migration in order to find seasonal work in capitalist agriculture. By 1900, however, the major trends in women's wage work in Lille were the decline of household production, the growth of large-scale capitalist industry and the increasing importance of service and distributive work. Within manufacturing, women's occupations continued to be limited to relatively few sectors – particularly textiles, garment-making, food and tobacco processing. Women's wages continued to be substantially lower than men's and their work roles frequently shaped by family and household position, whether as daughters or wives.

The nineteenth century was a time of far-reaching change in French cities. In Paris, Lyon and Lille, industrial capitalism extended its influence. Investment in manufacturing increased; units of production and distribution grew larger; occupations became specialized and differentiated; workers lost control over the conditions and rhythms of work. The French experience seems to have varied more decisively among cities than did the English. Most likely this was due to the fact that each city remained tied in reciprocal relations to regional hinterlands with distinctly different economies. For Paris, the hinterland was increasingly all of France, from which migrants flowed into the capital. As the capital of a nation-state that was highly centralized not only in government administration and bureaucracy but also in intellectual life, fashion and taste, it is not surprising that Paris continued to be a centre of consumer industry which innovated in the organization of distribution rather than production. The condition of agriculture and the relative strength of the peasantry in the hinterlands of Lille and Lyon strongly influenced urban developments there, as did the timetable of French industrial capitalism, in particular its second-place relationship to England manufacturing. It was difficult for the French to compete directly in cotton textiles. Lille industry depended in its early years on impoverished rural migrants driven from household industry by competition from England. Nevertheless, the industrial complex of the Nord, of which Lille was the centre, eventually turned away from cotton, to wool (in the satellite cities of Roubaix and Tourcoing) and to more diversified economic activity in Lille itself. Unlike England, cotton manufacture was relatively less important in the French textile industry. In the case of Lyon, French industry had to deal with strongly entrenched urban artisanal production and uncertain labour supply due to lingering peasant agriculture. In the silk industry, innovation was supplemented and often resisted by urban artisans, and the eventual outcome was not urban industrialization but decentralized industrialization which tapped non-urban work forces expelled from declining agriculture.

These suggestions about the particularities of French urban industrial capitalist development based on the crude comparisons among cities provided here require much fuller research and elaboration. Yet it is clear that the English experience of industrial capitalism does not provide a model for French experience except in the most abstract and generalized terms. Timing, texture, detail and the interrelations of city and country are quite different; French male workers' experience reflected the continuing importance of smaller units, artisanal production, decentralized industry and centralized distribution and development of taste.

The comparative position of French men and women can likewise only be suggested, for the experience of men is not examined in detail in this paper. Nevertheless, we can make some generalizations.

First, about occupations. Throughout the nineteenth century, women were limited to relatively few occupations, which varied according to the economic activity of the city in which they worked. The century started with women primarily working as servants, in petty commerce or in textile and clothing production in household units. At mid century, this continued to be the pattern in Paris, but in Lille and Lyon (and the Lyonnais), industrialized large-scale spinning, and later weaving, were major employers of women. By the end of the century, women were very likely to work in commerce and business, for the economy of all three cities had converged on that sector. Urban men worked in many more industrial occupations; over the century, they continued in productive work.

Second, about migration. Migration to the city both transferred men and women in space and placed them in new occupations. The mechanism by which this dual move occurred was often the network of kin and acquaintances that provided both the means for migration and assistance in finding a job. Men and women shared migration and the organization of migration; however, they entered very different job markets in the cities. Male migrants had limited choices and often did unskilled service and construction work. Female migrants to Paris were most likely to be servants; in Lyon and its region, women migrants entered unskilled auxiliary work in silk production; in Lille they were factory spinners. Their occupations were typically unskilled and poorly paid, and migrant women were particularly vulnerable to exploitation because of their great need for work. In addition, many were disadvantaged because of the absence of their immediate families, which could offer support and protection.[73]

Third, about families. Families could both help and hold back women. Their work for wages was shaped and often limited by their life-cycle stage and the family obligations incurred by each stage. Thus girls and young women often were obliged to aid their parents; they also saved for their own future marriage. Two families – their family of birth and their future family of marriage – pulled at young single women and affected their choices and goals. The *internats*, in which employers tried to control women's personal lives as well as their work lives, are the clearest example of young women's sacrifice of independence for either parents' goals or their own future, a sacrifice that went well beyond that expected of boys and men. Most women did not experience as clear a continuation of dependency in work as those of the *internats*, but late marriage and long residence in the parental household were the typical woman's lot. Independent living arrangements and enjoyment of one's own salary were still rare for a young woman in 1900. Even when her wages were adequate for independence, family claims made it unlikely that a woman would actually enjoy it.[74]

Married women had heavy responsibilities for household tasks and childcare which they had to reconcile somehow with wage work, whether they chose it or were obliged by economic need to do it. Family division of labour made few such demands on men. As place of work became separate from place of residence, married women often found it difficult to earn wages. Any work for wages they could do in their homes was especially poorly paid. Older women who had never married or who were widowed were the most disadvantaged workers. Many occupations, such as machine-tending in textile mills, were primarily for the young; older women had to be satisfied with sewing (as long as their eyes held out), or with work as cleaning women, laundresses and the like.

In what other ways did women's occupations differ from men's? Men's work was equally segregated, and 'male' occupations were as clearly designated as 'female' ones. Nevertheless, there was a much broader range of male occupations and they included many in which skill and experience could eventually bring good pay. For much of the nineteenth century, some skilled men workers owned their tools and enjoyed some control over the organization of their work, its rhythm and timing. This was rare for a woman; if she did work at home with her own sewing machine it was not because she was a skilled worker with something an employer would gladly pay for. Rather, she was a cheap worker that an employer could exploit to his profit. Thus girls and women both experienced proletarianization early and were quintessential proletarians – wage-earners with no control over the place or organization of their work.

Did industrial capitalism separate 'work' and 'life', as Edward Thompson puts it, for French women in the nineteenth century? Most male workers, their tasks physically removed from the household over the course of the century, did experience such a bifurcation. The experience of women differed. Some women's wage-earning continued to be based in the home. Other women earned in dependent situations, for example the *internats* and domestic servants in the employer's household. Still other young women's work was undertaken to help their parents or to save for marriage. This is not to suggest that no women were independent wage-earners but rather that wage work and 'life' were much more intertwined for most women than for men throughout the century. Industrial capitalism changed the setting of work for many women; it transformed the tasks that they did. Yet wage work in large-scale manufacturing, the prototypical experience of industrialism, was most often a stage in a woman's life; over her life cycle, the family continued to shape her work life. Further, the dominance of industrial manufacturing in French urban economies was transitory over the long run. Nevertheless, in all the cities, women's lives were changed, in common with men's, by the transformation of the scale of life – population concentration and urbanization; the scale of work – large units of production; and the new discipline of work. It was the often life-long claims of family which shaped the distinctively female encounter with French urban life and industrial capitalism in the nineteenth century.

8 Decazeville: company town and working-class community, 1826–1914[1]

Don Reid

The Decazeville strike of 1886 revealed to a shocked French nation that the newspaper serial (*feuilleton*) world of *Germinal* to which they had been introduced a year earlier had a real-life counterpart. In Zola's novel the angry townsfolk of Montsou lynched the lecherous merchant Maigret because, as an ally of the mine company, he manipulated the use of credit to restrict the workers' freedom. Decazeville strikers murdered the ascetic company engineer Jules Watrin, who had masterminded company efforts to control local commerce. Comparing the *watrinade* to *Germinal*, socialists expressed satisfaction that 'an official representative' of 'the capitalist bourgeoisie', rather than a shopkeeper, had been the victim of the workers' rage.[2] Zola was not so far off the mark, however, for Watrin's death, like that of Maigret, pointed up the interrelation and tension between capitalist industry and the working-class community in nineteenth-century company towns.

While industrial capitalism spurred the growth of existing cities, it also created new towns where only small rural villages had existed before. These *villes champignons* sprang up overnight to house and provide services for the labour demanded by large-scale coal-mining and iron production. 'Decazeville', a visitor commented, 'was born with large modern industry. Therefore it has no memory of the past'.[3] The boom-town atmosphere pervading these new settlements differed markedly from that in metropolises like Paris and Lyons or the aging textile centres of Lille and Rouen. Furthermore, the absence of an established bourgeoisie or a body of skilled craftsmen separated new towns dominated by a single company, such as Grand-Combe (Gard), Montceau-les-Mines (Saône-et-Loire) and Decazeville (Aveyron), from larger, more diversified and older industrial centres like Limoges and Saint-Étienne.[4] The relative weakness of these social groups both minimized and intensified management–worker conflicts in company towns. For if there was neither a community of artisans to pass on a radical tradition nor an entrenched bourgeoisie to lead opposition to the new industrialists, the independent middle class which might have served as a buffer between the *patronat* and labour was also missing.

The rapid growth of company towns, in addition to abridging, or at least postponing, the full development of intermediary social classes between workers and the representatives of industrial capitalism, often stunted the towns' development as urban centres. Writing in the early 1840s, during Decazeville's first flush of prosperity, the economist Michel Chevalier described Decazeville as a 'locality'; he would have called it a town 'had the municipal authorities taken the trouble to align the houses and to build roads'.[5] Louis Reybaud repeated this plaint thirty years later: 'everything is pell-mell; nowhere is there the shadow of an attempt at alignment'.[6] Decazeville never successfully handled the rapid changes in population caused by fluctuations in the economic wellbeing of the mines and forges. The town's size ranged from perhaps a few hundred inhabitants in the early 1820s, before the establishment of the commune, to 8842 in 1856; from 7106 in 1866 to 14,144 in 1911.

As the comments of Chevalier and Reybaud indicate, Decazeville was not graced with the well-ordered working-class housing developments found in northern French coal towns. The town's outline was established by the confines of the valley in which the early forges and foundries were built rather than by a company architect. It could be argued that such spontaneous urban geography makes the examination of Decazeville's political and economic institutions all the more important in determining what, to paraphrase Chevalier, made Decazeville a town with a municipal identity rather than merely a locality.

The answer to this question hinges on an analysis of the Decazeville workers' response to changing managerial strategies in the workplace and in the community. Until the final years of the Second Empire, management exercised authoritarian control over community institutions and experienced little collective resistance from workers. During the first decades of the Third Republic company attempts to increase supervision in the mines met with organized opposition at the workplace. Of particular importance was the development of political and economic responses within the community which were hostile to attempts to structure town life around company needs. The final period, the decades before the first world war, was marked by the withdrawal of management from participation in community life in order to concentrate on administration of the workplace. While this encouraged the growth of community institutions free from company control, it also forced workers to turn some of their energy from municipal politics to national corporate and political organizations in order to challenge the company.

The authoritarian presence

The Société anonyme des houillères et fonderies de l'Averyron (SHFA) was founded by the Duc Decazes in 1826 and established the first mines and forges at Decazeville soon thereafter. The SHFA placed a greater premium on the assumed imperatives of deference to authority than on actual close supervision in the community and in the mines, where the use of contractors was widespread. Because iron was the company's primary product, the SHFA asserted more control over work in the forges and foundries than in the mines themselves. Yet, even there, management's primary goal was to exert its authority over the highly skilled workers rather than to subject all forge-workers to strict surveillance.

In Decazeville the SHFA attempted to create a community in its own image, beginning with the name. That the town was to be an extension of the industrial complex is evident from the company director François Cabrol's request in 1832 to have Decazeville made a separate township:

There are few towns in the department where the National Guard would appear to be more necessary and to have more interests to protect than at Decazeville. All my efforts to organize a company [of the National Guard] here have been foiled by intrigues resulting from the relative positions of Aubin and Decazeville.

As fights are numerous in a population composed of workers, it is necessary to have a municipal authority on the spot which can stop serious disorders and which can often forestall unfortunate incidents that develop while one goes off looking for the mayor [of a nearby town] or his adjunct.[7]

The SHFA's need for authority in the town to back up that exercised at the workplace was a prime factor in the prefect's decision the following year to authorize the establishment of the commune of Decazeville. When, as mayor, Cabrol created a 600-man National Guard in 1848, he did so along company lines. Cabrol appointed the officers from the ranks of the SHFA; the assistant director was made batallion commander and the officers were chosen from among other managerial personnel. At the ceremony in which the new officers were sworn in, Cabrol used the occasion to explain to the workers 'the way in which he [understood] the duties of the National Guard and the citizen'. Twelve members of the National Guard always stood watch over the company cashier's office. An institution which could have worked to politicize local residents and to create ties to the republic was made a disciplinary tool of the company.

In fact, the history of the revolution of 1848 in Decazeville nicely illustrates the nature of SHFA power. During a severe breakdown of the managerial hierarchy, the company engineer Cadiat took advantage of Cabrol's absence in March 1848 to proclaim the republic. Cadiat called on workers to continue to work peacefully and to make the sacrifices necessary to ensure the success of the new government. On his return to Decazeville, the Orleanist Cabrol immediately seized control of events by publicly humiliating Cadiat and inflaming the assembled workers against him. His speech bore some resemblance to that given earlier by Cadiat, but in Cabrol's version the SHFA replaced the nation as the benefactor to which the workers owed allegiance and for which they had to make sacrifices in time of economic depression. When the republic's commissioner in Rodez sent a plenipotentiary to inform Cabrol that the local authorities wanted nothing better than to live in harmony with the SHFA, Cabrol replied curtly: 'I am more master here than any commissioner of the provisional government and more than the provisional government itself is in Paris'. Decazeville's workers were introduced to national politics as the result of a breakdown in company authority, not of grassroots politicization of the community. National political events like the revolution of 1848 were mediated through the company rather than through national political institutions.[8]

The church, a traditional source of moral authority in the community, was also drawn into the company's service. The local clergy strengthened their own position while working in the company's interest. In company-supported schools and in the community at large they helped to acclimatize rural migrants to life in an industrial centre. Decazeville's church, built with the aid of the SHFA, symbolized the company's presence in the town; it was, a visitor wrote at the turn of the century, 'a heavy classical building dear to the bourgeois period of King Louis Philippe'.[9]

Company efforts to control Decazeville were aided by the new town's demographic structure. Well into the Second Empire most workers were recent arrivals to Decazeville.[10] The absence of a strong independent community identity among the immigrants reinforced legal impediments to challenging company authority. There were few large-scale labour protests against the SHFA; disgruntled miners and forge-workers were far more likely to set off for the countryside or other industrial centres than to put up organized resistance in Decazeville.

Coercive paternalism

The SHFA went bankrupt in 1865, a casualty of the collapse of the market for southern French iron. After a three-year receivership, the Société nouvelle des houillères et fonderies de l'Aveyron (SNHFA), under the direction of Alfred Deseilligny, took its place. Deseilligny, son-in-law of Eugène Schneider and former director of Le Creusot, improved operations at Decazeville. In the 1870s the SNHFA renovated the industrial complex to make mining, rather than iron production, the town's primary industry. To improve productivity in the mines the SNHFA eliminated mine contractors and increased the number of piece-rate workers under direct company supervision.

These developments determined the course of worker–management relations under the SNHFA in the community as well as in the workplace. Municipal services improved as a by-product of the new company's investments. The SNHFA constructed pumping facilities to provide the factories and mines with much-needed fresh water from the nearby Lot River. The town received water from the same system. The erection of gas lights at the coal sorting and washing installation permitted work to continue after dark; in Decazeville it helped assure the maintenance of public order.[11]

While the SNHFA built little housing, what it did construct was done in accordance with its new approach to labour management in the mines. Under Cabrol the SHFA had constructed a limited amount of housing composed of adjoining lodgings. Reybaud commented in 1875: '[Cabrol's plan] is now condemned; it does not isolate households enough and leads to too much promiscuity. It has been shown decidedly that it is not good for workers to live too close to each other.'[12] In favouring individual homes, management projected into the community the separation of the piece-rate worker from the team under the direction of a contractor. The company also recognized the increased importance of supervisory employees when discussing the town layout. The general assembly of SNHFA stockholders resolved in 1880: 'The insufficiency and poor arrangement of the housing of our managerial personnel has required our attention for some time.... It is agreed to devote a certain sum each year to the construction of managerial employees' houses suitably arranged and grouped around the director's house'.[13]

At the heart of the SNHFA managerial strategy was an effort to confront the appearance of organized working-class movements, exemplified by the successful strike against the post-SHFA receivership in 1867. Deseilligny turned the workers' challenge to the SNHFA's advantage by actively involving them in electoral politics for the first time. In 1869 he mobilized SNHFA employees to campaign for him throughout the district in his successful bid for a seat in the Chamber. Although the personnel of the mines and forges worked to elect the traditional authority figure in the town, in so doing they expressed themselves politically as a group far more vociferously than they had ever done before. With the collapse in the late 1870s of the economic prosperity experienced under Deseilligny, workers used this new-found political power to mount a political challenge to company hegemony in Decazeville.

In 1878 the workers and shopkeepers of Decazeville voted in their first republican town government. The nature of the republicanism of the new Mayor Cayrade and his associates was determined by the position of the working-class community in the company-dominated town of Decazeville. Shortly after the republicans took office, miners struck over a wage reduction. Cayrade distanced himself from the republican government's co-operation in the repression of the strike by refusing to allow troops to bivouac in the centre of town. Actions such as this earned Cayrade the workers' respect and helped define the moderate republicanism which characterized his administration until his death in 1886. That year an informer working for the Paris police described the constant struggle between Cayrade's administration and the SNHFA:

Formerly, the Company controlled the whole town administration, while now it has been evicted from any share. Consequently, not a day passes when a conflict does not arise between the municipality which is moderately republican, and the Company, which is absolutely reactionary.[14]

The anti-republican sympathies of prominent members of the company board of directors gave national political significance to workers' struggles in isolated Decazeville. However, only when workers had wrested control of their town from company hands could they themselves participate freely in the national politics that their strike in 1886 had so influenced. The SHFA had long before assured the integration of the Decazevillois in the national economy. Local action on the part of town residents was a necessary precondition, however, to meaningful political integration on a similar scale.

Deseilligny's death in 1875 coincided with the onset of a lengthy depression in Decazeville. In the late 1870s and the 1880s the SNHFA instructed its supervisory personnel to use their positions to reduce the piece-rates paid to miners. Despite SNHFA disclaimers to the contrary, the company also used its managerial personnel to create a political climate conducive to the acceptance of these wage cuts. Just as the supervisory staff could apportion work more efficiently, it could also be used to get the vote out for anti-republican company candidates. The victory of republican candidates in 1884 and 1885 revealed a successful extension of the workers' struggle against the company from the workplace to the community.

Not all SNHFA managerial personnel thought that political hegemony was the most effective way to control Decazeville's workers. The ill-fated Watrin, head of the forges from 1880 to 1886, believed that intervention in the economic life of the town was a better means to bolster profits than winning the town hall. Workers hated Watrin for the strict attention that he allegedly devoted to the way in which they spent their money. For Watrin, however, such supervision complemented the care managerial personnel had to show in setting piece-rates. A trip to Longwy in 1885 convinced Watrin that the operation of company stores and restaurants not only permitted management to reduce wages to match a company-determined standard of living; it also allowed the re-creation of a community in the company's image: 'The goal [of the manufacturer] is to prevent business from establishing itself around his factory or to destroy it when it already exists there'. By 'free[ing] themselves from the servitude of commerce', companies could eliminate that element of the population which provided workers with political allies at election time and valuable support during strikes.[15]

The SNHFA management took a step in this direction during the mid 1880s by placing top managerial personnel at the head of a large, previously independent co-operative store in Decazeville. Company control of the town's retail trade was not a new idea, but the rationale for it had changed since it first appeared during the early years of the SHFA. When Cabrol set up a company store, one of his primary aims had been to eliminate company managerial employees from commerce. He had felt that the company's authority over its supervisors suffered when they dealt with workers as both producers and consumers.[16] Watrin reintroduced supervisory personnel – now part of a stronger managerial hierarchy – into the commercial life of the community in order to tighten the company's hold over the workers.

As of early 1886 a relatively small percentage of workers' wages were spent at the company-dominated co-operative bakery and butcher's shop, but the thriving enterprise had plans to expand into the sale of other goods. Only Mayor Cayrade's efforts forestalled the opening of a general store. As spokesman for the shopkeepers, Cayrade had never been enthusiastic about the co-operative, but the company takeover of its direction raised his ire and that of the whole community; the coal company of a similar town, Montceau-les-Mines, Cayrade told the SNHFA director, 'had paid dearly, very dearly, for its conflict with the town'. Cayrade argued that only under constraint would workers patronize a store run by the head mine engineer Blazy, a man as despised by the workers as Watrin. Company attempts to control local commerce threatened the very fabric of community life: 'one can hardly separate the worker from the shopkeeper', Cayrade explained, 'because a large number of [workers] have a son, a brother, an uncle or a cousin who is a businessman in the town'. The mayor estimated that the opening of the co-operative general store would force at least one-quarter of Decazeville's shopkeepers to close their doors:

[The general store] would ruin Decazeville without profiting the workers. They would not save as promised, and would be denied, by the suppression of small retail business, one means of earning their livelihood, a kind of pension when the company could no longer employ them.[17]

Many miners and forge-workers viewed the expansion of the company-dominated co-operative, like company attempts to replace the republican town government, as attacks on the community of small shopkeepers and workers which had grown up outside of company control since the 1860s.

The 108-day strike of 1886 was ostensibly fought over a change in the calculation of piece-rates which reduced miners' wages. By all accounts, however, company interference in community affairs built up tensions between workers and management which led to the walk-out. Watrin's murder lifted the strike out of the confines of a single town and temporarily made Decazeville's affairs those of the nation. The impact of the *watrinade* made it impossible for Cayrade to question the stationing of troops in Decazeville. On the contrary, the encampment of the soldiers gave General Boulanger, then minister of war, a chance to strut and pontificate before the Chamber on the advantages of the conscript army in a democratic nation. Boulanger even managed to make a virtue out of the fact that there were about as many soldiers as strikers in Decazeville: 'perhaps, as I speak, each soldier is sharing his soup and his ration of bread with a miner'.[18] Although this bit of whimsy won Boulanger the applause of admiring deputies, strikers in Decazeville could not forget the fusillade which had ended the 1869 strike in the neighbouring town of Aubin and which had served as one of Zola's sources for his description of the massacre of the strikers in *Germinal*.

The army was not alone in coming to Decazeville. The debates in the Chamber following the *watrinade* focused national attention on the isolated town for the first time in its history. Socialist and left-wing republican deputies and journalists came from Paris to Decazeville after Watrin's murder and assumed leadership of the movement. They related the workers' struggle in Decazeville to major political issues and underscored the national significance of the strike. An unprecedented outpouring of support from leftist groups throughout the country supplied the strikers with funds. Parisian newspapers that gave lengthy and sympathetic coverage to the strikers were widely read in Decazeville; it is not far-fetched to speculate that articles on Decazeville in *Le Cri du peuple* and *L'Intransigeant* put the town on the map, not just for readers throughout the country, but, in a sense, for the Decazevillois as well.[19]

While Decazeville's workers emerged victorious from the strike, the economic stagnation of the late 1880s brought layoffs and significant emigration from the town. The SNHFA board of directors took advantage of the workers' perilous situation to make a final effort to restore the type of company-controlled community over which Deseilligny had presided. Through the efforts of the company board, one of its officers, Jules Gastambide, came to dominate Decazeville in 1888. Gastambide turned the paternalism preached by Deseilligny into an unsystematic mixture of spendthrift management of the mines and forges and severe repression of the community's political and economic life. Although elected mayor, he was thwarted in his attempt to take back control of the co-operative, which had reverted to non-company management after the strike of 1886, and in his campaign to win a seat in the Chamber. In revenge, Gastambide launched an unprecedented attack on those communal institutions which remained outside of company control. The company's man juggled hiring practices and used the threat that the forges would close to manipulate public opinion in his favour. Soon after his election as mayor, Gastambide ordered the company, which controlled water distribution in the town, to cut off service to the outgoing republican mayor, a liqueur manufacturer. Foiled in his attempt to take over the co-operative store, Gastambide ordered those he could influence to withdraw from it, thereby dooming the enterprise. Before the legislative elections of 1889 he took advantage of the SNHFA's dealings with numerous merchants in the area to curry support for his candidacy. Yet, having made many enemies, Gastambide lost. He subsequently instructed the company's master-miners and foremen to organize a boycott of some twenty-odd merchants, landlords and barkeepers. Workers shunned the designated republican shopkeepers for over a month out of fear of losing their jobs.[20]

The division of control

Although Gastambide had hoped to create a loyal and disciplined labour force whose productivity would return the SNHFA to prosperity, his politically motivated operation of the mines and forges only accelerated the company's demise. The SNHFA was purchased in 1892 by the iron and coal conglomerate Société anonyme de Commentry-Fourchambault (SCF, and after 1899, Société anonyme de Commentry-Fourchambault et Decazeville [SCFD]). The new owners invested heavily in the aging industrial complex and some degree of prosperity returned to the town in the two decades before the first world war. Unlike the SHFA and the SNHFA, the SCFD owned several other mines and metallurgical plants in France. These multiple interests influenced the SCF to decide to forsake involvement in community affairs in order to devote full attention to the operation of a strictly disciplined and well-ordered workplace. Decazeville's moderate republicans prevailed upon the SCF to join it in an electoral alliance against Gastambide in 1892, but in future years the SCF generally remained aloof from active intervention in Decazeville's political as well as commercial life.[21]

Gastambide, now ironically running on a platform of communal autonomy from the new company, lost to the SCF–republican ticket in the municipal elections of 1892. The alliance dismayed socialists, many of whom had kept alive the radical issues of the 1886 strike, but they supported it in order to rid themselves of Gastambide. During the next two decades republicans and socialists in Decazeville challenged the traditions of local life inherited from the SHFA and the SNHFA. They took responsibility for many municipal services independent of company tutelage. The local correspondent of *La Dépêche* proclaimed on the eve of the Decazeville town council elections of 1900:

Until now public health has not particularly pre-occupied our various town governments. They have been content to live from day to day, without undertaking the major utilitarian projects which are needed.... It is true that it was impossible to undertake big projects before because of the duality which existed between the town and the company when they fought for municipal power. Fortunately, this duality no longer exists; the company undertakes productive industry and has no desire to go into politics, an enterprise in which its predecessors failed so miserably.[22]

Left-wing leaders also attacked the company's old ally, the church, opposing the clergy's right to hold public processions and to control the town's schools. During the strike of 1886 a journalist for *Le Cri du peuple* claimed that the procession following Sunday services was 'a surprising spectacle': 'The large road ... fills up with a veritable human river. You would think you were in a town of 500,000'.[23] Yet one of the first challenges to the church's public presence in the town had come during the strike of 1886. The well-attended civil burial of a forge-worker who had been deported after the coup d'état of December 1851 boldly challenged the church's monopoly of the public observance of such events.[24] The symbolic value of control of public thoroughfares maintained its importance through the turn of the century. Socialists elected to the Decazeville town council in 1900 fought unsuccessfully to prohibit public religious processions. In so doing they underscored their kinship with the major French anticlerical groups.[25]

The republican administrations of Cayrade and his successors supported the public schools in their struggle for financial aid and students against the company-backed church schools. Whereas Gastambide had fought the development of lay education in Decazeville, the general director of the SCF outlined an official policy of company neutrality on the issue during his first visit to Decazeville. He announced that the SCF intended to draw part of its personnel each year from both public and parochial schools.[26] However, the SCF provided financial assistance to the church schools, and a parochial education was looked on favourably when it came time to name master-miners and foremen. In spite of this, an increasing number of Decazevillois sent their children to public schools in the pre-war years. In 1900 the town council passed a resolution asking all municipal employees to enrol their children in public schools; by 1908 60 per cent of male children in Decazeville attended them.[27] The anti-clericalism of the early Third Republic represented at once a step in the creation of a new community separate from the company and a form of active participation in national political life.

Both the SHFA and the SNHFA had attempted to control local commerce. In the years preceding the first world war unions and other groups of residents reversed this tradition by establishing co-operative stores. These played an important role in the lives of Decazeville's workers who, on the average, spent at least half of their wages on food in the first decade of the twentieth century.[28] The miners' union founded the successful La Revanche Prolétarienne, while the forge-workers' union set up La Syndicale and lent it several thousand francs to finance its expansion.[29] Because the co-operative movement undercut some shopkeepers, commerce played an indirect role in the town's political life. In 1912

Bos, the republican mayor of Decazeville and a prominent wholesaler, was fined for having tried to avoid payment of taxes on a shipment of alcohol; Bos's opponents linked his corrupt business practices with poor management of town services.[30] Co-operatives successfully operated by workers and their political allies helped lay the groundwork for the election of the socialist and ardent co-operationist Paul Ramadier as mayor of Decazeville in 1919.

The SCFD's decision to withdraw from an active role in town politics brought conflicts between republicans and socialists to the fore. Opposing class interests were reinforced by organizational and ideological differences. Decazeville's early republicans acted within the context of national political developments, but received little direct outside assistance other than that provided, more or less unofficially, by the prefect. However, Decazeville's socialists saw themselves first and foremost as part of a national movement and viewed the major socialist leaders as their own. The republicans always drew their candidates for deputy from the local elite: Cayrade took a typical path in going from mayor to deputy. Through the turn of the century the socialists often selected as candidates major figures with whom they were familiar, both to avoid local squabbles and because socialist ideology stressed the national and international nature of the workers' confrontation with capital. The *guesdiste* Albert Duc-Quercy, who made his reputation in Decazeville as the popular reporter of *Le Cri du peuple* during the 1886 strike, was the local socialists' choice for deputy in 1893 and 1906; Jean Allemane accepted the nomination in 1898.

Allemanisme, a hybrid of revolutionary syndicalism and municipal socialism, provided the ideology closest to Decazeville's socialist leaders in the 1890s. Several associated themselves with Allemane's Paris-based Parti ouvrier socialiste révolutionnaire during this period. Union leaders, who predominated among Decazeville's socialists at this time, were attracted by the calls of the *allemanistes* for citizen control of municipalities and union control of industry. To achieve the first of these aims socialists allied with the town's left-wing republican forces at the turn of the century but, like the *allemanistes* in general, came to regret the decision later. Soon after winning the elections of 1900 the two partners diverged over the issue of which group was to hold the upper hand in the municipal council. As a result, the local socialist movement split in two along the lines of Guesde's Parti socialiste de France and Jaurès's Parti socialiste français. Decazeville's socialists, divided even after the formation of the SFIO in 1905 and disoriented by the constant influx of new workers during the prosperous pre-war years,[31] failed to win a majority on the Decazeville town council until after the war.

The failure of the municipal coalition in 1900 disenchanted many workers and led the Decazeville miners' union to renounce active participation in town politics in March 1901:

We had thought at one time ... that taking town hall was a great step in advance, but it isn't at all.

All this proves is that the workers of Decazeville made the mistake of many others. By not making their first priority the defense of their class interests on the economic turf, they renounced the principles of class struggle, going into politics where they have nothing to gain except to become suckers.[32]

Although union militants remained active in local politics, they realized that the municipality offered too limited a forum to achieve their goals. It is ironic that company towns, the insular nature of which the owners had tried so hard to protect, were generally dependent on industries with national and international markets. As the bonds tying the company town loosened, miners, in particular, looked to the efforts of left-wing deputies and to their national union federation to reduce the length of the work day and to raise pensions. The need for a national approach was especially evident to workers in Decazeville who experienced the change in management from the SNHFA, which had run just the industrial centre of Decazeville, to the SCFD with operations in central and eastern France.

Decazeville grew from a noble's dream during the restoration monarchy to a teaming industrial centre of almost 15,000 on the eve of the first world war. The SHFA (1826–65) exercised authoritarian control over the workplace and the town. The limited freedom given some workers, particularly miners, by the contract system, was restricted to non-institutional outlets, as Cabrol's handling of the 1848 revolution demonstrated. This event also illustrated the company's mediating role in relations between the working-class community and the state before the establishment of the Third Republic. The SNHFA (1868–92) saw Alfred Deseilligny's brief attempt to establish a community along the lines of Le Creusot founder when the company proved unable to fulfil its role as 'provider'. The SNHFA manipulated the very order it was committed to implementing in the workplace and the community, in a futile attempt to reassert hegemony over the working class. During this period workers began to act collectively. The workers' republicanism, shaped by their struggle with the SNHFA, helped anchor a working-class community independent of company and church. The SCFD, which operated the mines and forges of Decazeville throughout the first world war, reacted to the SNHFA's failure to reap benefits from its control of the town by retiring in large part from municipal life and devoting its attention to strengthening administration of the mines and forges. Under the banners of republicanism and socialism residents of Decazeville asserted at the turn of the century the independence of their community from company control.

The formation of the working-class community in a company town was the product of the conflict between workers and management. Nineteenth-century firms derived the strategies they applied in company towns from those they employed in the workplace. As a result, labour movements in the workplace and in the town were necessarily linked. In challenging the structure of the company town, workers joined their efforts to those of workers elsewhere in France and raised economic and political issues which were being hotly contested on the national level. Yet, although the freeing of local commerce and municipal government from company interference at the end of the century weakened the control of the *patronat* over workers in certain aspects of their lives, the same period saw the owners come to exert greater control in the workplace. Future working-class action in the mines and forges of Decazeville increasingly involved the participation of the town's workers in national syndical and political movements, the fruit of their earlier struggles for control of their community.

9 Urbanization, worker settlement patterns and social protest in nineteenth-century France[1]

Michael P. Hanagan

Strikes, protest marches and barricades, as well as machines and factories, marked the social transformation of France in the nineteenth century. The processes of industrialization and urbanization altered the spatial arrangements of both work and protest. As large-scale industrialization gradually changed the spatial organization of work, so too the spatial arrangement of protest shifted. The slogans and rituals of a protest march reveal the intention of its organizers; explanations as to why a revolutionary crowd preferred one parade route to another or why the inhabitants of some working-class and not others quarters participated have proved useful in understanding collective action.[2] In addition, existing spatial configurations had other obvious historical implications: the location of the royal court some distance from the capital city may have made it more difficult for the urban crowd and commercial middle classes to influence the political system, and the presence of adjacent coal and iron fields may have insured economic expansion.[3] Recent research by urban historians and geographers also suggests that a study of locational aspects of industrial and urban growth can shed light on nineteenth-century labour history.[4]

A look at the varieties of work and the types of worker that concentrated in the nineteenth-century French city can increase our understanding of the evolution of social protest. The growth of large factories, facilitating the supervision of labour and expediting the incorporation of new technologies into the production process, promoted the concentration of workers into cities. Where pre-industrial work created occupationally specialized areas in the city that were inhabited by merchants, artisans and apprentices engaged in the same trade, large-scale industrial work tended to place factories on the city's outskirts and, at least initially, scattered semi-skilled workers across the pre-industrial city while creating new industrial worker housing at the city's edges.[5] And not only did the transition from artisanal to industrial work shape the urban environment, but the structure of the artisanal city influenced the structure of the industrial city that succeeded it. Many French industrial cities, such as Amiens, Lyon and Rouen, had a rich artisanal past; the French urban proletariat grew up in a setting dominated by artisans.

The manner in which the shift from pre-industrial to industrial work structures influenced the urban background of social protest acquires added importance from the perspective of France, a country renowned for militant worker protest throughout the whole of the century. Historians of England and America have rediscovered the artisanal presence in the late nineteenth-century work-force; but, on the continent, the transition to industrial work was even slower and crested much later. In France, with an old artisanal tradition, the role of pre-industrial work, its effect on urban growth and development, and the relationship between urbanization and social protest assumed crucial importance.

How did the pace of French urbanization and its associated patterns of worker settlement affect working-class militancy in the second half of the nineteenth century? Several important aspects of this problem which will be discussed are: the relationship between French industrial development and urban growth, the influence of artisanal and industrial workers' settlement patterns on worker mobilization and, finally, the effect of urban structure on artisanal and industrial worker co-operation within the industrializing city. Most of the examples will be drawn from the industrial region around the city of Saint-Étienne in the department of the Loire. This region, the 'Stéphanois', provides a particularly rich area for the study of urban development and working-class protest.

The Stéphanois region of France, located on the eastern edge of the Massif Central about 40 kilometres from the city of Lyon, presents a variety of industrial and urban centres for analysis. The Stéphanois is named after its capital and largest city, Saint-Étienne, but there are several important industrial towns within its boundaries, namely Firminy, Le Chambon-Feugerolles, Rive-de-Gier and Saint-Chamond. In the course of the nineteenth century, Saint-Étienne and its tributary cities, lined along the streams flowing through the coal basin, participated in a dramatic industrial and urban growth. The region has been called 'the cradle of the industrial revolution in France'.[6]

The economy of the Stéphanois cities developed as a mixture of artisanal and industrial trades. Saint-Étienne, well known as a centre of metal construction, housed two important artisanal industries – luxury arms manufacture and artisanal ribbon-weaving, by far the city's largest employer. Firminy and Saint-Chamond were industrial towns, engaged in metal-working and textile production; while Le Chambon-Feugerolles and Rive-de-Gier were centres of artisanal file-making and glassblowing respectively, as well as the sites of industrial machine-construction.

The mountainous countryside surrounding the coal basin exemplifies the rural antecedents of urbanization and industrialization in nineteenth-century Europe. For most of the century, farmers in this region were engaged in subsistence agriculture supplemented by rural industry. The highland areas of the Stéphanois did not export grain but silk thread, lace, ironware, knives and wood products. The small villages nestled in the mountains had high rates of natural increase, and the spread of regional industrialization and urbanization was greatly facilitated by the relatively dense population of semi-skilled workers in the countryside who were willing to migrate to Saint-Étienne and the valley towns.[6] The relatively fertile plain of the Forez lay north of the east–west-looking Stéphanois valley; this marshy plain with its swamp fevers and resulting high mortality constantly demanded agricultural labour and contributed few workers to the Stéphanois. Only the Monts du Lyonnais which bordered the Forézien plain on the east and the Rhône valley on the west provided additional manpower but they also sent their labourers to the nearby urban centre of Lyon.[8]

The case of the Stéphanois, with its combination of urban industrial areas, rural industrial countryside and agricultural villages, may typify the overall course of French urbanization. From the perspective of contemporaries, the growth of French cities in the nineteenth century seemed extraordinarily rapid, but other European and American cities were growing even faster. In 1800, of all the large nations in Europe, only England was more urbanized than France, and the English lead was widened significantly by the remarkable size of London; the great metropolis, the only English city with a population over 100,000, contained almost 10 per cent of the nation's inhabitants. In contrast, the three French cities with over 100,000 population contained only a little under 3 per cent of the French population. Between 1800 and 1890 the percentage population in cities over 10,000 grew 2.5 times in France, from 10.5 to 25.9 per cent but in England, despite its already substantial urban population, the percentage grew three times, from 21.3 to 61.8 per cent and in the United States the percentage grew almost eight times, from 3.8 to 27.6 per cent.[9]

This relatively slower French urban growth had two distinctive aspects. First, French population itself grew much slower than in these other countries. The rise of cities was everywhere associated with the migration of workers from overpopulated rural areas and with positive rates of natural increase. And, during the nineteenth century, population growth occurred much faster in England, Germany and the United States than in France. Between 1800 and 1900 the population of France increased by half, but the population of England grew two and a half times, Germany one and a half, and in the United States, population grew almost fifteen times its 1800 size. Second, the French urban lag was greatest in the category of large cities, the fastest-growing urban sector in almost every European country. In 1800 only Paris, Lyon and Marseilles had populations over 100,000; and in 1890 there were twelve. By contrast, in England there was only one such city, London, in 1800; by 1890 there were twenty-four, in the United States there were none in 1800 and twenty-eight in 1890.[10]

The most important reason for France's more gradual urban growth was the nature of its economic transformation. In order to understand French economic evolution it is necessary to distinguish between factory production and economic development. Long-term indicators of the growth of national product in the nineteenth century show only a slight French lag; the growth of national product in France remained broadly similar to that of other advanced industrial countries.[11] But even over the course of a century the expansion of the factory system was much less rapid in France than in England, Germany, or the United States.

The disparity between the slow pace of factory development and economic growth can be explained by the differing forms of economic transformation in France. As in other European countries, French industrial development preceded urban expansion. However, unlike other European countries in the second half of the nineteenth century, the urban-industrial sector in France did not absorb the rural-industrial sector; and industrialization did not become co-extensive with urbanization. In France, throughout the whole of the century much industrial development took place in rural areas. Whereas English industrialists welded together unskilled workers into a proletariat inside factory walls, French entrepreneurs found a ready-made proletariat within the cottage. Undoubtedly, much of France's peculiar course of economic development can be attributed to the persistence of small-scale peasant proprietors in agriculture. With good reason, French men and women were loathe to give up claims on the land for the uncertain fate of propertyless proletarians. As a recent study by Keyder and O'Brien has demonstrated, French peasant proprietors were able to increase their productivity to respond to the needs of a growing market: yet French agriculture remained relatively backward, at least when compared with its traditional rival across the Channel, because of the inferior quality of much of French soil.[12]

The existence of a large population on the land, however, did mean that, except at harvest time, some family members were underemployed. Also, in the case of family farms the pressure of population increase acted to create a domestic work-force as docile and driven as that created with much greater effort in the factories.

By seeking out under-employed labour in the countryside and by hiring domestic and part-time labour on a more extensive scale than in other industrial countries, French capitalists in large part overcame the obstacles to capitalist development flowing from the existence of a substantial sector of peasant proprietors. Several centuries of economic growth had already prepared the way for industrial development in the nineteenth century. The industrialization of the countryside thus can be traced far back in French history. The introduction of fulling mills in the late Middle Ages paved the way for the invention of other water mills and, by the eighteenth century, many textile and metal shops were located next to fast-running streams. In an era of high transportation costs, many industries followed unwieldly factors of production like coal, sheep and silkworms into the countryside. Added impetus was given to this movement by attempts to circumvent urban guild regulations. But, above all, in early modern as in nineteenth-century France, industry sought out under-employed peasants where the climate prohibited year-round agriculture or where parcellization made survival by farming alone impossible.[13]

The existence of rural industry usually presumed the proximity of urban centres for the distribution of raw materials, the collection of finished products and the residence of middlemen in touch with final markets. But these urban nucleii of rural industrial networks were much smaller than the industrial towns which concentrated production in the factory. In the 1890s the author-traveller Ardouin-Dumazet visited the textile town of Tarare, a centre of rural industry in the department of the Rhône, only a few kilometres from the department of the Loire, and noted:

The number of workers working for Tarare actually surpasses 60,000; which including women and children represents the population of a city of 250,000, more than Roubaix and Tourcoing combined. But all these workers are scattered in the mountains of the Loire and Rhône; one even finds them as far as the Saône-et-Loire. Tarare is consequently a city of less than 13,000 inhabitants.[14]

French economic development represented more an industrial evolution than an industrial revolution. The gradually accelerating pace of economic growth that culminated in the industrial revolution affected France differently than England. While its neighbour was specializing in the mass-production textile trade and developing coal and iron production, France was specializing in quality and even luxury production, often associated with the famous *articles de Paris*. The English economist Alfred Marshall succinctly summarized the distinctive development of the French economy:

As the eighteenth century drew on, the extravagance of the French Court, and the selfish use which the privileged classes made of their power, pressed heavily on the people.... More and more did her best artisans specialize themselves in work that called for individual taste and thought as regards form, arrangement, and colour; meanwhile English artisans were specializing themselves rather on work that required strength, resolution, judgement, persistence, power to obey and to command, and withal an abundant use of capital....[15]

Even outside rural industry, traditional methods of production and small-scale industry persisted in France. In 1901 over 30 per cent of the industrial work-force described itself as working 'alone' or as 'self-employed' – admittedly a rather broad category including artisans, domestic production workers and day-labourers. In that same year of all French industrial establishments hiring one or more workers, 87.9 per cent employed between one and five; in 1900 in the United States, only 57.9 per cent of all manufacturing establishments belonged to this lowest category.[16] Anglo-American historians often assume that small-scale production was inefficient, but this is not necessarily so, as a very large number of skilled workers were available in France. C. K. Harley, a student of comparative industrial structure, has argued that, for at least several decades, non-mechanized English firms employing skilled workers successfully competed with mechanized American firms employing semi-skilled or unskilled workers.[17] To reiterate a well-known argument, mechanization served in part as a substitute for skilled workers.[18] This interpretation, frequently used to explain the persistence of skilled workers in England compared with the United States, may also explain the enduring presence of artisanal workers in France compared with England. Contemporaries candidly discussed this trade-off between skill and mechanization. After describing the artisanal work organization of the silk industry in Lyon in the 1890s, an American observer came to the conclusion that the Lyonnais silk industry had nothing to fear from factory-produced American goods:

> It seems to be settled in the minds of thoughtful observers that the system of work prevailing in the silk industry of Europe ... cannot be easily superseded. It offers to the manufacturer advantages which fully counter-balance the advantages accruing to him from the smaller rate paid per yard in power mills. First, the all-important fact that the manufacturer can employ all his capital as free and floating capital. He requires no fixed capital. He has not hundreds of thousands invested in brick and mortar and machinery. The looms belong to the weavers without any risk of ownership to the manufacturers....[19]

The disproportionate role of small-scale industry in the economy deprived French cities of a powerful force promoting urban concentration; instead, France's relatively limited industrial-urban concentration resulted from the aggregation of highly skilled work-forces. In 1896 France had only thirteen enterprises which employed more than 5000 workers.[20] In the 1890s Ardouin-Dumazet, passing through one small industrial town after another in the Loire, found the economy of each town dominated by its particular artisanal milieu; hat-making in Chazelles-sur-Lyon and Grigny, boots and blankets in Saint-Symphorien d'Ozon, and shoemaking and hat-making in Saint-Symphorien-sur-Coise.[21]

In sum, slow mechanization, the continued predominance of

small-scale artisanal production and dependence on part-time, rural, unskilled labour were the main features of many sectors of the French economy as late as the turn of the nineteenth century. As a result urban growth proceeded slowly, the urban population was heavily composed of artisanal workers, and factories only gradually appeared in the city. What were the effects of the particular patterns of French economic and urban growth on social protest? An investigation of the urban residential patterns of the large numbers of surviving French artisanal workers in the late nineteenth century, and a brief look at industrial workers who were divided between city and countryside, should provide an answer. Together the rural–urban division of labour and artisanal and industrial worker residential patterns contributed to artisanal militancy and industrial worker quiescence. Finally, the effects of the interplay of artisanal and industrial residential patterns in promoting worker solidarity will be discussed.

The French artisanal workers concentrated in cities were not simply the residue of workers who remained after semi-skilled and unskilled jobs had been distributed throughout the countryside. There were powerful reasons for artisanal concentration in towns and in special quarters of large cities. Before the revolution of 1789, governmental and guild regulations forced many trades within town walls. Access to raw material in which some cities were better supplied than others was another factor. But whatever the origins of employer concentration, strong reasons preserved the pattern once established. The whims of fashion shaped the fortunes of many luxury traders; such trends were most easily followed in the company of other employers in the same vicinity, as exemplified by the Lyonnais silk industry. The presence of a skilled work-force reinforced the tendency to concentration. Employers who considered moving elsewhere faced the alternatives of persuading workers to emigrate or of training unskilled workers in a new location. In these small-scale industries no single employer could afford the financial burden of training young workers; instead many of the costs were assumed by the artisanal community of parents and workmates.[22]

In centres of artisanal production, employers often tried to attract skilled workers by building housing which further strengthened the trend to concentration. As industry expanded in the nineteenth century, the housing market in small towns, where capital remained scarce, did not always expand to meet the need, and employers had to step in to fill the gap. A large minority of glassworkers, in Rive-de-Gier, one of the small towns in Saint-Étienne's hinterland, lived only a few blocks from the glass factory in apartments rented from their employer. The Claudinon company in nearby Le Chambon-Feugerolles built a housing project for skilled workers close to its major factory complex.[23]

Beyond all these factors other forces led artisans to gather together within town and city. As would be expected, artisanal workers often lived in the same neighbourhood, and so they could share a common leisure time. Their particular life styles brought them together in many ways. They frequently worked different hours from other local workers. In Rive-de-Gier glassworkers had won the eight-hour day and worked two hours less than other local adult male workers. Also glassworkers were involved in constant shift-work; those who laboured between four in the morning and midnight, and those in the midnight to eight shift were likely to find that the only people with leisure time to share were other comrades from work.[24]

A sense of prestige and dignity as skilled workers also brought artisans together and gave them a distinct identity. The individual or family wages of artisanal workers were higher than those of factory or rural workers. The glassblowers of Rive-de-Gier, for example, occupied the very pinnacle of the working-class occupational hierarchy, earning three times the wages of semi-skilled metal-workers by 1890.[25] The relatively skilled artisanal file-workers of Le Chambon as individuals earned less than metal-workers but there was more opporuntity for children and married women to work in file-making, providing them with higher family wages.[26]

Working-class songs illustrate the occupational pride of the artisanal worker and the relative occupational indifference of the semi-skilled or unskilled worker. Artisanal professions typically had songs which specifically mentioned their trades and singled out the best known characteristics of their work. A blacksmith's song composed by a Stéphanois worker went:

The rhythm of the song that he hums
Renders his heavy hammer lighter,
And soon the steel that he fashions
Is ready to pass to the anvil.
Will he fashion a weapon
Or a farming tool?

Hoe, lance or machine gun,
It is his children's bread.[27]

In contrast, industrial workers' songs rarely described work scenes and sometimes did not even identify their specific occupation. No metal-worker's song, but only a factory song, is found in a collection of working-class songs published in the Stéphanois:

It is the sepulchre of health,
Of strength and beauty:
It grabs hold of children,
Eats at them, makes them sweat, and weakens them,
And renders them old men at thirty
The Factory.[28]

Traces of this attitude of sad resignation can be found in the manuscript census. Skilled workers usually identified their trade specifically, even proudly: 'glassblower', 'file-grinder', 'puddler'; but semi-skilled workers usually listed themselves as 'metal-worker' or 'glassworker', sometimes only as 'day-labourer'. The infrequent exception to this rule among unskilled workers is sufficient to demonstrate that it is not a simple artifact of the census recorder's prejudice. As skill levels diminished so did occupational pride.

The prestige and high wages of the artisan ultimately rested on skill and jealously guarded autonomy. Furthermore, glass-workers, file-workers, forgers and ribbon-weavers largely controlled their own jobs. Teams organized by the skilled worker performed much artisanal work. These work teams had wide latitude in deciding work methods and in establishing work schedules. This remained true whether the artisanal teams worked in factories, small shops or domestic workshops. Because they owned their own tools, artisans were not inextricably bound to large-scale industries. Unlike unskilled workers they often could start their own shops or easily find employment in the multitude of small shops which survived the growth of factories; the file trade in Le Chambon provides a classic example of the co-existence of large- and small-scale production.[29] The presence of highly skilled workers with considerable autonomy inside factory and small workshop, has been insufficiently remarked and appreciated.

Let us look more closely at the characteristics of the artisanal worker who played a key role in shaping the environment of the nineteenth-century French manufacturing city. Figure 4 places the

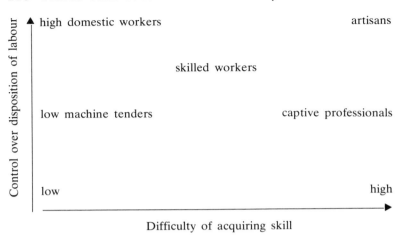

Figure 4 *Workers' control over the labour process*

urban artisan within a framework which includes other nineteenth-
and twentieth-century workers. The common types of nineteenth-
century workers – the artisan, skilled worker and machine tender
– all differed with respect to both skill and autonomy. The
differentiation between 'artisan' and 'skilled worker' is based on
the distinction between the craft-trained worker who possessed
many skills and the 'skilled worker' whose job was often created
by subdividing artisanal work among several new categories of
workers and creating a supervisor to co-ordinate these workers.[30]
Also, the category of 'skilled worker' frequently resulted from the
mechanization of key artisanal skills and the introduction of a shop
foreman. Domestic workers provide an example of labourers who
possessed considerable job autonomy but lacked skill. As long as
they earned a survival wage, domestic workers could determine
their work methods and schedule at their own discretion. And the
small cost of looms and forges meant that domestic workers had
considerable flexibility in choosing an occupation; the Stéphanois
and Lyonnais regions provide many instances of whole rural areas
shifting from one domestic industry to another. Some mid-
twentieth-century workers, the so-called 'captive professionals,'
such as petroleum technicians and plant engineers, possess great
skill without much autonomy. Their university training equips
them with considerable skills but they are supervised by

university-trained superiors, and they are at the mercy of large-scale industry because their talents are only relevant to a few specially designed factories.[31]

The strategic importance of the artisan in nineteenth-century social protest stems from his combination of skill and job autonomy. Since all training in glassblowing, skilled metal-working and file-making took place on the job, artisans faced with a new task often needed to consult one another on the shop floor; these contacts reinforced friendship links with other artisans in the same profession. The kind of bonds that were formed by artisans in the same profession could be described as 'tight knit', because of the frequency of over-lapping relations within a given group.[32] To illustrate, let us start with the example of an individual artisan who consults several other artisans on the shop floor daily. Outside the job these same artisans may be linked together by informal ties more complicated than their friendship with the first artisan; several drink together at a café while others may see each other on the street corner where they live. The same forces which promoted artisanal concentration within the city also encouraged the formation of tight-knit friendship groups.

The precise friendship networks of men long dead are difficult to document, but there is evidence of the overlap between work, recreation and neighbourhood among artisanal workers. A novelist described the café haunts of the glassworkers of Rive-de-Gier in the pre-war period: 'in a narrow, obscure room, tiny tables were lined up. Every table was occupied by a young glass-worker, cane changer, bottle carrier, or *gamin*'.[33] Information about residential patterns is more conclusive. Samples drawn from the manuscript census show that in Rive-de-Gier and Le Chambon-Feugerolles, artisanal glassworkers and file-workers were more urbanized than industrial workers and concentrated in distinct sections of the city.[34]

The close world of artisanal workers provided great potential for them to act collectively in their interests. Informal contact not only deepened acquaintanceships formed in the shop and provided opportunities for discussing work issues, but it also furnished a natural means of enforcing collective decisions. Evidence from strike actions suggests that artisanal workers who might be tempted to ignore the demands of an impersonal strike committee or union organization found it almost impossible to resist the collective will of their neighbours and drinking mates. An individual artisan holding out against the community by refusing to join his striking companions invariably faced threats of violence from fellow workers. Sometimes these threats were carried out. On several occasions non-striking artisans in Rive-de-Gier and Le Chambon-Feugerolles found it necessary to leave town in the wake of a successful strike.[35]

Artisans were particularly susceptible to militant appeals because of the fear of mechanization. Too often historians confuse artisans with the 'labour aristocracy' which arose in England in the late nineteenth century. Nothing could be more misleading. The distinguishing characteristic of the English labour aristocracy was not its skill or high wages but the security of its position; labour aristocrats came from that segment of the artisanal community not facing any challenge to its control over skills. Many artisanal workers in nineteenth-century France were neither proletarians nor labour aristocrats, but highly skilled workers whose positions were increasingly threatened by the advent of industrial capitalism. The very slowness of industrial change in France gave artisans time to prepare themselves to respond to mechanization. As industrialization impinged on their lives, many of these workers turned to militant protest. File-workers and glassworkers led mass strike protests in both Le Chambon-Feugerolles and Rive-de-Gier at the turn of the century.[36]

In particular, those artisans strategically located in factories were in the vanguard of worker protest; the urbanized artisans' position 'inside the belly of the beast' favoured such actions. The existence of a large plant and costly machinery which could be forcibly shut down gave artisans considerable leverage over their employers. Within the factory artisans obtained information about the state of the market and the financial position of their employer – invaluable information for deciding when to strike. In addition, they were familiar with the state of the existing machinery, whether it could replace them, and for how long. Finally, artisans lived in cities that were also political units and, after the establishment of genuine universal suffrage at the municipal level in 1870, a large working-class population could hope to influence the political authorities. The spread of socialist municipal administrations throughout France in turn facilitated urban protest. While socialist mayors occasionally feared the political consequences of militant strikes, they depended on the working classes for their constituency and usually provided political support.

The advantageous position of artisanal workers within the city contrasts with that of unskilled or semi-skilled workers, many of whom were only temporarily members of the labour market or who were scattered over town and countryside. The urban-dwelling, adult, male factory worker pictured in the revolutionary posters was, in fact, not typical, representing only a minority of the non-artisanal labour force in industry. Estimates of the size and militant potential of the nineteenth-century proletariat are misleading if they rely on the strength of numbers alone and fail to account for the many hundreds of thousands of workers who were part-time, domestic and rural labourers. Because of its great dependence on domestic industry and child labour the French economy employed a larger percentage of the female population in industry than the English.[37] Women made up 38.5 per cent of the French manufacturing work-force in 1901; women composed 34.7 per cent of the English manufacturing work-force in the same year. The proportion of women was greatest in industries most strongly affected by the first industrial revolution, the textile revolution; in the garment industry, 87.1 per cent of the work-force was feminine, and in textiles 51.4 per cent.[38] Moreover, a large portion of the female labour force was only temporarily engaged in factory production; many women left the factory when they were married or had children and thus had no long-term industrial commitment. Even in cases where adult male industrial workers were brought together inside factories, their homes often remained in the country or dispersed throughout the city.

The plight of the rural industrial worker reveals the problems of industrial worker mobilization most clearly. Rural households provided industrial labour in a variety of ways which can be classified, following James Vance, Jnr, as 'time segmented labour' or 'family segmented labour'.[39] By 'time segmented labour' is meant that whole families worked for a period of time in industry; the best example of time-segmented industry in the Stéphanois were the *montagnard* families who made crude furniture, wooden shoes and farm implements when the weather made herding, lumbering and sawyering impossible. The small number of wood-working *montagnards*, combined with their isolated location, scattered among the various mountain ranges, and their limited production, confined to cheap consumers goods, largely condemned this population to silence. In any case, these rural workers often sold their products directly to the consumer, eliminating the need for both employers and distributors.

'Family segmented labour', where the members of the same household engaged in different employments, was a much more important force in the Stéphanois economy. Two interesting studies of late nineteenth-century rural industrial labour in the Stéphanois furnish examples: a local archivist describes a mountain village, La Fayette, to the south-west of the coal basin; and a follower of Le Play undertook a study of a single family living in an isolated mountain enclave, situated to the south of the basin in the commune of Saint-Genest-Malifaux.[40] The inhabitants of La Fayette were principally involved in some kind of industrial work, as most men made nails while women wove ribbons; agricultural pursuits such as sheep and goat-herding were only supplementary activities. Many farmers' wives owned a loom for ribbon-weaving, although by 1892 the shift to dairy production, in response to the growing population of the coal basin, had been so rapid that many women were abandoning their looms to devote their full time to butter-making.

The difficulties of mobilizing rural industrial workers like the nailmakers and ribbon-weavers seem enormous, particularly when keeping in mind the previous discussion of urban artisans. The rural labour force was dispersed over many kilometres, making communication and co-ordination difficult. Workers scattered over such a wide terrain could not meet together to discuss common grievances or form a united organization. Nor could rural workers create the kind of environment in which collective decisions could be enforced: dissident rural workers were not forced into daily contact with others in the same occupation. The place of residence of rural workers was not determined by their work but by their inheritance and the opportunity to supplement industrial incomes by cattle-raising, dairy production and gardening. And workers continued to live in the countryside even after the agricultural contribution to the family income was no longer primary.

For both the villagers of La Fayette and the family of Saint-Genest-Malifaux, the centre of industrial work remained the home. In these villages, as in other Stéphanois towns, the combined home-workshops of the nailmakers lined the twisting, narrow streets. The typical nailmaker's home consisted of two stories, the first given over completely to the forge, the second possessing a bedroom and a kitchen. Although work was concentrated in the home, a kind of solidarity did exist among village nailmakers who often met under a clump of trees to take their breakfast and lunch. But local solidarity could not overcome the dispersion of the trade over a whole series of distant villages and to isolated cottages on the edge of the Stéphanois towns. Silkweaving characterized Stéphanois rural industry in the nineteenth century. Even in La Fayette, the second-floor bedroom of the nailmaker's home often held a loom, and while the nailmaker worked on the forge his wife wove silk. But the case of Saint-Genest-Malifaux presents the most typical mix of industry and agriculture in the rural areas immediately surrounding the Stéphanois coal basin. One family owned only a few hectares of land; the head of the household, the father, raised grain and tended four or five cows. The family's oldest sons who were old enough to work were employed as shepherds. The eldest daughter worked at a rural textile plant in order to accumulate money for her dowry. The mother worked at butter-making but engaged in ribbon-weaving during the wintertime. Although ribbon-weaving was declining in this region, the number of looms having fallen from 4000 to 400, it remained important in regions less accessible to the Stéphanois basin. In a radius of 100 kilometres from the city of Lyon, tens of thousands of women worked at looms for part of the year. The size of this work-force was enormous, yet its location made it practically impossible to organize.

In Saint-Genest-Malifaux, the case of the oldest daughter working in a local textile plant presents a problem of classification which also sheds light on industrial worker quiescence. The eldest daughter worked at a rural factory and boarded in a company-owned dormitory, supervised by nuns. Except for a company-supplied soup stock, the daughter received all her food from her family during her weekly visits home. Should such a 'commuter' be classified as belonging to the family household? It hardly matters what classification is used as long as it is noted that this woman who lived five and a half days in a factory environment remained in some important ways a member of a rural household. There were thousands of such cases in the Stéphanois region.

But even if nailmakers and silkweavers had been able to band together to overcome their physical separation, the obstacles to their political mobilization would still have been great. Disgruntled rural workers lacked a clear focus for their protest; their employers did not have a large investment in equipment which could be immobilized by striking workers, and those who profited most from cottage industry were often too far away to reach. The nailmakers of La Fayette received their orders from merchants in Firminy who supplied the nail blanks and paid the workers by the batch; these merchants were only middlemen between the merchants and distributors in Saint-Étienne. The merchant who commissioned silkweavers played a similar intermediate role; he furnished workers with material and a loom but received his orders from firms in Lyon. The employer of rural workers was attached to his work-force by a gossamer thread of personal knowledge and past commitment, not by the iron fetters of costly investment in plants and machinery. The small fixed capital in rural industry made it entirely feasible for an employer to desert one area for another relatively easily.

Also, whether industrial workers' wages played a primary or supplementary role within the family economy, they were not very great. Like almost everything else in a nineteenth-century worker's life, serious protest required cash; mass protest generally demanded organization which, in turn, depended upon paid leaders and rented halls. And rural workers lacked resources; although not paying rent and growing most of their own foods, they did not have the extra funds to gather together with distant fellow workers or to survive on strike, deprived of wages for a sustained period.[41]

The concentration of labour into factories in the second half of the nineteenth century did not automatically provide industrial workers the same potential for mobilization as artisans. Well into the century, many factory workers retained the peasant homestead and small plots that made rural industry so attractive. Since many industrial labourers working in the city lived in the countryside, the journey to work for some could be extremely long. And the trek to work was liable to be longer in country towns which drew a large proportion of their work-force from the countryside than in larger cities like Paris or Lyon which drew mainly on their own densely packed population or that of an adjoining suburb. In large nineteenth-century American cities most workers lived within a mile of their workplace; in Philadelphia the vast majority lived within six-tenths of a mile from their place of work in 1850 and within a mile in 1880.[42] But in the small town of Le Chambon-Feugerolles several hundred bolt-workers walked 2 or 3 kilometres, about a mile and a half, to work and many metal-workers walked 5 kilometres, over 3 miles.[43] This long journey to work was nothing outstanding in France: in Carmaux the mine owners fought to limit the journey to work to 5 kilometres, because they feared that energy lost during the journey would tell in the mines.[44]

A pattern of considerable dispersion also characterized city-dwelling industrial workers. In the city, too, many industrial working-class families engaged in family segmented labour. Usually the working-class family lived as close as possible to where the male head of household could find employment; other family members sought work within the radius allowed by adult male employment. Many women engaged in industrial work until their marriage or before the arrival of their first child. This was typically the case in braidmaking in Saint-Chamond where the overwhelming majority of workers were teenagers, either the daughters of local metal-workers living at home or the daughters of peasants residing in company-owned dormitories.[45] Sons who were too young to perform the heavy physical labour involved in metal-working or coal-mining also found employment as machine tenders in factories. Many young bolt-workers in Le Chambon-Feugerolles were only counting the days until they could perform 'adult' work.[46] Thus, for a large portion of the industrial working class employed in supplementary jobs, city location was not determined by *their* friendship networks, distance from work or income; rather the location needs of the household head were dominant.

The forces tending toward concentration were weaker even among adult male industrial workers than among artisanal workers. Adult male industrial workers established households within working-class neighbourhoods, often among fellow factory workers, but not near to their shopmates. In Saint-Chamond, metal-workers showed some tendency to live in the same *quartier* as other metal-workers, but adjusters and turners who worked in the same large shops did not concentrate any more closely together than metal-workers in general.[47] Industrial work did not require or even allow the kind of consultation that underlay the fraternity enjoyed by artisanal workers. Instead of being clustered together inside the city, industrial plants were dispersed on the edge of town where land was cheap enough to permit the building of large factories; added impetus to this trend was provided by the desire to escape the octroi, an urban toll levied mainly on consumers' goods, which added to the cost of labour. Moreover, most industrial work was sufficiently similar that only minor distinctions existed in the pay or work schedule of semi-skilled or unskilled labourers; the wages and hours of even the 'skilled industrial worker' were closer to those of the semi-skilled worker than those of the artisan. Thus, industrial workers were not drawn together outside the job and formed more 'loose knit' social groups than artisans. An individual worker might have some friends at work but these friendships were often too casual to push workers to live in the same neighbourhoods or to frequent regularly the same bars.

Yet if urbanization did not bring the ability of industrial workers to protest up to the high standards of urbanized artisans, still it increased their ability beyond that of rural industrial workers. If urbanized industrial workers did not live next to their shopmates, they were close enough to attend common meetings when the issue was sufficiently compelling. In contrast with rural workers, factory work provided industrial workers a clear enemy to rally against and permitted them the leverage of shutting down the plant. The wages of adult male metal-workers and ribbon-weavers in factories were higher than those of nailmakers and silkweavers in the country, although it is difficult to say to what extent uniformly low women's wages for industrial work differed between city and country.[48] In any case, urbanized male industrial workers were better able than their rural counterparts to afford to organize and to financially support strikes.

So far, the urban characteristics of artisanal and industrial worker life have been examined separately, but these two groups often inhabited the same urban territory. Industrial workers seeking factory employment found a mass of artisans that had preceded them; militant protest was among the lessons learned from these artisans. Both urban growth and the industrial worker protest in the nineteenth century were built upon strong artisanal foundations. The mass industrial strikes that swept Rive-de-Gier in 1893 and Le Chambon-Feugerolles in 1910 and 1911 were based on coalitions between powerful artisanal organizations and a nascent industrial workers' movement.[49]

David Ward's demonstration of how the interaction of artisanal and industrial housing needs engendered labour solidarity in mid nineteenth-century England may apply to late nineteenth-century France.[50] It is worth repeating that the close relationship between home and work among artisans led them to value an occupationally specialized environment where glassworkers lived next to glassworker shopmates, and file-workers lived next to file-workers. As a result of this pattern of housing, small artisanal neighbourhoods formed within the city, but considerable space existed between these neighbourhoods: the existence of unused space inside the city explains why mid nineteenth-century English social critics seldom complained about overcrowding but concentrated their fire on the quality of housing and the need for proper sanitation. As the map shows, the conspicuous availability of land in a Stéphanois artisanal town seems to suggest that Ward's argument may work in France.

The growth of an industrial workforce in artisanal towns acted to fill this empty space. Because factories grew up on the outskirts of town and industrial worker employment opportunities often shifted, industrial workers were not so much interested in proximity to the factory as in rental expense. Thus, as industrial workers filled in empty spaces within the still existing pre-industrial city, occupationally heterogenous neighbourhoods were created made up of the residents of the pre-industrial city, in our case mainly artisans, and the new industrial work-force.[51]

In the Stéphanois the clear consequence of the appearance of industrial workers in artisanal towns was a gradual filling in of urban space and the creation of a new layer of industrial worker housing on the edges of the city enveloping the artisanal centre. As a result industrial workers became neighbours of artisans. Although artisanal and industrial workers continued to differ from one another in many ways, the emerging social geography of the nineteenth-century city encouraged mutual co-operation. While political reasons were certainly important, the interaction of artisanal and industrial workers within the city contributed to the formation of the coalition of artisanal and industrial workers which played an important role in Stéphanois politics in the late nineteenth century.

In conclusion, the pace of urbanization and the structure of nineteenth-century French cities were strongly influenced if not determined by the particular evolution of the economy. The enduring presence of large numbers of artisanal workers in French cities continued their distinctive pattern of urban life throughout the century. The tight-knit character of French artisanal life offered skilled workers the means to defend themselves against

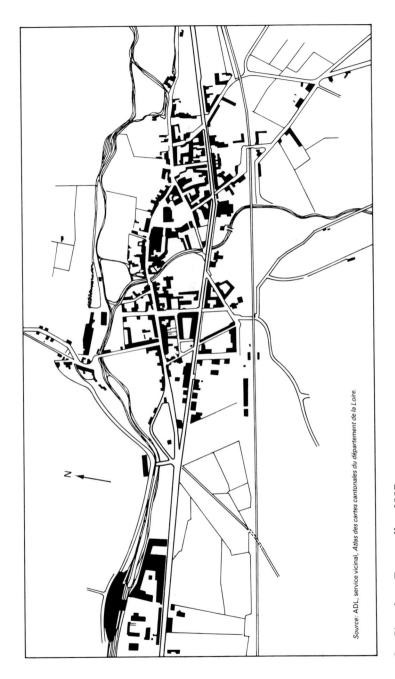

Le Chambon-Feugerolles, 1887

Source: ADL, service vicinal, *Atlas des cartes cantonales du département de la Loire.*

technological change. The same economic developments – the greater tendency of small-scale industry to concentrate, the higher wages of skilled workers and the larger amount of on-the-job interaction among skilled workers – which created conditions favourable for artisanal resistance weakened the chances for industrial worker militancy. Much industrial work remained scattered over the countryside or was dispersed throughout the city until late in the century. A disproportionately large fraction of the French work-force remained composed of women engaged in domestic work or only occupied temporarily in the factory. But over the long run of a century of social change and conflict the industrial worker was not left entirely to his own devices. Because of the continued artisanal presence in industrializing cities, artisans and industrial workers were thrown together. Together all these changes in worker settlement patterns help explain the increased organization and militancy of French industrial workers in the late nineteenth century.

10 Mayors versus police chiefs: socialist municipalities confront the French state[1]

Joan W. Scott

> The commune can become an excellent laboratory of decentralized economic life and, at the same time, a formidable political fortress for the use of local socialist municipalities against the bourgeois domination of the central power, one time when serious autonomy can be realized.
>
> *Edouard Vaillant*

As 1 May 1892 approached, anticipation heightened in every political camp in France. 1 May was international labour day, marked by work stoppages and demonstrations in cities and towns across Western Europe and the United States. Begun in 1886 as part of the American Federation of Labour's campaign for an eight-hour day, May Day by 1892 had become the symbol of the internationalism of the working-class movement.

French workers had observed May Day for the first time in 1890. Met by brigades of police and charged by the cavalry, they paraded none the less and their leaders delivered to the Chamber of Deputies petitions bearing thousands of signatures in favour of an eight-hour day. In 1891, local authorities prohibited demonstrations in some towns and arrested leaders in others. But events at Fourmies, where troops fired on a peaceful crowd, killing eleven people (mostly women and children) and wounding many others, heightened the enmity of French workers for the Third Republic.[2]

The legacy of the 'massacre at Fourmies' – fear of another one and of an angry reaction from French workers – was enough to worry politicians in 1892. But there was another reason for their concern. Since passage of the municipal law in 1884, granting the right to all municipalities (except Paris) to elect their councils, municipal elections were held every four years on the first Sunday in May. In 1892 that day fell on 1 May. Eager to capitalize on the coincidence, socialists had for months directed their efforts to capturing local government. The turnout this year, they urged, must be at the ballot box. Victory at the polls would enable workers to avenge the deaths of their comrades at Fourmies because 'the municipal elections put in your hands the legal means of enacting justice'. The call of the Parti Ouvrier (POF) incorporated participation in the elections into the original goals of May Day: 'To the ballot box and long live the eight-hour day! Long live the workers' party! Long live international solidarity!'[3]

In the Chamber of Deputies someone moved that the date of the elections be advanced to 3 April to avoid conflict with the workers' demonstration. Some feared a socialist landslide; others predicted revolution. But after discussions of the legal and administrative problems of changing it, the Chamber let the official date stand. The argument of M. Magnien, deputy from the department of Saône-et-Loire, offered a penetrating assessment of the situation:

> For my part ... I see no disadvantage in letting the May 1 demonstration coincide with the municipal elections. To hold the elections early would perhaps give the demonstration a significance it doesn't have: we would seem to be recoiling [in fear] from it. They say May 1 is a celebration of labour. An election is a celebration of universal suffrage. The two will become comingled and that will be all to the good![4]

M. Magnien's prediction that the association of the two fêtes would serve to integrate workers into French politics has become the standard interpretation of the socialist victories in 1892 and of the experiences of French socialist municipalities after that. There is, of course, no question that 1892 was a turning point in the socialists' electoral success and in their political strategy. On 1 May 1892, Guesdists won a majority on twenty-three municipal councils, among them those of Toulon, Roubaix, Montluçon and Narbonne. Victories by Independents, Possibilists, Allemanists and members of the Comité central révolutionaire brought the total to sixty communes.[5] In the legislative elections the following year socialist candidates polled over half a million votes. Thirty-seven socialists were elected and Jules Guesde entered the Chamber as one of six of his party to win a seat. By 1896, socialists held a majority in 150 municipalities and were among the minority in 75 others. Socialist mayors presided in the cities of Marseille, Lille, Dijon, Limoges and Roanne as well as in a host of smaller towns. In 1896, close to 1.5 million votes were cast for socialists of one tendency or another.[6]

Socialist spokesmen defined their victories as 'revolutionary'.

Jules Guesde, whose Parti Ouvrier had long denounced the reformism of other socialist factions, now defended 'the legal terrain of suffrage' as the battleground for socialist revolution.[7] The point was to capture the state, not necessarily to transform it, since it was merely the mechanism by which a majority could impose its will. Guesde told his fellow deputies in 1894 that

> The revolution of 1789 was completely accomplished when the Third Estate, majority at Versailles, took over political power. . . . If the Bastille fell, if gunpowder was used, if there were corpses and guillotines all of that was the revolution *illustrated*, not the revolution itself. . . . I am saying that all the drama was not the revolution, that the revolution was made when the Third, master of the Estates-General, began to make law.[8]

Guesde argued that the evolution of socialism was inevitable and that it would come by legal, parliamentary means. He did not believe that socialism in the towns and cities was the first step in a successful movement for communal autonomy. For him the commune was a training ground for electoral participation at the national level. It prepared workers for the eventual seizure of state power by means of the vote. Evolution and revolution became increasingly synonymous. The socialist revolution would be enacted by a parliament whose elected majority adhered to socialist doctrine.[9]

Guesde's own evolution was typical of a more general development in French socialism, indeed among Western European socialists in this period. When one looks at party histories and at the statements of other leaders in the 1890s, Michelle Perrot's characterization of the significance of socialist municipalities seems apt: 'A slow process of integration began which continued in the parliamentary hemicycle. The citizen replaced the comrade; and municipal fanfare replaced the trumpets of the last judgement.'[10] French socialism exchanged revolution and the bloodshed associated with Fourmies for a legal and peaceful transition to a new organization of society. Elation and triumph on 2 May 1892 replaced the shock and anger of the previous year. French workers, once bloodied and defeated by the Fourmies massacre, now celebrated victory. The use of the vote brought an unprecedented sense of power. The lesson of 1 May 1892, was, as M. Magnien had foreseen, that workers could voice demands and win them by participating in the politics of the French state.[11]

But is this an accurate characterization? From one perspective it is; clearly municipal victories gave workers a sense that they could use the vote to their immediate advantage and, perhaps in the long run, even to create socialism. But it does not necessarily follow that voting meant integration and *positive* acceptance of membership in the French nation-state. That conclusion is drawn from hindsight, by historians attempting to explain why a socialist revolution did not occur in France and by those who, still caught up in old ideological battles between reformists and revolutionaries, retrospectively assign blame.[12] Such an interpretation examines the national politics of formal organizations and the ideas of prominent national leaders, ignoring the motives of and the dilemmas faced by local leaders as well as the experiences of their followers.[13] Another look at the history of socialist municipalities in the 1890s leads to a re-evaluation of earlier interpretations. Socialists used the vote subversively at least at the local level. The Fourmies massacre had epitomized the entrenched power of capitalism and the state. Thus socialists adopted a defensive strategy. They attempted to build enclaves of resistance in their city halls and to perpetuate a sense of working-class non-acceptance of, if not active opposition to, bourgeois republican France.

Socialists first formulated in 1881 the programme that swept them into municipal office in 1892. A far-reaching statement, which took some of its inspiration from the Paris Commune of 1871, called for communal autonomy in matters of administration, police and justice; the municipalization of public services (gas, water and transportation); communal funding in the areas of medical care, legal services, unemployment assistance and trade union activity. The programme was endorsed by the Fédération des travailleurs de France, the Broussist or Possibilist party.[14]

Throughout the 1880s the 'possibilist' programme was the object of attack by Jules Guesde who had split with Paul Brousse in 1882 and founded the Parti Ouvrier Français. Guesde particularly objected to the decentralist notion of communal autonomy and the reformism of municipal socialism. The ownership of gas and water by a city, Guesde thundered, was not the same as the expropriation of capitalist property or the seizure of state power, nor would it ever lead to that.[15] None the less, by November 1891 (seven months after Fourmies) the POF at its congress in Lyon adopted a municipal programme of its own which carefully omitted references either to communal autonomy or municipalization, but listed fourteen reforms similar to those in the federation's programme.[16]

At the same time, a new group, the Parti Ouvrier socialiste révolutionnaire, led by Jean Allemane, split from the Broussist camp. While objecting to the federation's loss of emphasis on violent revolution, the Allemanists – a more militant working-class group – retained most aspects of the Possibilist municipal programme. Other socialist factions, such as the one led by Édouard Vaillant and Benoît Malon, endorsed municipal programmes as extensive as that of Paul Brousse and insisted as well on the 'necessity of conquering public power in the communes of the State'.[17]

'Commune, commune,' cried the bourgeoisie after the twelfth century and they freed themselves. 'Social commune!' ought to repeat the modern proletarians, and they too will trimph by this cry.[18]

Each group differed about the ultimate importance of municipal power for achieving socialism, but after 1891, all directed their efforts to winning votes in the commune. Municipal elections became an important focus for political activity in this period, the more so as first council seats and then city halls fell into socialist hands.

Contests by socialists for municipal control were part of a larger movement by working-class organizations in France. Edward Shorter and Charles Tilly refer to the years 1880–1914 as 'the period of the great mobilization of the working class for participation in national politics'.[19] During that time national unions and political parties emerged to co-ordinate what earlier had been sporadic, local efforts. Centralized, increasingly bureaucratized organizations directed working-class collective action towards the levers of state power. Shorter and Tilly examine patterns of strike activity, but their comment applies as well to political efforts. From this perspective the municipal elections were, at the very least, *les écoles de guerre* which familiarized local populations with 'struggles in the public arena'.[20] Following strategies and programmes devised by national organizations, local leaders appealed to constituencies on issues of immediate concern.[21] Once mobilized, socialists expected that an electorate would continue to vote for their candidates whether they ran for the district (*arrondissement*) or departmental councils or the Chamber of Deputies.[22]

National organizations could devise programmes appealing to a variety of localities because, despite great economic and social diversity, workers confronted common problems. From 1873–96 the French economy was in a depression. Low prices and an increase in wages did improve the buying power of some French workers, but a stagnant economy also made employment unstable. Competition for jobs increased as steady streams of peasants migrated from the countryside. In some of the larger industries mechanization reduced the wages and power of skilled workers, making them more vulnerable to under-employment and un-employment. Mechanization also led to changes in the organiza-tion of production that intensified the rhythm of work and diminished workers' control over processes of production and labour markets.[23] Employers gained increased power at the work-place and they also began to form national industry-wide organiza-tions which lobbied for favourable legislation and co-ordinated resistance to collective actions by their employees. By the 1890s it was clear that French capitalism was entrenched economically and that it had great political power. In addition, industrial develop-ment concentrated increasingly large numbers of workers in cities or in their suburbs; as a consequence, workers often formed the overwhelming majority of inhabitants (and voters). They were concerned locally with the price of food, taxes, housing, water supply and the cost and availability of medical and legal services. As the employment of children in industry declined and with the passage of compulsory primary education laws in the 1880s, the quality of teachers and schools and the ability of their children to secure education became issues of concern for working-class people. Union organization, which became legal in 1884, also flourished in cities. Workers sought municipal protection and financial support for their activities, especially during strikes. In effect, the law of 1884 (and a subsequent law on arbitration passed in 1892 which permitted justices of the peace to negotiate strike settlements) admitted working-class interests and organizations into the political arena. Defence of those interests then became a political, as well as a strictly union matter.[24]

Socialist attempts to influence municipalities to act on these issues were made possible by the law on municipal organization of 5 April 1884. Under the new law, all eligible voters directly elected the municipal councillors of their commune. The councillors then elected one of their number as mayor. (Paris – the rebellious capital – was excluded from the law until 1977, having been denied municipal government since the end of the French revolution.) Since 1848 voters had chosen municipal councillors, but mayors usually were appointed by the prefect or minister of interior and were viewed as agents of the state, not representatives of municipal interests. After 1884, voters effectively chose the mayor as well as the councillors. And though municipal powers were carefully circumscribed and most actions ultimately subject to prefectoral veto, the potential for a unified assertion of local demands now existed in the town halls.

The fact that the laws extended new rights to unions and municipalities moved conflict into a different arena but did not end working-class opposition to capitalism or the bourgeois republic. Indeed, the 1880s and 1890s saw increasing numbers of voters turn from the bourgeois politicians of the Third Republic to socialists. Throughout the Second Empire, the hopes of working-class groups had been tied to republicanism. Many expected significant social improvement would follow the introduction of genuine universal manhood suffrage and parliamentary democracy. But as the years wore on with few concessions to working-class needs and with local *notables* firmly implanted in the Chamber and in town halls, workers became disillusioned. Many began to speak of the need for a new kind of republic, a social republic. 'If the workers' hopes are disappointed', wrote a future socialist mayor of Carmaux in 1889, 'they will turn either to reaction or revolution'.[25] Like him, many turned to revolutionary socialists who promised social justice, equality and an end to poverty and exploitation. The revolutionary syndicalists turned entirely away from electoral strategies, urging use of the general strike as an ultimate revolutionary weapon. The socialists advocated the use of political rights to gain economic justice and equality. Indeed, they looked to a long tradition in French history in which workers democratically represented in the Commune of Paris had saved the republic during the French revolution and defended it again in 1870–1, instilling it with revolutionary purpose. If the strike demonstrated the fact that workers were essential to production and the economy of the nation, voting represented citizenship, the right, won during the French revolution and now enjoyed by all men, to exercise influence over the laws. The republican form of government, socialists said, made possible the realization of the revolutionary transformation of social and economic relationships implied in the phrase 'the social republic'. Socialism, with its emphasis on class struggle, was the ideology of the great mobilization of 1880–1914, but it was socialism within a republican context. 'If from an economic point of view we are socialists', wrote a Guesdist municipal councillor from Montluçon in 1898, 'we are above all republicans'.[26]

Political strategies implied that the sovereign people could make their will felt by voting. The municipal strategy had an additional purpose: to create within the bourgeois state an alternative model of government. In the town hall socialists claimed they had installed a new political system that exemplified the practices and values of the economic system they would one day create. It was a living alternative, albeit a limited one, to the status quo.[27]

Socialism at the municipal level offered an opportunity for the concrete implementation of rhetorical phrases and abstract theory.[28] It gave workers a powerful sense of belonging to a community united around its interests as a class. Although Possibilists disagreed with Guesdists about the efficacy of reform in a capitalist society, both groups enacted similar measures when they conquered a Hôtel de Ville.

These measures have been classified under four rubrics: revamping municipal finances; creation of municipal enterprises; encouraging and protecting organizational efforts of workers; and reforming and extending public assistance.[29] State authorities usually prohibited planned transformations of the basis of taxation, as well as municipalization of gas, water and transportation. And the Conseil d'État usually overruled as violations of free enterprise attempts to use city funds to set up free pharmacies or to provide free legal consultation. Thus most efforts of local socialists were directed to the third and fourth areas listed above: working-class organization and welfare.

When a town hall fell to the socialists, all forms of working-class activity were encouraged.[30] In some cities, municipal funds were used to purchase a building for a Bourse du Travail, thus guaranteeing its members against eviction by a landlord who disapproved of their politics. During strikes socialist municipal councils donated money to workers and their families. They underwrote the appearance in town of national socialist celebrities. And they encouraged the formation of study groups, clubs and unions. Above all, they provided protection from the police, the repressive arm and most immediate exemplification of state power. The speeches and political actions of socialists reiterate the theme of opposition to the police and so demonstrate its importance. At public meetings held to rally voters, build morale during strikes or explain socialist doctrine and recruit new followers, socialist orators invariably lashed out at the police. As if following a script, a speaker would interrupt his talk to mock the self-importance of the police commissioner and reveal his identity.

Pointing to the back of the room, a speaker in Riom announced, 'That *mouchard* is here simply to spy on us.'[31]

As cries of 'Vive la Commune' filled a hall in Roubaix, Jules Guesde egged his audience on: 'Monsieur le commissaire de police can mention this in his report. . . . At least it will show he has done something useful.'[32]

When, during a speech in Nouzon by Jean-Baptiste Clément, someone warned that the police were there taking notes, he proclaimed defiantly that he was not afraid.[33]

At Castres, the birthplace of Jean Jaurès, in 1895, A. Briant 'spoke of policemen, of decorated spies and terrorist prefects. . . . He described the Prefect of the Tarn as a grotesque imbecile, an evil puppet, valet to the rich and aggressor against the poor. . . . And he complained of the presence of three *commissaires de police* in the room'.[34]

The remarks generally provided relief during an otherwise serious exposition. Crowds hooted and laughed, hurled epithets at the commissaires in the room and defiantly shouted revolutionary slogans in unison. These moments, repeated in town after town, welded the audience and speaker in a ritual denunciation of their enemy. There was a sense of outrage and solidarity as socialists and their followers verbally attacked the police and displayed their determination to keep them from invading working-class terrain – in this case the public meeting hall.

The experience in the lecture hall was re-enacted on the streets, frequently during strikes. Municipal councillors and mayors then used the authority of public office to prevent or challenge invasions of workers' rights by agents of the state. Events in Montluçon on 20 August 1893 exemplify the nature of the challenge.

As the commissioner of police of the metal-working city rode past a bar on the trolley, someone shouted an insult at him. 'Do you see that pig of a police commissioner?' The commissioner jumped off the tramway and strode up to the group he believed responsible. Among the men assembled was the newly elected socialist mayor, Jean Dormoy. Dormoy stepped in front of him, as if to block his way and asked, 'What are you doing? Leave these people alone. You are disturbing the peace.' General hilarity followed, most of it at the expense of the dignity of the commissioner – at least that was what he reported to the prefect. None of the seventeen witnesses questioned seemed to remember the incident clearly and the government had to drop its charges against the mayor for 'insults to a state functionary in the exercise of his office'.[35]

Later that same day, the mayor again confronted the police agent. This time it was at the office of the subprefect at 10.30 in the evening. A crowd that had gathered was being dispersed by the commissioner and someone shouted at him 'dirty pig' (*'cochon et salop'*). Hardly had the police chief grabbed the man by his collar when Dormoy appeared, his official mayoral insignia (*écharpe*) in his hand. Dormoy, asserting his formal power, ordered the police chief to let the man go. The chief told the mayor not to interfere with his job, which he was fulfilling under orders from the subprefect. The mayor replied that he, not the subprefect, was the legal superior of the police chief. Then Dormoy and others pushed (*'foncèrent'*) against the commissaire, forcing him to release his grip on the prisoner. Dormoy told the man to 'beat it' (*'va-t-en'*) and he vanished into the crowd. The policeman turned to the mayor and accused him of violently assisting a prisoner's escape. Despite conflicting testimony, Dormoy was this time convicted of a violation of the penal code.

These incidents were part of an ongoing dispute between Dormoy and the police commissioner. They typify as well a more general pattern of conflict in other socialist municipalities. The commissaire embodied the power of the state in the commune. In challenging police authority, the mayor insisted on his own legitimacy, on his right to assert the will of the people. Dormoy's mayoral sash signified that he was a representative elected by the people. It demonstrated to his constituents his willingness to use the power of his office to serve and protect their interests. Moreover Dormoy claimed that he, not the subprefect, had the right to give orders to the police. Like him, other socialist mayors insisted that the police commissioner was under their jurisdiction and that any such defiance was illegal. Dormoy's actions dramatically conveyed both a political and a personal challenge to the agent who spied on workers, broke up their meetings and arrested them during strikes. The confrontations between socialist mayors and the police agents gave human form to the abstract entities of justice and injustice, universal suffrage and the state, rights of association and repression. The mayor was the collective voice of the workers who had elected him and he provided a new line of defence within the town against state repression.[36]

The workers themselves sometimes carried the words of orators and the actions of mayors even further. In Carmaux, for example, in 1893, miners and glassworkers threw garbage at and insulted policemen who were patrolling the streets. Wrote the Prefect of the Tarn:

Carmaux believes itself to be a state within the state. The gendarmes are the objects of grave violence ... a policeman's life is in danger.... There is no longer safety for representatives of the law nor for agents of the mining company. They are deluged by a multitude which lacks all respect for them.[37]

Popular democracy, here again, challenged the right of the state to intervene in local affairs. Workers mobilized to protect their rights within the town whose government they controlled. In each case they deliberately chose the police as a target. Policemen were the immediate obstacles to working-class collective action and to the expression of the popular will.

The sense of the socialist municipality as a protector of working-class organization, evident in confrontations with the police, was even more explicit in social welfare policies. When socialists took office they allocated more money than had been spent by previous administrations for various forms of public assistance including maternity hospitals, nurseries, sanitoria for sick children, food and clothing for the offspring of the poor, strike benefits for workers, public baths and old age homes. In addition to financial assistance, the councils tried to give the workers some control over urban institutions by, for example, appointing workers in place of clerics to the boards of charitable institutions.

Not only did the socialists expand public assistance, they redefined their reasons for insisting on its development. In contrast to what they deemed the humiliating paternalism of previous administrations, they saw themselves fulfilling the obligations of society to guarantee the health, education and subsistence of its members. The obligations were likened to those of parents to children, of one family member to another. Indeed the 'socialist conception' the municipalities tried to realize was that of the rights and duties of family members.[38]

When, for example, the socialist municipal council of Roubaix offered free clothing and hot lunches to school children, it defined its action as that of a surrogate family, substituting its functions for those of 'the ruined and poor individual family destroyed by capitalist rule'.[39] In discussing the creation of a sanatorium at the seashore for sick children, a Roubasien socialist editor evoked the intimacy of parental emotions (*'vos petits'*, *'vos bébés mamans'*, *'nos chers marmots'*) and attributed them to the socialist council: 'Only the socialist commune can put into practice such generous ideas, because socialism in the commune transforms the commune into a big family.'[40]

The family implied egalitarianism and a willingness to share resources with those who needed them, unselfish devotion and loyalty to one's kin and the recognition of reciprocal duties and rights. In its idealized version at least, 'the social family' remained something one could turn to and depend on when all else failed: a place of last resort where personalized concern replaced the bureaucratic disdain of the state. By depicting socialism in these terms local leaders supported an extension of resources and control to workers over decisions affecting the welfare of their families.[41]

In France discussions of a need to protect the working-class family intensified during the 1880s and 1890s. If bourgeois reformers and socialists often used the same language, their purposes differed. While legislators of the Third Republic wanted a strong family to instil morality and discipline in the working class, socialists and trade unionists saw the family as a unit of economic protection and political resistance. The family was a co-operative, humanizing institution, a school for socialist values and class consciousness in a capitalist society.

Of course, working-class ties long had been depicted in family or kinship terms. *Fraternité*, which depicted class relations as family relations, was the slogan of the French working-class movement throughout the nineteenth century. Still in the 1890s, at the civil baptisms favoured by socialist militants, godparents solemnly pledged to instil in a child collectivist principles. Then 'the lips of the child were wet with wine – the wine of fraternity'.[42] *Fraternité* was the cry of the working class in 1848 and in the 1890s, but the image conjured up had evolved during that period. In 1848 *fraternité* was meant literally as brotherhood, the fraternity of craftsmen, the members of trade corporation. The emphasis was on male bonds and trade ties. Working relationships were like family relationships, but it was the association of workers that was projected as the basis for an alternative social order. The workshop would become the social workshop. By the 1890s, capitalism had conquered the organization of the workplace and socialists looked to the family, with its collectivization of resources and co-operative division of labour in the interests of group welfare, as a concrete example of their own principles. If the *fraternité* of 1848 implied an assault on contemporary society, references to family in the 1890s signified protection of workers from capitalism and the state. That was suggested in the socialists' use of family metaphors that stressed the ties between parents and children. They spoke of solicitous care, the provision of necessities and the protection of individuals from the ravages of ill-health or destitution. Like a working-class family, but on a larger scale, the socialist commune was depicted as a shelter against the ultimate alienation and impoverishment of capitalism.

A campaign song for the municipal election of 1896 in Roubaix summed up the significance of socialist victories. It addressed a local capitalist:

You are stuffed with riches gained by the sweat of the worker
You have houses and mistresses
You are the king at the factory.
Alas, what vexes you despite your wealth and your gold:
You are nothing at the city hall and you never will be.[43]

The song reflects the sense of autonomy and control workers could have when they ran the city hall. It was to be their domain. As they did in the domestic *foyer*, so they reigned in the Hôtel de Ville, though the capitalists continued as undisputed kings of the factories. The autonomy and control were limited and narrow, local and protective, not national or offensive. Indeed, local political control was an alternative to, perhaps consolation for, the economic wealth and power of factory owners. The municipality in socialist hands represented a base for organizing opposition to the bourgeois republic.

Plate 14   *A Socialist Baptism*

State authorities recognized the subversive potential of these municipalities and joined local anti-socialists in extensive campaigns to stem the socialist tide. Mayors were fined and arrested for 'outrages against public authority'. They were suspended and then sometimes disqualified from running for office because they had been convicted. After the elections of 1892, for example, the socialist mayors of Narbonne and Montluçon were suspended, as were four deputy mayors in Marseille. In 1896, the socialist mayor of Lille was temporarily removed from office. Two years later the same fate befell the socialist mayor of Roanne.[44] In Narbonne in 1896, authorities used charges of electoral fraud (brought by defeated moderate republicans against the victorious socialists) as a reason to annul the election; the voters returned the socialists to office in a new election, but it was not until 1899 that charges were finally dropped for lack of conclusive proof.[45] In Carmaux, Mayor Jean-Baptiste Calvignac was charged with various kinds of misconduct and suspended several times during his early years in office. In 1896, the prefect reduced the mayor's expense account. The municipal council of Carmaux protested the action and one councillor, M. Toulze, charged the prefect with misconduct. In response, the prefect filed charges against Toulze. His explanation for this action to the Minister of the Interior reveals how calculated was the campaign to weaken socialist power in the municipalities:

My only purpose ... was to awaken in M. Toulze a salutary fear of the law. A simple legal investigation should have sufficed ... to attain this result, and would not have been without advantage in an environment such as Carmaux. The ever increasing audacity of the socialist party, the scorn it shows for the government and its representatives seem to me to require repression even in the least of their manifestations. The example was that much better because Toulze is one of the most militant and most agitated of his party.[46]

Voters often defied higher authorities and re-elected their socialist mayors, only to have them arrested again for another infraction of the law. In what Rolande Trempé describes as an atmosphere of 'civil war' in Carmaux, the authorities managed to 'strike the most active and esteemed militants and to decapitate the municipality as well as organizations and unions'.[47]

Socialists were not everywhere eliminated from municipal office, but their power was weakened and their actions increasingly circumscribed by vigilant prefects and their aides. In this way, the potential of socialist cities to shelter working-class populations was underscored even as it was limited and sometimes destroyed. Indeed, it is in the interaction of socialist municipalities and state authority that some of the explanation for the success of the socialist appeal as well as the failure of revolution must be sought. The socialist political strategy – at the local and national levels – reveals not the limits of socialist imagination but the power of French capitalism and the state.

A close examination of the words and actions of socialist municipal councillors in the 1890s calls into question the integrationist thesis. Some deputies clearly were 'infatuated' with parliamentary politics. But workers who voted for socialists in municipal elections were not necessarily being asked to 'buy in' to French politics so they could assert their claims as a new interest group. That was how the state ultimately defined their actions; that was the lesson M. Magnien, the deputy of the Saône-et-Loire cited earlier, hoped to teach. Socialists, however, were using the vote as a challenge to, not an endorsement of the bourgeois republican order. Especially at the municipal level, a socialist political victory could have tangible results. Capturing a city hall meant enlarging the domain of resistance to capitalism and creating a protected enclave within which resistance might be organized.

In one sense, the strategy failed, for it never won political power at the national level and certainly never fulfilled the professed revolutionary aspirations of the leaders. In another sense, however, it had noteworthy success. The extraordinary longevity of socialism in many municipalities and the strength of working-class culture in France stem, at least in part, from the efforts begun in the 1890s by socialists in the communes to improve the lives of their constituents.

Their experience suggests the need to re-examine the socialists' municipal strategy, not as a phase in the long-term evolution of ideology and formal national organizations, but in the context of the 1890s. The local experience deepens and complicates our understanding of the national experience. It perhaps also calls for a conceptualization of *le mouvement social* which thinks not in linear evolutionary terms, but in terms of different forms of struggle at different times by workers against capitalism and the nation-state.

Notes and references

Abbreviations

AD	Archives Départementales
ADA	Archives Départementales de l'Aveyron
ADHV	Archives Départementales de la Haute Vienne
ADL	Archives Départementales de la Loire
AG	Archives de la Guerre
AML	Archives Municipal de Limoges
AN	Archives Nationales
BSAHL	*Bulletin de la Société Archéologique et Historique du Limousin*
CSD	Commissaire spécial de Decazeville
DCMD	Délibérations du conseil municipal de Decazeville
PA	Prefect of Aveyron
PG	*procureur général*
PGL	*procureur général* of Limoges
PHV	Prefect of Haute Vienne

Chapter 1: Images of the nineteenth-century French city

1 I thank Judy Coffin, Peter Gay, Ted Margadant and Carol Payne for their comments on this essay.
2 Louis Bergeron and Marcel Roncaylo, 'De la ville preindustrielle à la ville industrielle: Essai sur l'historiographie française', *Quaderni Storici*, no. 27 (1974), p. 828.
3 ibid., p. 836.
4 The so-called 'human' geographers, disciples of Vidal de la Blanche and Albert Demangéon, undertook systematic studies of individual cities – in the words of Raoul Blanchard, to 'explain the origins and the development of the town as a function of physical conditions and location'. They first 'defined' the city by its physical surroundings and then determined its economic functions (agricultural, commercial, industrial, military, administrative). The format of their

studies was consistent, but the quality of their presentation and analysis varies considerably. Among the most important such studies were those of Antoine Vacher (Montluçon), Raoul Blanchard (Grenoble), Albert Demangéon (Paris) and Jacques Levainville (Rouen). These have much to tell us about patterns of land use, the geography of work, changing shape of the city, migration and neighbourhoods. They have almost nothing to say about politics: the human geographers believed that, in the words of Levainville, 'populations cannot, in any case, free themselves from the yoke of nature. Societies can never escape the power of physical conditions, not only because of the mark they receive from the climate and the soil, but especially because these conditions are the first causes of their origin and their development'. Blanchard thus expresses amazement at Grenoble's continued economic growth in the nineteenth century in the face of imposing physical obstacles, 'a geographic paradox which can only be explained by human initiative, full of daring, and constantly regenerated and rejuvenated'. Levainville's thorough analysis of changes in work structure in Rouen and its region does leave the impression, however, that this and the concentration of the working class in Rouen could have political implications and that the workers would be heard from. This generation of urban geographers is particularly interested in urban networks; see, for example, Michel Rochefort, *L'organisation urbaine de l'Alsace* (Paris 1960).

5 Daniel Roche, 'Urban history in France: achievements, tendencies and objectives', *Urban History Year Book 1980* (London 1980), p. 14. See especially Manuel Castells, 'Structures sociales et processus d'urbanisation', *Annales: Économies, Sociétés, Civilisations*, no. 25 (1970), pp. 1155–99.

6 See Kingsley Davis, 'The urbanization of the human population', in Charles Tilly (ed.), *An Urban World* (Boston 1974), pp. 160–75.

7 Cited by Georges Dupeux, 'La croissance urbaine en France au XIXe siècle', *Revue d'histoire économique et sociale*, no. 52 (1974), pp. 173–4. For a scathing critique of Pouthas, see Paul G. Spagnoli, 'The demographic work of Charles Pouthas', *Historical Methods Newsletter*, vol. 4, no. 4, pp. 126–40.

8 The decline in urban population between 1866 and 1872 was due to the loss of Alsace-Lorraine to Germany in the Franco-Prussian war.

9 Dupeux, 'La croissance urbaine', p. 183.

10 J. F. Gravier, *Paris et le desert français* (Paris 1947), p. 38.

11 Flora Tristan, *Tour de France: journal inédit, 1843–44* (Paris 1973), pp. 132–3.

12 AG MR 1266, 'Notice sur la ville de Saint-Étienne et de ses environs' (1846), by Joseph Brignan.

13 AN C 956, canton of Saint-Étienne.

14 AG MR 1184, 'Mémoire sur la reconnaissance de la route Petites Loges à Reims' (1828), by M. Lefebvre; AN C 958, canton of Reims.

15 Yves Lequin, *Les ouvriers de la région lyonnaise, 1848–1914*, vol. 1, *La formation de la classe ouvrière régionale* (Lyons 1977), p. 45.

16 See T. Margadant, *French Peasants in Revolt: The Insurrection of 1851* (Princeton, NJ 1979), for a thoroughly brilliant analysis.

17 AG MR 1298, 'Mémoire sur les environs de Châtellerault' (1841), by M. Thiebault.

18 Alexis de Tocqueville, *The Old Regime and the French Revolution* (Garden City, NY 1955).

19 J. F. Gravier, *Paris et le desert français* (Paris 1947), p. 22.

20 ibid., p. 14.

21 ibid., pp. 21–2.

22 See Lewis Greenberg, *Sisters of Liberty: Marseille, Lyon, Paris and the Reaction to a Centralized State, 1868–1871* (Cambridge, Mass. 1971).

23 AG MR 1234: 'Quelques réflexions sur la feuille de Bourbon Vendée' (1840), by A. Goguel; 'Mémoire sur les environs de Bourbon-Vendée' (1842), by M. Leclerc; 'Mémoire descriptif et militaire de Napoléon Vendée' (1853), by Feraud; Pierre Lavedan, *Histoire de l'Urbanisme (Epoque Contemporaine)* (Paris 1952), pp. 34–7.

24 AG MR 1234, 'Mémoire sur les environs de Bourbon-Vendée' (1842), by M. Leclerc.

25 M. A. Legoyt, *Du progrès des agglomérations urbaines et de l'émigration rural en Europe et particulièrement en France* (Paris 1867), p. 195.

26 See Susanna Barrows, 'After the Commune: alcoholism, temperance, and literature in the early Third Republic', in John M. Merriman (ed.), *Consciousness and Class Experience in Nineteenth-Century Europe* (New York 1979), pp. 205–18, and her forthcoming *Distorting Mirrors* (New Haven, Conn. 1981) for a discussion of the attitudes of the early crowd psychologists and of the bourgeoisie toward crowds.

27 Paul Meuriot, *Des agglomérations urbaines dans l'Europe contemporaine* (Paris 1897), pp. 406–7. Meuriot's study recalls the pioneering work of Adna Weber, *The Growth of Cities in the Nineteenth Century* (Ithaca, NY 1967), first published at the turn of the century.

28 George Rudé, *The Crowd in History* (New York 1964); David H. Pinkney, *The French Revolution of 1830* (Princeton, NJ 1972); Charles Tilly and Lynn Lees, 'The people of June 1848', in Roger Price (ed.), *Revolution and Reaction: 1848 and the Second French Republic* (London 1975), and many others.

29 Quoted from Fernand Braudel and Ernest Labrousse (eds.), *Histoire économique et sociale de la France*, vol. 3, pt 2 (Paris 1976), p. 792.

30 Charles Tilly, Louise Tilly and Richard Tilly, *The Rebellious Century* (Cambridge, Mass. 1975), p. 46.

31 Martin Nadaud, *Mémoires de Léonard, ancien garçon maçon* (Paris 1947).

32 See John M. Merriman, 'Incident at the statue of the Virgin Mary: The conflict of old and new in nineteenth-century Limoges,' in Merriman, *Consciousness and Class Experience in Nineteenth-Century Europe.*

33 For a somewhat different approach to the problem of urban and rural antagonisms, see Gravier, *Paris et le desert français.*

34 Cited in Jean-Paul Brunet, *Saint Denis, la ville rouge, 1890–1939* (Paris 1980), p. 15.

35 Lavedan, *Histoire de l'urbanisme*, the title of ch. 5.

36 See Christopher H. Johnson, *Utopian Communism in France: Cabet and the Icarians, 1839–51* (Ithaca, NY 1974).

37 See David H. Pinkney, *Napoleon III and the Rebuilding of Paris* (Princeton, NJ 1958).

38 Important exceptions include Anthony Sutcliffe, *The Autumn of Central Paris* (Paris 1970), and Louis Chevalier, *L'Assassinat de Paris* (Paris 1977).

39 Richard Cobb, *Promenades* (Oxford 1980), p. 1; see also his *Paris and its Provinces* (London 1975), *A Second Identity* (London 1969), *Reactions to the French Revolution* (London 1972) and *A Sense of Place* (London 1976).

Chapter 2: Changing urban politics in industrializing Limoges

1 This essay is part of an ongoing larger study of the city of Limoges during the nineteenth century; see also John M. Merriman, 'Incident at the statue of the Virgin Mary: the conflict of old and new in nineteenth-century Limoges', in J. M. Merriman (ed.), *Consciousness and Class Experience in Nineteenth-Century Europe* (New York 1979), pp. 129–49, and J. M. Merriman, *Agony of the Republic: The Repression of the Left in Revolutionary France, 1848–1851* (New Haven, Conn. 1978), chs. 1, 6.

2 On the revolution of 1830, see David H. Pinkney, *The French Revolution of 1830* (Princeton, NJ 1972). See also John M. Merriman, (ed.), *1830 in France* (New York 1975), particularly James Rule and Charles Tilly, 'Political process in revolutionary France, 1830–1832', Christopher H. Johnson, 'The revolution of 1830 in French economic history', and J. M. Merriman, 'The *Demoiselles* of the Ariège, 1829–1831'.

3   *Annales de la Haute Vienne*, 23 January 1829; AG MR 1300, 'Mémoire sur les environs de Limoges', by M. A. Joinville; Monique Lachtygier, 'Tableau de la vie ouvrière à Limoges de 1800 à 1848' (Mémoire pour le diplôme d'Études supérieurs, Université de Poitiers 1959).

4   *Nouvelles Ephémérides du ressort de la cour royale de Limoges* (Limoges 1837); Lachtygier, 'Tableau de la vie ouvrière', p. 106. The excess of deaths over births (average of 1206 to 1136 births between 1820 and 1835) was at least partially attributable to sizeable charitable institutions with notoriously high mortality rates.

5   A. Fray-Fournier, 'Balzac à Limoges', *Bibliophile Limousin*, no. 13 (1898), p. 51.

6   ibid.

7   ADHV 1M 243, letter of minister of interior, 4 July 1825; A. Fray-Fournier, 'Limoges et les bonnes villes', *BSAHL*, no. 52 (1903), pp. 281–352; AML, 'D', letters of Prefect of Haute Vienne (PHV), 6 December 1816 and 4 July 1825.

8   AG MR 1300, Joinville.

9   J. J. Juge, *Changements survenues à Limoges depuis cinquante ans* (Limoges 1817); Henri Ducourtieux, 'Les statues dans les carrefours de Limoges', *Limoges illustré*, 15 May 1906; Lachtygier, 'Tableau de la vie ouvrière', pp. 125–6.

10   Juge, *Changements survenues*; Louis Guibert, 'Les Confrèries de Pénitents en France et notamment dans le diocèse de Limoges', *BSAHL*, no. 27 (1879); *Almanach Limousin* (1863), 'Les Ostensions'.

11   AN F7 9711, PHV, 6 May 1819; Juge, *Changements survenues*, pp. 46ff.

12   AN F7 9711, PHV, 6 May 1819; ADHV 3M 57, electoral lists.

13   Pierre Cousteix, 'La vie ouvrière dans la Haute Vienne sous la Restoration,' *L'information historique* (Novembre 1952); Lachtygier, 'Tableau de la vie ouvrière'; Camille Grellier, *L'industrie de la porcelaine en Limousin* (Paris 1908).

14   ADHV 4M 44, police reports of 10 February and 30 June 1820.

15   AN F7 9711, PHV, 18 and 19 June 1816; ADHV 1M 133, 19 June 1816; ADHV 4M 53, daily reports for restoration.

16   AML, *procès-verbaux* of municipal council deliberations.

17   Registered voters increased by a remarkable 250 per cent between 15 August and 30 September 1827, by far the largest percentage in all of France: Sherman Kent, *The French Election of 1827* (Cambridge, Mass. 1974), p. 117; AN F7 6772, PHV, 31 July 1827, etc.; AN BB18 1150, letter of PGL, 5 July 1827; AN F7 6741, PHV, 30 November 1827; AN F1cIII Haute Vienne 4, PHV, 20 September 1827.

18   F1cIII Haute Vienne 4, PHV, 9 September 1827.

19   n.n., 'François Alluaud,' *BSAHL*, no. 60, *procès-verbaux* of 15 July 1910 session.

20   F1cIII Haute Vienne 4, PHV, 18 November 1827; AN F7 6777, PHV, 31 July 1827; AN BB18 1155, PGL, 5 February 1828; AN BB18 1157, PGL, 23 April 1828; AN F7 6741, PHV, 30 November 1827; *Les Annales de la Haute Vienne*, 30 November 1827; AN F7 6772, PHV, 31 July 1827.

21   F1cIII Haute Vienne 4, *procès-verbaux* of election and *profession de foi* of Dumont St Priest; AN F19 5682, Bishop, 7 May 1828; minister of interior, 7 and 21 May 1828; ADHV 2M2, *fonds de l'évêché*, letter of mayor, 21 March 1828; 1T 86A, Bishop of Limoges, 6 May 1828.

22   AN F7 6772, PHV, 2 July 1828.

23   ibid., PHV, 6 February, 5 August, 8 November, 13, 14 December 1829, etc.

24   ibid., PHV, 8 March 1822, 6 November 1829.

25   The editor was Aimé Mallevergne, who had won a first for rhetoric six years earlier in school; Abria, a clerk for a local merchant, was the managing director; other collaborators included Peyramont, later an Orleanist deputy, and Dumas, a very popular liberal retired army officer who assumed command of the National Guard after the revolution of 1830.

26   *Annales de la Haute Vienne*, 16 April 1830, spoke of '*les ordures vomies par une bouche immode*'; 14 May 1830; AN F7 6772, PHV, 16 September 1829 and 1 March 1830.

27   Lists of eligible voters, F1cIII, Haute Vienne 4.

28   AN F7 6772, PHV, 16 September 1829.

29   ibid., 26 January 1830. The Chambre Consultative had been created in 1804 as the Chambre des Manufactures et du Commerce, but left no traces until 1822. It initiated a Conseil des Prud'hommes and organized a school of design in 1825; the former was charged with a moralizing function and its inauguration description refers to 'mistakes of bad faith' and 'exaggerated demands arising from their [the workers'] wrongly perceived interests': *Annales de la Haute Vienne*, 5 July 1825.

30   Arthur Young, *Travels during the Years 1787, 1788 and 1789* (London 1791), p. 14.

31   J. C. Parot, '1830 à Limoges' (Mémoire complémentaire pour le diplôme d'Études supérieur, Université de Poitiers 1964), pp. 10–11, quoting the bishop's letter to the minister of foreign affairs, 23 February 1830.

32   AN BB18 1149, PGL, 7 June 1827; ADHV 4M 53, police report of 20–21 April 1828; *Annales de la Haute Vienne*, 19 and 26 February 1830.

33 AN F7 6772, PHV, 9 January 1830; ADHV 3M3, *fonds de l'évêché*, letters of PHV, 28 December 1829 and 1 January 1830; *Annales de la Haute Vienne*, 1 January 1830.

34 AN F7 6772, 9 January 1830; *Annales de la Haute Vienne*, 1, 12, 22 January, 19 March 1830; *Le Contribuable*, 12 May 1830.

35 *Le Contribuable*, 12 May, 1830; De la Bastide had also been accused of financial irregularities in 1824 by Descoutures, who became a leading liberal after being denounced by the municipal council: *Réponse de M. Descoutures à M. le Bon de la Bastide, maire de cette ville, juillet, 1824* (Limoges 1824), claiming that the mayor allocated a large sum of money for his friend, the secretary of the town hall.

36 See John Merriman, 'Incident at the statue of the Virgin Mary', pp. 138–45.

37 AN F7 6772, PHV, 14 December 1829; 21 July 1830.

38 *Le Contribuable*, 19 May 1830; Coster noted on 1 March 1830 that Limoges businessmen blamed the ministry for its policies: AN F7 6772.

39 *Annales de la Haute Vienne*, 11 June and 16 July 1830.

40 *Le Contribuable*, 12 July 1820; Parot, '1830 à Limoges', p. 12, notes that the newspaper helped register eighty new voters for the election. Evidence of the bishop's part in the election may be found in 2M3, *fonds*; Victor Alluaud noted as the most important liberal organizer in F7 6772, PHV, 16 September 1829.

41 F1cIII Haute Vienne 4; Coster had noted, on 1 March that 'the people take no part in the debate': AN F7 6772. Dumont St Priest's electoral statement had promised to call the king's attention to the interests of business. *Le Contribuable*, referring to Bourdeau-Lajudie's election, expressed delight to have a deputy who would 'defend the public liberties because they are in danger; a celebrated manufacturer, whose useful work gives bread to people and glory to France'. Execution described in *Le Contribuable*, 12 July 1830; the fall of Algiers, 26 July.

42 AN F9 733, letter of Dumas, appointed as commander of National Guard, 11 September; lockout rumoured, AN BB18 1187, PGL, 1 September, and referred to during the 1837 strike by porcelain artisans: ADHV 1M 130, 'Précis sur la situation véritable des ouvriers et artistes en porcelaine, sans travail'; *Le Contribuable*, 9 August; ADHV 1M 127, *affiches*; AML, deliberations of the municipal council. Parot, '1830 à Limoges', also describes the reception of the news of the events of Paris; *Le Moniteur*, 29 July, reported that 3000 'workers' gathered in every quarter shouting 'Long live Liberty!', but no local sources substantiate this; AN F7 4215/14, gendarme reports noted that Limoges 'was in a great state of effervescence'.

43 The first days of the revolution may be followed in AN F7 4215/14 and in the daily reports of the war ministry, Archives de la Guerre, E/5 1 and 2.

44 ADHV 1M 127, PHV, 1 and 6 September; AN BB18 1187, PGL, 1 September; ADHV U Cour 174 and 190, trial and statements of the accused. The bakers received an indemnity: AML, municipal council session of 1 September 1831.

45 ADHV, U Cour 190; Alluaud convoked the wealthiest businessmen of the town to organize a loan of 60,000 francs to purchase grain; this sum helped Limoges through the winter by financing the municipal workshops until a royal loan was granted.

46 ADHV 1M 127, letter to the minister of finance, 1 October; PHV, 23 September; Alluaud letter, 23 September, relating the complaints against the indirect taxes to 'le changement que la glorieuse révolution de juillet ont fait naître dans les idées'. The PHV requested that Limoges garrison be maintained, 5 September: ADHV 4M 105 and 4M 86. Alluaud's two elderly deputy mayors resigned to allow more vigorous men to aid him maintain order: *Le Contribuable*, 30 August. See also 1M 100, PHV, 26 March 1831, reporting that the *boissons* tax was not collected at all in August. Early in 1831, 1600 of the 2400 porcelain workers in the region were unemployed; the Chambre Consultative, its role enhanced by the revolution, was active in dealing with the economic crisis: Alfred Leroux, 'Délibérations de la Chambre Consultative des arts et manufacturers de Limoges', *BSAHL*, no. 52 (1903), pp. 197–279.

47 *Le Contribuable* believed that the most important specific change brought by the revolution was the admission of many more voters: 15 November 1831. These men were 'grateful' for the economic action of the government on their behalf after the election, helping to prevent bankruptcies: F1cIII Haute Vienne 10, PHV, 31 October 1832; F1cIII Haute Vienne 4, 'Tableu du collège électoral de la Haute Vienne en 1831'. In the following table, the first column lists eligible voters in 1834 who would have qualified to vote by the laws of the restoration (that is, those paying at least 300 francs in taxes). The second column lists those voters who would have been added to the register by virtue of contributing between 200 and 300 in taxes, enfranchised by the revolution.

	300 francs or more	*200–99*
propriétaires	56	16
négociants/industriels	68	35
commerçants	84	55
professions liberales	36	17
fonctionnaires du roi	18	6

	300 francs or more	*200–99*
fonctionnaires/maires	6	2
officiers	4	2
dignitaires	3	0
électeurs adjoints	1	0
clergé	0	0
divers	26	6
Total	302	139

Source: Jean Léger, 'Étude des listes électorales du département de la Haute Vienne sous la monarchie de juillet (1830–48)' (Mémoire sécondaire diplôme d'études supérieur, Université de Bordeaux, n.d.).

48   *Almanach Limousin* (1864), 'Limoges depuis cent ans', pp. 80–93. The municipal elections of 1832 were hotly disputed, with *Le Contribuable* (now *Nouveau*) supporting a list of candidates, thirteen of thirty-seven of whom were *industriels* (10 May 1832); it declared that 'the council places should in no way be perpetuated in the same families . . . the leading inhabitants of the town should be called upon, in turn, to serve and pay the tribute of their enlightenment and their devotion to their fellow citizens in the discussion of common interests.' The number of annual meetings of the council: 1826, 11; 1827, 7; 1828, 8; 1829, 10; 1830, 32; 1831, 30; 1832, 33; 1833, 33; 1834, 34. The correspondence between the butchers and the municipality is extremely interesting: ADHV 4M 54, 55; 123 0 7(24); *Limoges et le Limousin* (Limoges 1865); AN BB18 1218, and others. The Chambre Consultative considered general reforms that would place business in Limoges on a sounder footing; it demanded less taxes and sound commercial legislation, to protect honest and hard-working entrepreneurs against unscrupulous speculators: see Leroux, 'Délibérations de la Chambre Consultative'.

49   National Guard correspondence in AN F9 733 and ADHV R 161; the Guard, entirely composed of the bourgeoisie of Limoges, remained loyal to the Orleanists, despite occasional signs of republican influence: *Le Contribuable*, 23 and 30 August 1830.

50   *Le Contribuable*, 6 and 21 June 1831. Dumont St Priest was born on 24 March 1786, and in 1834 paid a tax of 315.99 francs, only the 137th leading taxpayer; crowds protested his receiving the légion d'honneur: AHDV 1M 128, PHV, 2 June 1831; F1cIII Haute Vienne 4, PHV, 18 October 1833.

51   *Le Nouveau Contribuable*, 25 April and 19 May 1832. On 25 October 1830, the same paper had warned that 'we will be republicans, if necessary' and printed the statutes of the '*Aide-toi*' association.

52 *Le Nouveau Contribuable*, 17 March and 14 July 1832, welcoming the establishment of a *banque de secours* and publishing a series of articles explaining its operations and reduced interest rate. See Johnson, 'The revolution of 1830 in French economic history'.

53 ADHV 1M 128, various reports on republican activities; *Le Contribuable*, 21 March 1831; ADHV 4M 54, police reports. The arrival of Polish refugees in 1832 was an occasion for republican gatherings and the increasingly frequent shouts of 'Down with the *juste milieu*!': 4M 54, police report of 12–13 April 1831, noting celebration of the news of a Polish victory over the Russians; ADHV 4M 55 and AN F9 733 contain correspondence on the election of two republican National Guard officers; F1cIII Haute Vienne 10, PHV, 31 October 1832. The only evidence of Napoleonic attachment during the entire period was one cry of 'Long live Napoleon II!' in June 1832. On the Saint-Simonian missions, see F7 4215/14, gendarme report, 6 December 1831; 4M 54, 24–25 May 1831; *Le Contribuable*, 30 August, 8 and 15 November 1831; ADHV 1M 128 and 4M55, various reports.

54 F1cIII Haute Vienne 4, PHV, 11 January and 18 October 1833; ADHV 1M 128, PHV, 14 June 1832; of 366 eligible voters who were expected to exercise their franchise (of 455 eligible), at least 184 would support the government on all issues and another 60 or more formed the dynastic or moderate opposition. Another 32 were Legitimists; but there were also about 90 *'démocrates'* or republicans, of whom 40 were pronounced in their systematic opposition: see Merriman, *Agony of the Republic*, pp. 1–13, 141–54.

55 AN F7 6784, PHV, 25 and 27 July; gendarme report, 27 and 29 July; AN F9 733, report of mayor, 31 July; AN BB18 1217, PGL, 27 and 28 July 1833. Mourgnes was born in 1772 in Montpellier; a former military diplomat and secretary general in the office of the ministry of the interior, he had also been prefect of the Haute Marne and the Dordogne.

56 ADHV 4M 55, police report, 24–25 June and 23–24 September; AN BB18 1218, PGL, 16 September, 15 October, and letter of minister of interior, 4 November 1833; J.-P. Aguet, *Les grèves sous la monarchie de juillet* (Geneva 1954), pp. 101–2; France, Direction du Travail, *Les Associations professionnelles ouvrières*, vol. 3 (Paris 1903), pp. 523–4; Grellier, *L'industrie de la porcelaine en Limousin*, p. 240.

57 ADHV 4M 55, 17 and 18 June 1833, police report.

58 F1cIII Haute Vienne 4, PHV, 2 and 3 April and 18 October 1834; AML, 'D', Alluaud proclamation, 27 July 1833. During the next several years, it was difficult to find anyone willing to take time from business to be mayor; for example, Juge St Martin, cited 'the need to

consecrate all my time to the family business': ADHV 2M 59, correspondence.

59 The bridge was first discussed at the municipal council meeting of 30 September 1830, after having originally been proposed in March 1829 (ADHV 1M 209); PHV, 25 July 1832; Alluaud became very involved in municipal projects, such as the quarter around the Champ de Juillet: ADHV Z25, *fonds Alluoud*. AG MR 1300, Joinville, 1840, noted that 'Since 1830, authorities and the ambitious, that is, the greatest part of what one refers to as "the Haute Vienne" have abandoned [the penitents].'

Chapter 3: Charivaris, repertoires and urban politics

1 This is a revised version of a paper presented to the Fourth Annual Colloquium on Nineteenth-Century French Studies, East Lansing, Michigan, October 1978. Under the title 'The routinization protest in nineteenth-century France', the earlier version appeared as Working Paper 181 of the Center for Research on Social Organization, University of Michigan (September 1978). The National Science Foundation and the Canada Council supported the research reported in this paper. The work reported here is part of a broader analysis of changes in the character of popular collective action in France from 1600 to the present, with special reference to Anjou, Burgundy, Flanders, the Île de France and Languedoc. Recent reports of that research appear in Charles Tilly, 'Getting it together in Burgundy,' *Theory and Society*, no. 4 (1977), pp. 479–504; *From Mobilization to Revolution* (Reading, Mass.: Addison-Wesley 1978); 'Collective violence in European perspective', in Hugh Davis Graham and Ted Robert Gurr (eds.), *Violence in America: Historical and Comparative Perspectives* (Beverly Hills, Ca: Sage 1979), as well as in a number of Working Papers of the Center for Research on Social Organization, available from the Center. I am grateful to Ronald Aminzade for the communication of notes concerning events in Toulouse, and to Sheila Wilder for help in producing the paper.

2 AD (Archives Départementales) Maine-et-Loire 21 M 162, report of February 1826.

3 Alain Faure, *Paris Carême-prenant: Du Carnaval à Paris au XIXe siecle* (Paris: Hachette 1978), pp. 114–21.

4 ibid., p. 167.

5 Nor are these the only possibilities. To take only one more, Eugen Weber sees the disappearance of customary forms of celebration and daily practice in the nineteenth century as a consequence of the incorporation of many local peasant cultures into a common, urban, national culture: *Peasants into Frenchmen: The Modernization of*

Rural France, 1870–1914 (Stanford: Stanford University Press 1976). See also Norbert Elias, 'On transformations of aggressiveness', *Theory and Society*, no. 5 (1978), pp. 229–42, and Michel Foucault, *Surveiller et punir. Naissance de la prison* (Paris: Gallimard 1975).

6   These generalizations rest especially on my unpublished compilations of 'contentious gatherings' – occasions on which people gathered in publicly accessible places and visibly made claims bearing on other people's interests – in Anjou, Burgundy, Flanders, the Île-de-France and Languedoc during the eighteenth and nineteenth centuries.

7   AD Somme, Mfv 80926, letter of 6 February 1836.

8   Weber, *Peasants into Frenchmen*, p. 402.

9   AN BB18 1183, letter of 22 April 1830.

10   AN BB18 1183, letter of 24 April 1830.

11   AN BB18 1183, enclosure in letter of 2 May 1830.

12   AN BB18 1183, letter of 30 May 1830.

13   AD Haute-Garonne 4 M 49, letter of 22 December 1831.

14   AD Haute-Garonne 4 M 49, second letter of 22 December 1831.

15   For general surveys of the revolution, including a good detail of detail on local collective action, see David H. Pinkney, *The French Revolution of 1830* (Princeton: Princeton University Press 1972), and John M. Merriman (ed.), *1830 in France* (New York: New Viewpoints 1975).

16   AN BB18 1215, letter of 2 May 1833.

17   AN BB18 1215, letter of 3 May 1833.

18   AD Haute-Garonne 4 M 50, report of police to mayor, 27 June 1833.

19   i.e. with the anniversary of the July revolution: AD Haute-Garonne 4 M 50, report of 2 July 1833.

20   AN BB18 1395A, letter of 25 August 1841. Guizot was the 'man of Ghent' because during the Hundred Days, in May 1815, the constitutional royalist faction of Paris had sent him to Ghent to meet Louis XVIII in exile, and to persuade Louis to turn away from the Ultras. During the opening debate of the 1840–1 session of the National Assembly, opposition deputies had taunted Guizot with his mission to Ghent, and Guizot had replied vigorously. For the 1815 mission, see Charles-H. Pouthas, *Guizot pendant la Restauration* (Paris: Plon 1923), ch. 3; for the 1840 debate, see Elias Regnault, *Histoire de huit ans, 1840–1848* (Paris: Félix Alcan 1884), pp. 22–5.

21   AN BB30 423, letter of 2 August 1860.

22   Weber, *Peasants into Frenchmen*, p. 403.

23   For a convenient summary, see John R. Gillis, *Youth and History* (New York: Academic Press 1974), pp. 30–1.

24   The events in question consist of every occasion involving at least one

group of fifty persons or more in some minimum of violence (seizure or damage of persons or objects over resistance) encountered by trained readers of two national newspapers for each day from 1830 through 1860 and for a random three months per year from 1861 through 1929. For more details, see the appendix to Tilly, *From Mobilization to Revolution.*

Chapter 4: Proto-urban development and political mobilization during the Second Republic

1 On traditional peasant revolts see Yves-Marie Bercé, *Croquants et nu-pieds: Les soulèvements paysans en France du XVIe au XIXe siècle* (Paris 1974); on peasants in the early Third Republic, see Eugen Weber, *Peasants into Frenchmen: The Modernization of Rural France, 1870–1914* (Stanford, Ca. 1976), pp. 195–374.

2 For a review of theories of urbanization, see Charles Tilly, *An Urban World* (Boston 1974), pp. 1–54; on the rural impact of urban growth, see Charles Tilly, *The Vendée: A Sociological Analysis of the Counterrevolution of 1793* (Cambridge, Mass. 1964), pp. 16–57; on proto-industrialization, see Frank Mendels, 'Proto-industrialization: the first phase of the industrialization process', *Journal of Economic History*, no. 32 (1972), pp. 241–61; for a long-term view of small towns and bourgs, see Georges Duby, 'L'Urbanisation dans l'histoire', *Études rurales*, no. 49–50 (1973), pp. 10–13.

3 On the political role of small towns and bourgs, see Maurice Agulhon, *La République au village* (Paris 1970), pp. 207–84, 376–403; and Roger Price (ed.), *Revolution and Reaction, 1848 and the Second French Republic* (London 1975), pp. 37–64.

4 On the contrast between commercial cities and market towns, see Edward Whiting Fox, *History in Geographic Perspective: The Other France* (New York 1971), pp. 33–71; for a general analysis of local market centres within urban networks, see G. William Skinner, 'Marketing and social structure in rural China', *Journal of Asian Studies*, no. 24 (November 1964), pp. 3–44, 195–228, 363–400; for data concerning 'urban communes' in nineteenth-century France, see Georges Dupeux, 'La croissance urbaine en France au XIXe siècle', *Revue d'histoire économique et sociale*, no. 52 (1974), pp. 173–189.

5 On fragmentary urban networks in early nineteenth-century France, see Michel Rochefort, *L'organisation urbaine de l'Alsace* (Paris 1960), pp. 175–211; Bernard Barbier, *Villes et centre des Alpes du Sud: étude de réseau urbaine*, pp. 18–24; and Michel-Jean Bertrand, 'Les rapports entre villes et villages du Bas-Livradois,' *Annales de Géographie*, no. 79 (1970), pp. 560–80. On the precocious development of an urban network in Mediterranean France, see Raymond

Dugrand, *Villes et campagnes en Bas-Languedoc* (Paris 1963), pp. 427–44.

6 For a theoretical discussion of this point, see Skinner, 'Marketing and social structure', pp. 195–228. For an example of the proliferation of markets in previously isolated areas as commerce expanded, see Georges Frêche, 'Études statistiques sur le commerce céréalier de la France méridionale au XVIIIe siècle', *Revue d'histoire économique et sociale*, no. 49 (1971), pp. 5–43.

7 Estimates of markets, fairs, and urban communes based on sources given in Table 2.

8 On town markets and fairs, see Jean Vidalenc, *Le département de l'Eure sous la Monarchie constitutionnelle, 1814–1848* (Paris 1952), pp. 378–80, 499–506; on the demographic growth of small towns, see Dupeux, 'La croissance urbaine', pp. 180–5; on disputes over new markets and fairs, see the correspondence in national and departmental archives, such as AN F/12 1244–76; on the periodicity of urban and rural markets, see the tables published in departmental *annuaires* during the 1850s, in series Lc 30 of the *Bibliothèque Nationale*.

9 On village fairs, see André Allix, 'The geography of fairs: illustrated by old-world examples', *Geographical Review*, no. 12 (1922), pp. 532–69; Roger Brunet, *Les campagnes toulousaines* (Toulouse 1965), pp. 258–68; and Pierre Bozon, *La vie rurale en Vivarais* (Valence 1961), pp. 121–9. On the substitution of village fairs for town markets, see also Jean-Claude Claverie, 'Les cadres spatiaux de la vie de relation dans le sud-oeust de la France durant la première moitié du XIXe siècle', *Revue géographique de l'Est* (1974), pp. 335–51.

10 On Mediterranean settlement patterns, see Maurice Agulhon, 'La notion de village en Basse-Provence vers la fin de l'ancien régime', *Congrès national des sociétés savantes, actes, section d'histoire*, no. 90, vol. 1 (1965), pp. 277–302.

11 See the departmental *annuaires* for the Ardèche, the Drôme, the Hérault and the Gard, which published information in the 1850s about the distribution of markets and shopkeepers.

12 For a national analysis of upper-class reactions to the Parisian revolution, see André-Jean Tudesq, *Les grands notables en France (1840–1849)*, vol. 2 (Paris 1964), pp. 992–1114; on conservative politics in the Paris region, see Louis Chevalier, 'Les fondements économiques et sociaux de l'histoire politique de la région parisienne, 1848–1851' (thèse de doctorat, University of Paris 1951).

13 On the June Days in Paris, see Rémi Gossez, 'Diversité des antagonismes sociaux vers le milieu du XIXe siècle,' *Revue économi-*

que, vol. 1 (July 1956), pp. 436–57; and Pierre de la Gorce, *Histoire de la Seconde République*, 2nd edn. (Paris 1898), vol. 1, pp. 329–404.

14 On this earlier repression at Rouen, see John M. Merriman, *The Agony of the Republic: The Repression of the Left in Revolutionary France, 1848–1851* (New Haven, Conn. 1978), pp. 13–18.

15 *Circulaire* cited by Jean Vidalenc, 'La province et les journées de juin', *Études d'histoire moderne et contemporaine*, vol. 2 (1948), p. 101.

16 For evidence about the scale of this provincial mobilization, see Vidalenc, 'La province', pp. 103–20, 142–4.

17 *The Recollections of Alexis de Tocqueville*, trans. Alexander Teixeira de Mattos (Cleveland 1959), p. 183.

18 ibid., p. 182.

19 Vidalenc, 'La province', pp. 134–40.

20 On the electoral campaign of the Party of Order, see Tudesq, *Les grands notables*, vol. 2, pp. 1116–226; on conservative victories in northern France, see also J. Bouillon, 'Les Démocrates-socialistes aux élections de 1849', *Revue française de science politique*, no. 6 (1956), pp. 70–95.

21 For a general analysis of these mobilizations, see Ted W. Margadant, *French Peasants in Revolt: The Insurrection of 1851* (Princeton, NJ 1979), pp. 8–39.

22 ibid., pp. 3–8.

23 AN C 951 (Drôme). Concerning the economic foundations of insurgency, see Margadant, *French Peasants in Revolt*, pp. 40–103.

24 For events at Bourdeaux, see Margadant, 'The insurrection of 1851 in southern France: two case studies' (Ph.D thesis, Harvard University 1972), pp. 376–83; for St Sauveur, see Merriman, *Agony of the Republic*, pp. 210–12.

25 Census list, AD Vaucluse, M26–5.

26 Interrogation of Fr. Bourne, in AD Vaucluse, 4M 56, no. 33. For these events, see also the testimony of witnesses in AD Vaucluse, 4M 74–76, dossier Roussillon.

27 Report of the mayor of Cliousclat, 10 December 1851, in AD Drôme, M 1353, dossier Cliousclat. For analysis of village mobilizations, see Margadant, *French Peasants in Revolt*, pp. 228–64.

28 Bercé, *Croquants et nu-pieds*, pp. 165–221; Alain Corbin, *Archaïsme et modernité en Limousin au XIXe siècle, 1848–1880*, vol. 1: *La rigidité des structures économiques, sociales et mentales* (Paris 1975), pp. 496–512; and Rémi Gossez, 'La résistance à l'impôt: les quarante-cinq centimes', *Études, La Société d'histoire de la Révolution de 1848*, ed. P. Angrand (Nancy 1953), pp. 89–132.

29 See the reports of PGs in AN BB18 1462; and the evidence in Gossez, 'Résistance', pp. 102–123, 132.

30 Gabriel Vauthier, 'A propos de l'impôt de 45 centimes', *La Révolution de 1848*, no. 27 (1930–1), pp. 246–8. For other examples of local riots, see Robert Schnerb, 'Le département du Puy-de-Dôme d'avril à septembre 1848', *La Révolution de 1848*, no. 28 (1931), pp. 87–8; and the correspondence cited in n. 29.

31 In the cantons of Mirambeau and St Jean-d'Angély (Charentes-Maritimes), Nay (Basses-Pyrénées), Miélan (Gers), St Martory (Haute-Garonne), Marcillac (Aveyron), Ahun (Creuse) and Gourdan (Lot). Sources cited in n. 29.

32 Letters from PG Agen to the minister of justice, 3, 9, 10 and 27 June 1848, in AN BB18 1462.

33 Letter from PG Poitiers, 9 November 1848, in AN BB18 1462.

34 Letters from PG Agen, 20 and 26 January 1849, in AN BB18 1462.

35 Corbin, *Archaïsme et modernité*, vol. 2, pp. 502–9; and Gossez, 'Résistance', pp. 104–108.

36 See Bercé, *Croquants et nu-pieds*, pp. 208–14.

Chapter 5: Industrialization and republican politics

1 I am grateful to Ann-Louise Shapiro and Paul Gallis of Brown University for their helpful comments and criticisms during the writing of this paper. Place of publication Paris unless noted.

2 E. J. Hobsbawm, *The Age of Capital, 1848–1875* (New York 1975).

3 The *mutation après décès*, the national probate of wills, was established by a law of 1794. Recent studies of social structure based on the use of this source, and on the more abbreviated *Tables des Successions et Absences* have included: Adeline Daumard, *La bourgeoisie parisienne de 1815 à 1848* (1963), and *Les fortunes françaises au XIXième siècle: Enquête sur la répartition et la composition des capitaux privés à Paris, Lyon, Lille, Bordeaux, et Toulouse d'après l'enregistrement des droits de succession* (1973); M. C. Aboucaya, *Les structures sociales et économiques de l'agglomération lyonnaise à la veille de la Révolution de 1848* (1963); Felix Codaccioni, *Lille, étude sociale, 1850–1914* (thèse de doctorat d'état, Université de Lille 1971); Jesus Ibarolla, *Structure sociale et fortune mobilière et immobilière à Grenoble en 1847* (Grenoble 1965); and Pierre Léon, *Géographie de la fortune et structures sociales à Lyon au XIXième siècle, 1815–1914* (1974).

4 Daumard, *La bourgeoisie parisienne de 1815 à 1848*, and *Les fortunes française au XIXième siècle*.

5 In *The Communist Manifesto* Marx traced the transition from the manufacturing bourgeoisie employing artisan labour to a newer industrial group whose introduction of 'steam and machinery revolutionized industrial production. The place of manufacture was taken

by the giant, modern industry, the place of the industrial middle class, by industrial millionaires – the leaders of whole industrial armies, the modern bourgeoisie': Karl Marx, *The Communist Manifesto* (New York 1947), p. 10.

6   Theodore Zeldin, *The Political System of Napoleon III* (Oxford, 1958).

7   Lynn A. Hunt, *Revolution and Urban Politics in Provincial France: Troyes and Reims, 1786–1790* (Stanford, Ca. 1978), pp. 10–11; and Georges Boussinesq and Gustave Laurent, *Histoire de Reims depuis ses origines jusqu'à nos jours* (Reims 1933).

8   Flora Tristan, *Le tour de France: Journal inédit, 1843–1844* (1845).

9   Sherman Kent, *Electoral Procedure Under Louis Philippe* (New Haven 1937), p. 30. The four taxes were the *contribution foncière sur propriété bâtie et non-bâtie*, the *contribution personelle et mobilière*, the *impôt des patents* and the *contribution des portes et fenêtres*.

10   Fortunes in the *mutation après décès* were counted as including the *communauté des biens*, the combined wealth of a husband and wife, which was also a standard practice for determining tax qualifications for voting under the July monarchy. 'Fictive credits' (such as the remaining portion of a dowry owed a husband by his wife) were not counted.

11   Although the *mutation* provides a detailed survey of investments, stock companies, bonds and real property owned by the *notables* at the time of their death, there are certain problems involved with the use of these registers. These include the age differences between the *notables* listed in the 1847–8 electoral lists, when many were still active in business affairs, and the sample of the bourgeoisie taken from the registration of wills, which contains a much larger proportion of older retired people. A certain number of younger notables of the middle to late years of the empire have inevitably escaped detection. A comparison of the ages of the 1848 *notables* at Reims and Saint-Étienne shows the heaviest concentration of men on the electoral lists to have been in their 40s and 50s, while the sample taken from the *mutation* shows the heaviest concentration among men in their 60s. It is difficult to know how people described their occupations after retirements, and a large number of *rentiers* and *propriétaires* among formerly active businessmen would have made the occupations reported in the *mutation* deceptive. However, the elderly were less likely to 'retire' in mid nineteenth-century France than they are today and were still known by their active professions until their deaths.

12   There were already 63 mechanized wool-combers in the city in 1853 when Isaac Holden, an English entrepreneur who had helped perfect the process, completed the construction of a giant combing factory in

the city. Because of the competition with the Holden factory, most of the remaining wool manufacturers had been forced to modernize their combing operations: see Boussinesq and Laurent, *Histoire de Reims*, p. 720; and Claude Fohlen, *L'industrie textile au temps du Second Empire* (1956), p. 344.

13 Fohlen, *L'industrie textile au temps du Second Empire*, pp. 124–5. David Landes has discussed the difficulties faced by 'new men' in nineteenth-century France in their search for financial support with which to finance new businesses: David Landes, 'French entrepreneurship and industrial growth in the nineteenth century', *Journal of Economic History*, vol. 9, no. 1 (May 1949).

14 Tihomir J. Markovich, 'Le revenue industriel et artisanal sous la Monarchie de Juillet et le Second Empire', *Économies et sociétés* (April 1967), pp. 91–3.

15 Cesar Poulain, *L'agriculture et les traités de commerce* (1879), Tables synoptiques de l'industrie lainière, 1789–1879.

16 Fohlen, *L'industrie textile*, pp. 335–6.

17 Boussinesq and Laurent, *Histoire de Reims*, p. 720.

18 In 1854 a new commercial bank, the Comptoir d'escompte de Reims, was established in the city with an initial capital fund of 1,500,000F raised by the sale of 3000 shares to the local elite, and also helped finance industrial development: *Le Comptoir d'escompte Chapuis et Cie, 1854–1924* (1925), p. 49.

19 Roger Price, *The Economic Modernization of France, 1730–1880* (London 1975), p. 147.

20 J. Turgan, *Les grandes usines: études industrielles en France et à l'étranger*, vol. 8 (1871), pp. 121–2. The enthusiasm of investors also benefitted other joint stock companies, including Fortel-Villeminot, a large wool-combing factory employing 60 mechanical combers, the Victor Rogelet company, and the Villeminot-Huard company. The latter company, having been founded in 1855 and equipped with 5000 spinning bobbins, was entirely refitted in 1866 with 19,000 mechanized spinning bobbins through the flotation of a stock issue: Fohlen, *L'industrie textile*, pp. 335–6.

21 In the 1840s the industry employed 32,000 workers on 18,000 looms, and through the period of the Second Republic continued to account for most of the manufactured wealth produced in the city, the value of ribbon production in 1848 being 45 million francs, compared with only 5 million in arms, 6,500,000F in coal, 6 million in small metallurgy and 8 million in iron and steel. In the 1850s, at the height of its prosperity, the number of manufacturing houses within the industry had increased from 258 in 1848 to almost 300 by 1860: *Statistique de la France*, 1835–73, premier série, vol. 13; AD Loire, *L'enquête industrielle de 1848, arrondissement de St Étienne*;

and Lucien Thiollière, 'Rubannerie', *Association française pour l'avancement des sciences*, twenty-sixth session, vol. 2 (August 1897), p. 70.

22 ADL, 'Rapport de la commission chargé de réchercher les causes de la décadence de la quincaillerie', 1850.

23 Louis J. Gras, *Histoire économique de la metallurgie de la Loire* (Saint-Étienne 1908), p. 217.

24 Turgan, *Les grandes usines*, vol. 4, p. 207.

25 Gras, *Histoire économique de la métallurgie*, p. 251.

26 The Terrenoire company had been founded in 1819 by the Lyonnais banker Frèrejean as the Compagnie des founderies et forges de la Loire et l'Ardèche: ADL, 80M5, letters of Jullien, the director of Terrenoire, to the prefect, 21 August and 4 December 1872.

27 In 1861 the Firminy company employed 750 workers; the Holtzer company employed 500: Gras, *Histoire économique de la métallurgie*, pp. 223–4.

28 Darmancier, 'Material de guerre', *Association française pour l'avancement des sciences*, twenty-sixth session (August 1897), vol. 2, pp. 214–16.

29 Price, *Economic Modernization of France*, p. 74.

30 The level of investment in local industry is found under 'French businesses' in Figure 3.

31 AN BB30 384, report of the *procureur général* to Garde des Sceaux, January 1866.

32 The masonic lodge, headed by the republican leader Dr Thomas, was also a centre for the newer and more dynamic group: AD Marne 30M19, report of the subprefect to the prefect, 8 October 1865.

33 AD Marne 30M19, report of the subprefect to the prefect, 8 October 1865.

34 AD Marne 87M61, La Société Industrielle, report of the mayor to the subprefect, 11 September 1866. One of the Société's secretaries, Houzeau, had also helped in 1867 to found the Ligue d'enseignement, an organization to promote free, compulsory lay education. In this way he and other liberals created links with the working class that would prove valuable in 1869 and during the period of transition to the Third Republic: see Gilles Derrole, 'L'anticléricalisme à Reims de 1870 à 1906' (mémoire de maitrise, Municipal Library of Reims), pp. 10–11.

35 The willingness with which the steel manufacturers who backed *L'Éclaireur* and *La Loire* made use of labour unrest during the last years of the empire was due in part to the relatively untroubled labour–management relations in the steel industry.

36 Dorian had gone to the École des Mines and subsequently started a sickle factory at Pont Solomon in the Haute Loire; following his

marriage to the daughter of Jacob Holtzer he became a director of the Holtzer company at Unieux. Sanford Elwitt has written of the 'separate threads of enlightened capitalism, the Protestant ethic, and a Saint-Simonian faith in the historic mission of the industrial bourgeoisie' which made up Dorian's character: *Le Courrier de St Étienne*, 16 May 1863; Sanford Elwitt, *The Making of the Third Republic* (Baton Rouge, La 1975), pp. 83–4.

37 Francisque Balay had inherited the government's patronage as well as his fortune from his uncle, Jules Balay, who had been the government's first offical candidate in 1852.

38 Others included Dorian's brother-in-law Jules Holtzer and Thomas Henry Hutter of the Montrambert coal company.

39 AN BB30 379, reports of the *procureur général* to the Garde des Sceaux, 8 January and 22 October 1866.

40 AN BB30 379, report of the *procureur général* to the Garde des Sceaux, 27 June 1863.

41 Theodore Zeldin believes that the emergence of a new type of candidate, who virtually bought their seats in the Corps Législatif through lavish expenditures of money on political campaigns, was one of the most important political developments of the 1860s. This development was especially important for the bourgeois opposition, which faced the additional problem of overcoming government hostility in the elections: Theodore Zeldin, *The Political System of Napoleon III*, p. 97.

42 AN BB18 1775, *L'Éclaireur* (1868–71), report of 11 August 1868. The directors of Terrenoire supported the Legitimist cause because of family ties with leaders of the party. Jullien, for example, was married to a grand-daughter of De Pommerd, a royalist deputy during the period of the restoration: AN BB/18 1776, *La Loire*, report of 24 August 1868.

43 AN BB18 1775, *L'Éclaireur*, reports of 13 and 22 February 1869.

44 Derrole, 'L'anticléricalisme à Reims', pp. 10–11.

45 Similarly, businessmen all over France gave their support to Thiers's conservative republic as the best means of coming to terms with the republican movement while avoiding any possibility of social revolution. At a national level the Third Republic forestalled social measures for almost fifteen years. In 1872 Gambetta told the nation 'there is no longer a social question', while in 1877 Thiers said, 'One no longer speaks of Socialism and that is good. We have been divested of Socialism': Jean Bouvier, 'Les banquiers devant l'actualité politique en 1870–71', *Revue d'histoire moderne et contemporaine*, vol. 5 (April–June 1958), p. 138; and Claude Fohlen, 'Bourgeoisie française: Liberté économique et intervention de l'état', *Revue économique*, no. 3 (May 1956), pp. 424–5.

46 AD Marne 12M237, *Conseil municipal* (1870–80). Results of the municipal council election of 1871.

47 Antide Martin, 'Élections générales de 1869: Devoirs des citoyens électeurs' (1868), Municipal Library of Saint-Étienne.

48 The Alliance républicaine replaced the Union démocratique as the directing political organization of the liberal elite following the overthrow of the empire, but the emphasis on the need for the bourgeoisie to control the republican movement remained constant. In June of 1871 *L'Éclaireur* wrote that it was the duty of the elite to fill the ranks of the republican organizations with its own members, thus freeing the government from dependence either on the support of the Monarchist Assembly or on the working class. Only the bourgeoisie, it concluded, had the education and leisure necessary to prevent excesses by formulating a moderate programme for the development of free institutions: *L'Éclaireur*, 23 June 1871.

49 Heavy industrialists had in the past depended on coercion as well as high wages to induce their workers to vote as their employers desired. In 1869 *Le Sentinelle populaire* complained of the way industrial workers at Terrenoire were influenced by their employers to support the Legitimist opposition, while *L'Éclaireur* declared that the political support of Euverte, a director of Terrenoire, guaranteed the votes of several hundred industrial workers for a candidate.

50 Although Lucien Arbel ran in 1871 on the conservative electoral list, he subsequently voted with the republican left: Jacques Gouault, *Comment la France est devenue républicaine, 1870–75* (1954), p. 214.

Chapter 6: Industry in the changing landscape from Daubigny to Monet

1 This does not mean that abstract art itself depends upon a false teleology, but that patterns of historical thought, addressed to all periods of art, unwittingly absorbed twentieth-century attitudes and set subject matter aside in favour of the formal components of art.

2 Daubigny's illustrations are the subject of the dissertation by Madeleine Fidell, *The Graphic Art of Charles François Daubigny* (New York 1974); Michel Melot has provided a new catalogue of Daubigny's prints, *L'Oeuvre gravé de Boudin, Corot, Daubigny, Dupré, Jongkind, Millet, Théodore Rousseau* (Paris 1978). The standard biography of the artist remains that of Étienne Moreau-Nélaton, *Daubigny raconté par lui-meme* (Paris 1925); new information and excellent reproductions are found in the best recent monograph, Madeleine Fidell-Beaufort and Janine Bailly-Herzberg, *Daubigny* (Paris 1975).

3   In *l'Artiste*, cited in Moreau-Nélaton, *Daubigny raconté par lui-même*, p. 69.

4   For Lachambeaudie, see Carel Lodewijk de Liefde, *Le Saint-Simonisme dans la poésie française entre 1825 et 1865* (Haarlem 1927). The best known edition of the *Fables* was published by Bry in Paris, in 1855. In this essay translations of excerpts from Lachambeaudie have been made in quite a literal fashion, without any attempt to provide equivalents of his poetic language.

5   Lachambeaudie was exiled in 1851, but the 1855 edition of his *Fables* was given a prize citation by the Académie Française.

6   Cited in Moreau-Nélaton, *Daubigny raconté par lui-même*, p. 63.

7   Cited in ibid., p. 65.

8   Raymond Williams, *The Country and the City* (New York and London 1973), is the most brilliant treatment of this theme.

9   My own interest in Argenteuil as an especially revealing case history began in 1964, and thereafter entered into my lectures. The present essay is in substance the sixth of ten Slade Lectures delivered at Oxford University in the winter of 1978. My work, however, has been based on available secondary sources and guide books for Argenteuil. Paul Tucker, in his recent dissertation, 'Claude Monet at Argenteuil' (Yale University 1979; to be published by the Yale University Press), has gone far beyond my preliminary study and has used archival and contemporary sources to document a very persuasive interpretation both of Monet's paintings and of changing Argenteuil. For Monet in the context of his generation, the unrivalled work is still that of John Rewald, *History of Impressionism* (New York 1946 *et seq.*), and the basic monograph is Daniel Wildenstein, *Claude Monet, biographie et catalogue raisonné*, vol. 1: *1840–1881* (Lausanne and Paris 1974).

10 Such compositions have been traced to Japanese prints and to Whistler's paintings, but this is one of the countless instances of art historians limiting themselves by staying within known traditions and looking only for the purely visual. In actuality the prototype for Monet's compositional structure can be found in earlier illustrations of rail and highway bridges. The artists of these illustrations frequently chopped off the two ends of a bridge to heighten the sense of its leaping across the page. See, for example, Eugène Chapus, *De Paris au Havre* (Paris 1855), a railroad guide in which more than one bridge is shown in that fashion, with one or more boats on the water underneath. (Daubigny did some of the illustrations for this book, but those of the bridges are not signed.)

11 Tucker, 'Claude Monet at Argenteuil', now supplies abundant proof of this; much evidence can be found in successive editions of guide

books to Paris and its environs, in which boating at Asnières and Argenteuil looms ever larger as the century progresses.

12 See Émile de Labédollière, *Histoire des environs du nouveau Paris* (Paris 1861); in addition to its text about boating, this book is graced by amusing illustrations by Gustave Doré.

13 Old guide books and maps make this clear but again, Tucker, 'Claude Monet at Argenteuil', has provided detailed and new information.

14 *View of Argenteuil, Winter* (1874), Nelson Gallery-Atkins Museum, Kansas City.

15 Wrongly dated 1872 by Wildenstein, *Monet, biographie et catalogue raisonné*, no. 227; the date of 1874 is confirmed by comparison with dated pictures, and by the fact that it is this painting on Monet's easel in the picture by Manet of 1874, *Claude Monet in his Studio Boat*, in the Neue Pinakothek, Munich.

16 Rodolphe Walter, 'Les maisons de Claude Monet à Argenteuil', *Gazette des Beaux-Arts*, vol. 6, no. 68 (December 1966), pp. 333–42, recapitulated and extended (with many letters of the period) in Wildenstein, *Monet, biographie et catalogue raisonné*, pp. 58 ff.

17 *De Paris à Saint Germain, à Poissy et à Argenteuil* (Paris 1856), pp. 5f.

18 'Du sentiment de la nature dans les sociétés modernes', *Revue des Deux Mondes*, no. 63 (15 May 1866), pp. 352–81 (p. 377).

19 See map in Walter, 'Les maisons de Claude Monet à Argenteuil'.

20 Concluding lines of Lachambeaudie's *Les deux rivages*.

Chapter 7: Three faces of capitalism: women and work in French cities

1 Many thanks to Leslie Page Moch, Elizabeth Pleck, Joan W. Scott and Charles Tilly for their thoughtful and helpful comments.

2 E. P. Thompson, 'Time, work-discipline and industrial capitalism', *Past and Present*, no. 38 (1967), 93.

3 See Louise A. Tilly and Joan W. Scott, *Women, Work and Family* (New York 1978).

4 Louis Villermé, *L'État physique et moral des ouvriers employés dans les manufactures de coton, de laine et de soie* (Paris 1840).

5 Jules Simon, *L'Ouvrière* (Saint-Pierre de Salerne 1977), pp. i, iv-v. Jules Michelet, *La Femme*, 2nd edn. (Paris 1860).

6 Paul Leroy-Beaulieu, *Le Travail des femmes au XIXe siècle* (Paris 1873).

7 ibid., pp. 437–43.

8 Richard Mowery Andrews, 'Paris of the great revolution: 1789–1796', in Gene Brucker (ed.), *People and Communities in the Western World* (Homewood, Ill. 1979), p. 57; Jean-Jacques Rousseau, *Les Confessions* (Paris 1968), pp. 146–7, quoted in Jeffry Kaplow, *The*

Names of Kings: The Parisian Laboring Poor in the Eighteenth Century (New York 1972), p. 3.

9   See the discussion of expenditures of the wealthy noble family of Saulx-Tavanes in Paris and the provinces in Robert Forster, *The House of Saulx-Tavanes: Versailles and Burgundy, 1700–1830* (Baltimore, Md. 1971), pp. 125–8.

10 B. C. Gournay, *Tableau général du commerce . . . années 1789 et 1790* (Paris 1789), quoted in Kaplow, *The Names of Kings*, p. 172.

11 N. E. Restif de la Bretonne, *Les Nuits de Paris* (Paris 1788–94), vol. 8: *1806–1807*, quoted in Kaplow, *The Names of Kings*, p. 55.

12 Kaplow, *The Names of Kings*, p. 35.

13 ibid., p. 56.

14 Schulz and Kraus, *Beschreibung und Abbildung der Poissarden in Paris* (Weimar and Berlin 1978), p. 8, quoted in Kaplow, *The Names of Kings*, p. 46.

15 Emile Zola, *L'Assommoir* (Paris 1877).

16 Victorine B[rocher], *Souvenirs d'une morte vivante* (Paris 1976), p. 61.

17 Frédéric Le Play, *Les ouvriers européens*, vol. 4: *Les ouvriers de l'occident*, 2nd edn. (Tours 1877), p. 424; and Pierre Du Maroussem, *La question ouvrière: cours libre professé à la Faculté de Droit de Paris* (Paris 1891–6), vol. 1, pp. 234–53.

18 Great Britain Board of Trade, *Cost of Living in French Towns: Report of an Enquiry by the Board of Trade into Working Class Rents, Housing and Retail Prices, together with the Rates of Wages in Certain Occupations in the Principal Industrial Towns of France*, Cd 4512 (1909), pp. 6–7.

19 Mouillon, Marthe-Juliette, 'Un exemple de migration rurale de la Somme dans la capitale: Domestique de la Belle Époque', *Études de la Région parisienne*, vol. 44 (1970), pp. 1–9.

20 Theresa M. McBride, *The Domestic Revolution: The Modernization of Household Service in England and France, 1820–1920* (New York 1976), p. 53.

21 ibid., *passim*.

22 Jeanne Bouvier, *Mes mémoires, ou 59 années d'activité industrielle, sociale et intellectuelle d'une ouvrière* (Poitiers 1936), pp. 1–59.

23 Claudie Lesselier, 'Employées de grands magasins à Paris (avant 1914)', *Le Mouvement social*, no. 105 (1978), pp. 109–110. See also Theresa M. McBride, 'A woman's world: department stores and the evolution of women's employment, 1870–1920', *French Historical Studies*, no. 10 (Autumn 1978), pp. 664–83.

24 André Lainé, *La situation des femmes employées dans les magasins à vente à Paris* (Paris 1911), p. 30.

25 Quoted in Lesselier, 'Employées de grands magasins', p. 109.

26 ibid., pp. 112–13; Emile Zola, *Au bonheur des dames* (1883).

27 Fernand and Maurice Pelloutier, *La vie ouvrière en France* (Paris 1900), pp. 102–3.

28 L'Abbé Expilly, *Dictionaire géographique historique et politique des Gaules et de la France* (Amsterdam 1766), quoted in Maurice Garden, *Lyon et les lyonnais au XVIIIe siècle* (Paris 1970), p. 6.

29 Jean-Claude Déglize, 'Observations particulières et générales sur un projet de loi relative aux manufactures et aux gens de travail de toutes les professions' (report done in An X [1804] but based on documentation from before 1789, manuscript number 2401, Bibliothèque municipale de Lyon), quoted in Garden, *Lyon et les lyonnais*, pp. 316–18.

30 Garden, *Lyon et les lyonnais*, pp. 52–3; Daryl Hafter, 'The programmed brocade loom and the decline of the draw girl', in Martha Trescott (ed.), *Dynamos and Virgins Revisited* (Metuchen, NJ 1980), *passim.*; Louis Trénard, 'The social crisis in Lyons on the eve of the French revolution', in Jeffry Kaplow (ed.), *New Perspectives on the French Revolution: Readings in Historical* Sociology (New York 1965); George J. Sheridan, Jnr, 'Household and craft in an industrializing economy: the case of the silk workers of Lyon', in John M. Merriman (ed.), *Consciousness and Class Experience in Nineteenth Century Europe* (New Haven, Conn. 1979), pp. 107–28.

31 Trénard, 'The social crisis in Lyons', p. 71.

32 Hafter, 'The programmed brocade loom', *passim.*

33 Olwen Hufton, 'Women and the family economy in eighteenth-century France', *French Historical Studies*, vol. 60 (1975), p. 8.

34 Garden, *Lyon et les lyonnais*, pp. 295–6, 304–5.

35 Olwen Hufton, *The Poor of Eighteenth Century France* (Oxford 1974), p. 115.

36 Garden, *Lyon et les lyonnais*, pp. 103–5.

37 Frédéric Le Play, *Les ouvriers européens* (1855 edn, p. 15), quoted by Yves Lequin, *Les ouvriers de la région lyonnaise (1848–1914)*, vol. 1: *La formation de la classe ouvrière régionale* (Lyon 1977), p. 44.

38 Leguin, *La formation de la classe ouvrière*, p. 44. There was a comparable situation in Nîmes, as discussed in Armand Cosson, 'Industrie de soie et population ouvrière à Nîmes de 1815 à 1848', in Gerard Cholvy (ed.), *Économie et Société en Languedoc-Roussillon de 1789 à nos jours* (Montpellier 1978), pp. 202–7.

39 Armand Audiganne, *Les populations ouvrières et les industries de la France: Études comparatives*, 2nd edn. (Paris 1860), p. 44.

40 Dominique Vanoli, 'Les ouvrières enfermées: Les couvents soyeux', *Les révoltes logiques*, no. 2 (1976), pp. 19–39; see also Louis

Reybaud, *Études sur le régime des manufactures* (Paris 1859).

41 Leroy-Beaulieu, *Le travail des femmes*, pp. 411, 425.

42 Lequin, *La formation de la classe ouvrière régionale*, p. 174; Laura S. Strumingher, *Women and the Making of the Working Class: Lyon, 1830–1870* (Eden Press, 1979), pp. 17–32, provides excellent descriptions of the various silk occupations.

43 Norbert Truquin, *Mémoires et aventures d'un prolétaire à travers la révolution* (Paris 1977), pp. 133–4.

44 Robert J. Bezucha, 'The "preindustrial" worker movement: the *canuts* of Lyon', in R. J. Bezucha (ed.), *Modern European Social History* (Lexington, Mass. 1972), p. 107.

45 Lequin, *La formation de la classe ouvrière régionale*, p. 45.

46 ibid., p. 122.

47 ibid., p. 186.

48 Chambre de Députés, *Enquête sur l'état de l'industrie textile et de la condition des ouvriers* (1906), quoted in Lequin, *La formation de la classe ouvrière régionale*, p. 189.

49 Lequin, *La formation de la classe ouvrière régionale*, pp. 200–1.

50 Lucie Baud, 'Document: le témoignage de Lucie Baud, ouvrière en soie', *Le Mouvement social*, no. 105 (1978), p. 141.

51 Vanoli, 'Les ouvrières enfermées', p. 21.

52 Christophe Dieudonné, *Statistique du départment du Nord*, (Brionne [1804]), vol. 1, p. 107.

53 ibid., vol. 1, pp. 530–51.

54 ibid., vol. 1, p. 522.

55 Georges Lefebvre, *Les paysans du Nord pendant la Révolution française* (Bari 1959; first publ. 1924), p. 307.

56 Dieudonné, *Statistique*, vol. 1, pp. 436–7.

57 ibid., vol. 2, pp. 448–9.

58 ibid., vol. 2, pp. 310–15.

59 Adolphe Blanqui, *Des Classes ouvrières en France pendant l'année 1848* (Paris 1848), and François Chon, *Promenades lilloises* (Lille 1888), quoted in Pierre Pierrard, *La vie ouvrière à Lille sous le Second Empire* (Paris 1965), p. 43.

60 Pierrard, *La vie ouvrière*, pp. 65–6.

61 ibid., p. 70.

62 ibid., pp. 72–3.

63 In fact, at any moment in time, most female factory workers were unmarried, as Pierrard notes elsewhere: ibid., p. 168. See also Louise A. Tilly, 'The family wage economy of a French textile city: Roubaix, 1872–1906', *Journal of Family History*, no. 4 (1979), pp. 381–94; and Tilly and Scott, *Women, Work and Family*, *passim*, for comparative information on Roubaix, a wool textile city, neighbour to Lille. Most married women probably worked sometimes and they were

most likely to work in a mill when they were young mothers of one or two children only.

64 Pierre Pierrard, *La vie quotidienne dans le Nord au XIXe siècle* (Paris 1976), pp. 142–4.

65 Ardouin-Dumazet, *Voyage en France* (1899), quoted in Pierrard, *La vie ouvrière*, p. 168.

66 Pierrard, *La vie quotidienne dans le Nord*, pp. 136–7.

67 Pierrard, *La vie ouvrière*, pp. 191 ff.

68 Felix-Paul Codaccioni, *De l'inégalité sociale dans une grande ville industrielle: Le drame de Lille de 1850 à 1914* (Lille 1976), pp. 88–92; Ernest Labrousse, Introduction to Codaccioni, *De l'égalité*, p. v.

69 Codaccioni, *De l'inégalité*, pp. 384–7.

70 cf. Tilly, 'The family wage economy'.

71 Serge Grafteaux, *Mémé Santerre*, pp. 10–11.

72 For comparison of a textile industrial town and a mining metal-working town, see Louise A. Tilly, 'Occupational structure, women's work, and demographic change in two French industrial cities, Anzin and Roubaix, 1872–1906', in Jan Sundin and Erik Soderlund (eds.), *Time, Space and Man: Essays on Microdemography* (Atlantic Highlands, NJ 1979), pp. 107–132.

73 See Leslie Page Moch, 'Migrants in the city: newcomers to Nîmes, France, at the turn of the century' (unpublished Ph.D dissertation, University of Michigan 1979), ch. 5. Evidence provided by Moch suggests that the migration of young women often followed the dissolution of their natal family through the death of a parent, usually the father.

74 The fact that working women often lived with their parents or husbands or in other socially dependent situations, such as the *internats*, should not be taken to mean that such dependence was necessarily paralleled by passivity in work roles. Under some conditions, particularly when they were relatively skilled workers, when they had the chance to build careers out of their work and when they were able to develop solidarity due to circumstances of work, women did mobilize to protect and advance their interests as workers. Lucie Baud, whose work life in silk mills was described above, became an activist in the silk textile workers' union and the leader of a strike. She decried the lack of militance of migrant women workers who were less eager to organize and resist. The precariousness of their jobs and their commitment to save, even if it meant self-exploitation, explains their lack of interest in the strike. See also Louise A. Tilly, 'Women and collective action in France, 1870–1914', forthcoming in Louise A. Tilly and Charles Tilly (eds.), *Class Conflict and Collective Action* (Sage, 1981).

Chapter 8: Decazeville: company town and working-class community, 1826–1914

1 I would like to thank the Georges Lurcy Charitable and Educational Trust, the Whiting Foundation, Stanford University and the Harvard University Society of Fellows for support which permitted me to research and to write this article.

2 *Le Socialiste*, 6 February 1886, p. 2.

3 Ardouin-Dumazet, *Voyage en France* 35e série (Paris 1904), pp. 22–3.

4 Major studies of owners' attitudes toward their workers in company towns include: Serge Bonnet, with the aid of Étienne Kagan and Michel Maigret, *L'Homme du fer: Mineurs de fer et ouvriers sidérurgistes lorrains, 1889–1930* (Nancy 1976); Lion Murard and Patrick Zylberman, *Le petit travailleur infatigable* (Fontaney-sous-Bois 1976); René Parize, 'Les militants ouvriers au Creusot pendant les grèves de 1899–1900', *Le Mouvement social*, no. 99 (April–June 1977), pp. 97–108; Louis Reybaud, *Le fer et la houille* (Paris 1874); Peter Stearns, *Paths to Authority: The Middle Class and the Industrial Labor Force, 1820–48* (Urbana, Ill. 1978); Rolande Trempé, *Les mineurs de Carmaux* (2 vols., Paris 1971). See also the comments on company towns in Michelle Perrot's illuminating article: 'The three ages of industrial discipline in nineteenth-century France', in John M. Merriman (ed.), *Consciousness and Class Experience in Nineteenth-Century Europe* (New York 1979), pp. 149–68.

5 Michel Chevalier, *Visite de Mgr. le Duc de Montpensier* (Paris 1843), p. 19.

6 Louis Reybaud, 'L'Établissement de Decazeville', *Journal des économistes*, 3e série, vol. 39 (September 1875), p. 335.

7 Archives of Société des Lettres, Sciences et Arts de l'Aveyron (Rodez): Fonds Daudibertières, carton 16, Cabrol to prefect of Aveyron (hereafter cited as PA), 30 June 1832.

8 *Journal de l'Aveyron*, 11 March 1848; 22 March 1848. AN 84AQ26, Decazeville management to SHFA board of directors, March 1848 (letters nos. 232 and 233); 28 March, 10 April, 18 April and 5 May 1848.

9 Ardouin-Dumazet, *Voyage*, p. 23.

10 More than half (52.3 per cent) of the men who married in Decazeville between 1860 and 1864 were born more than 25 kilometres away. This figure dropped by almost one-half, to 27 per cent, by the years 1881–5; the percentage of grooms born in Decazeville or in a contiguous town rose during this period from 24.1 to 41.8 per cent.

11 Reybaud, 'L'Établissement', pp. 336–9. DCMD, 11 May 1873.

12 Reybaud, 'L'Établissement', p. 336.

13 AN 59AQ489, general assembly of SNHFA stockholders, 28 February 1880.

14 Archives de la Préfecture de Police de Paris, BA 186, 'Grève de Decazeville, Février 1886', Agent '26', no. 101, 5 February 1886.

15 AN 110AQ7 (4), 'Notes de M. Watrin sur une visite faite à Longwy' [1885].

16 AN 84AQ24, Cabrol to SHFA board of directors, 18 January 1841.

17 ADA U Watrin VII, no. 582, Cayrade to president of SNHFA, 7 December 1885; U Watrin VII no. 580, report of SNHFA director Petitjean, 23 November 1885.

18 France, *Journal Officiel*, Chambre des Députés, Débats Parlementaires, vol. 16 (13 March 1886), p. 508.

19 Well before the Third Republic Decazeville's workers saw themselves as full-fledged Frenchmen whose livelihood depended on the vagaries of the national and international iron and coal market. However, the SHFA had prevented workers from actively participating in the political life of the Second Republic when workers and peasants in many parts of France had done so. The strikes of the early Third Republic permitted Decazeville's workers both to join forces with republicans throughout the country and, through the repercussions which the strike of 1886 had in the Chamber, to spur the growth of an autonomous socialist movement. On the second point, see Alexandre Zévaès, *La grève de Decazeville (janvier-juin 1886)* (Paris 1938).

20 Information on Gastambide's tenure at Decazeville (1888–92) is drawn from ADA 5M15; ADA 5M18; ADA 11 M5 4; AN BB18 1823, and from the Decazeville newspapers, *Le Pays noir* and *Le Bassin houiller de l'Aveyron.*

21 AN 110AQ1(7), Paris management of SCF to Decazeville management, 13 April, 20 April and 16 May 1892; ADA 8M74, Commissaire spécial de Decazeville (hereafter cited as CSD) to PA, 16 April, 18 April, 27 April and 6 May 1892; Commissaire de police de Decazeville (hereafter cited as CPD) to PA, 16 and 29 April 1892; ADA 68S6, CSD to PA, 2 and 4 February 1892; ADA 5M15, CSD to PA, 25 March and 16 May 1892.

22 *La Dépêche* (Toulouse), Aveyron edition, 27 March 1900.

23 *Le Cri du peuple*, 28 April 1886.

24 *Le Matin*, 8 May 1886, and *Le Cri du peuple*, 10 May 1886.

25 DCMD, 29 November 1900; ADA 11M5 7, CPD to PA, 30 November 1900. The socialists disassociated themselves from local republicans on whose ticket they had been elected.

26 ADA 11 M5 4, CSD to PA, 9 March 1892.

27 Archives de l'Évêché de Rodez, *visite pastorale* to Decazeville, 18 June 1908.

28 Patrick Couffin, 'Aspects de la vie ouvrière à Decazeville au début du

XXe siècle (1892–1914)' (mémoire, Université de Paul Valéry [Montpellier III] 1975), p. 109.

29 Archives of the Confédération générale du travail (Decazeville), general assembly of miners' union, 7 February 1909 and 25 February 1912; general assembly of forgeworkers' union, 23 September 1909; Dentraygues, secretary of the forgeworkers' union to Brune, secretary of 'La Syndicale', 30 July 1909. AN 110AQ50(5), company guard to local SCFD management, 16 January 1911. *La Dépêche* (Toulouse), Aveyron edition, 26 November 1913.

30 *L'Éclaireur*, 4 February, 18 February, 21 February, 3 March 1912.

31 See the material on the mobility of Decazeville forgeworkers in the pre-war period in Rolande Trempé's excellent article, 'Pour une meilleure connaissance de la classe ouvrière: L'utilisation des archives d'entreprise: le fichier du personnel', in *Mélanges d'histoire sociale offerts à Jean Maitron* (Paris 1976), pp. 249–63.

32 Archives of the Confédération générale du travail (Decazeville), general assembly of miners' union, 31 March 1901.

Chapter 9: Urbanization, worker settlement patterns and social protest

1 I would like to thank for their helpful comments and criticisms, Miriam Cohen, John Merriman, Charles Tilly, and David Ward.

2 For example, Mona Ozouf, 'Le Cortège et la Ville: les itinéraires parisiens des cortèges révolutionnaires', *Annales: Économies, Sociétés, Civilisations*, no. 26 (September–October 1971), pp. 889–916, and Lynn Lees and Charles Tilly, 'Le peuple de juin 1848', *Annales: Économies, Sociétés, Civilisations*, no. 29 (September–October 1974), pp. 1061–91.

3 See E. J. Hobsbawm, 'Cities and insurrection', in *Revolutionaries, Contemporary Essays* (New York 1973), pp. 222–3, and Walter Isard, 'Some locational factors in the iron and steel industry since the early nineteenth century', *Journal of Political Economy*, no. 56 (3 June 1948), pp. 203–17.

4 Some important works by urban geographers and historians of interest to students of social protest are: Sam Bass Warner, Jnr, *The Private City: Philadelphia in Three Phases of Its Growth* (Philadelphia, Pa. 1968); James E. Vance, Jnr, 'Housing the worker: determinative and contingent ties in nineteenth-century Birmingham', *Economic Geography*, no. 43 (April 1967), pp. 95–127; James E. Vance, Jnr, 'Housing the worker: the employment linkage as a force in urban structure', *Economic Geography*, no. 42 (October 1966), pp. 294–325; and David Ward, 'Victorian cities: how modern?', *Journal of Historical Geography*, no. 1 (1975), pp. 135–51.

5 The 'heterogenous city' of early industrialization was not the only urban environment created by industrial capitalism. According to Ward at a later period, as artisans disappeared, as the size of the white-collar working class grew, and as income differentials increased within the industrial working class, income-stratified residential areas began to develop. Thus, industrial capitalist expansion first caused urban neighbourhoods to become more heterogenous and finally less heterogenous. In France this later stage of greater homogenization would have occurred in the twentieth century: David Ward, 'Environs and neighbors in the "Two Nations" residential differentiation in mid-nineteenth-century Leeds', *Journal of Historical Geography* (1980).

6 On the Stéphanois background: Maxime Perrin, *Saint-Étienne et sa région économique* (Tours 1937).

7 Jacques Schnetzler, *Les industries et les hommes dans la région Stéphanoise* (Saint-Étienne 1973), and Jean Merley, 'Elements pour l'étude de la formation de la population stéphanois à l'aube de la révolution industrielle', *Bulletin du centre d'histoire économique et sociale de la région lyonnaise*, no. 8 (1977), pp. 261–75.

8 Yves Lequin, *Les ouvriers de la région lyonnaise (1848–1914)*, vol. 1 (Lyon 1977), pp. 132–9.

9 Urban growth in Germany was also faster than in France but information is only available on German towns for the period after 1818. On urbanization in England, France and the United States see Adna Ferrin Weber, *The Growth of Cities in the Nineteenth Century: A Study in Statistics* (Ithaca, NY 1899).

10 For population statistics see *European Historical Statistics, 1750–1970*, ed. B. R. Mitchell (New York 1976), and Department of Commerce, *Historical Statistics of the United States: Colonial Times to 1970* (Washington, DC 1975).

11 Maurice Lévy-Leboyer, 'La croissance économique en France au XIXe siècle: résultats préliminaires', *Annales: Économies, Sociétés, Civilisations*, no. 23 (1968), pp. 788–807; J. Marczewski, 'Le produit de l'économie française de 1789 à 1913', in J. Marczewski, *Introduction à l'histoire quantitative* (Geneva 1965), pp. 81–184.

12 Patrick O'Brien and Caglar Keyder, *Economic Growth in Britain and France 1780–1914: Two Paths to the Twentieth Century* (London 1978), pp. 137–9. The older view of a French peasant agriculture, largely stagnant in the first half of the nineteenth century, seems no longer tenable: see W. H. Newell, 'The agricultural revolution in nineteenth-century France', *Journal of Economic History*, no. 33 (1973), pp. 697–731, and the magnificent collection edited by Maurice Agulhon, Gabriel Désert and Robert Specklin, 'Apogée et

crise de la civilisation paysanne, 1789–1914', vol. 3 of *Histoire de la France rurale*, ed. Georges Duby and Armand Wallon (Paris 1976). Two important attempts to re-evaluate the role of agriculture in French economic growth are Richard Roehl, 'French industrialization: a reconsideration', *Explorations in Economic History*, no. 13 (1976), pp. 233–81, and Roger Price, *The Economic Modernization of France* (London 1975).

13   Herman Kellenbenz, 'Rural industry in the west from the end of the Middle Ages to the eighteenth century', in Peter Earle (ed.), *Essays in European Economic History 1500–1800* (Oxford 1974).

14   Ardouin-Dumazet, *Voyage en France – La région lyonnaise*, 7eme série (Paris 1902), pp. 225–6.

15   Alfred Marshall, *Industry and Trade: A Study of Industrial Technique and Business Organization*, 4th edn. (London 1921), pp. 225–6.

16   Cahen, 'La concentration des établissements en France de 1896 à 1936', *Études et conjoncture*, no. 9 (September 1954), pp. 855, 859 and 862; and Bureau of the Census, *Abstract of the Twelfth Census of the United States 1900* (Washington, DC 1904), p. 327.

17   C. K. Harley, 'Skilled labor and the choice of technique in Edwardian industry,' *Explorations in Economic History*, 2nd series, no. 11 (Summer 1974), pp. 391–414.

18   See H. J. Habakkuk, *American and British Technology in the 19th Century* (Cambridge 1962).

19   J. Schoenhof, *The Economy of High Wages* (New York 1893), p. 55. See also George J. Sheridan, Jnr, 'Household and craft in an industrializing economy: the case of the silk weavers of Lyon', in John M. Merriman (ed.), *Consciousness and Class Experience in Nineteenth Century Europe* (New York 1979).

20   Cahen, 'La concentration des établissements', p. 855.

21   Ardouin-Dumazet, *Voyage en France – La région lyonnaise*, pp. 148, 163.

22   See Marshall, *Industry and Trade*, pp. 271–3. The classic presentation of why some industries concentrate in centre cities and other industries or segments of industries disperse is Max Hall (ed.), *Made in New York, Case Studies in Metropolitan Manufacturing* (Cambridge, Mass. 1959).

23   On housing in Rive-de-Gier, see Archives départementales de la Loire (ADL) 92/M/54 and for Le Chambon-Feugerolles, Petrus Faure, *Histoire de la métallurgie au Chambon-Feugerolles* (Le Chambon-Feugerolles 1931).

24   A description of work on the Ripagerien glassworkers in the early 1890s can be found in ADL 92/M/52 and in Leon de Seilhac, *Une enquête social: La grève de Carmaux et la verrerie d'Albi* (Paris 1897), pp. 29–31.

25 On glassworkers' wages, ADL 92/M/152 and 10/M/101.

26 On file-workers' wages, Faure, *Histoire de la métallurgie*, and Michael Hanagan, 'The logic of solidarity: social structure in Le Chambon-Feugerolles', *Journal of Urban History*, no. 4 (August 1977), pp. 409–26.

27 J. F. Gonon, *Histoire de la chanson stéphanoise et forézienne* (Saint-Étienne 1960), p. 465.

28 ibid., p. 462.

29 See Faure, *Histoire de la métallurgie*.

30 For a further elaboration of the distinction between 'artisans' and 'skilled industrial workers' see 'Artisan and skilled worker: the problem of definition', *International Labor and Working Class History* (November 1977), pp. 28–31.

31 For a discussion of the 'captive professionals': Serge Mallet, *Essays on the New Working Class* (St Louis 1975), and Edward Shorter and Charles Tilly, *Strikes in France 1830–1968* (Cambridge 1974).

32 The distinction between 'tight knit' and 'loose knit' work groups used here was adopted from J. A. Barnes, 'Networks and political process', in Marc J. Swartz (ed.), *Local Level Politics: Social and Cultural Perspectives* (Chicago 1968).

33 Michel Fournier, *Le roman d'un petit verrier* (Paris 1925), p. 88.

34 Analysis of the manuscript census for 1891 shows that glassworkers were disproportionately concentrated in tenements in two districts of the city. In 1891 a sample of individuals living in different sections of the city of Rive-de-Gier shows that 63 per cent of all glassworkers lived in two neighbourhoods which were occupied by 27 per cent of the total population.

   Among file-workers in Le Chambon, in a semi-rural commune where half of the population lived in the countryside, 73.5 per cent of all file-workers lived in the city of Le Chambon.

35 On violence by workers against strike-breakers see particularly ADL 92/M/186–188 for Le Chambon and ADL 91/M/59 for Rive-de-Gier.

36 For an analysis of the mass strike process in these two towns see Michael Hanagan. *The Logic of Solidarity, Artisans and Industrial Workers in Three French Towns, 1871–1914* (Urbana, Ill. 1980).

37 See Louise A. Tilly and Joan W. Scott, *Women, Work, and Family* (New York 1978), and C. E. V. Leser, 'Trends in women's work participation', *Population Studies*, pt. 2 (November 1958), pp. 100–10.

38 See P. Bairoch, *The Working Population and Its Structure*, vol. 1 (Brussels 1968), and Madeline Guilbert, *Les femmes et l'organisation syndicale avant 1914* (Paris 1966), pp. 13–14.

39 James E. Vance, Jnr, *This Scene of Man: The Role and Structure of*

the City in the Geography of Western Civilization (New York 1977), p. 281.

40 Albert Boissier, 'Essai sur l'histoire et sur les origines de l'industrie du clou forgé dans la région du Firminy', *Revue de folklore française*, no. 12 (April–June 1941), pp. 65–101, and Pierre Du Maroussem, 'Fermiers montagnards du Haut-Forez (Loire-France)', in *Les ouvriers des deux mondes*, 2eme série, no. 4 (1892).
    James R. Lehning's study examines the economy of silkweaving in a small Stéphanois village in fascinating detail, *The Peasants of Marlhes: Family Organization and Economic Development in 19th Century France* (Chapel Hill, NC 1980).

41 Wages of domestic workers are notoriously hard to estimate. Boissier notes that 'there is no doubt that the income of nailmakers in the seventeenth through nineteenth centuries was extremely low': 'Essais sur ... le clou forgé,' p. 94. A survey of workers' wages in the *arrondissement* of Saint-Étienne, an area largely coterminous with the Stéphanois region, which was carried out between 1861 and 1865 shows that nailmakers were the lowest paid adult male workers in the region; the wages of an average adult male metal-worker were 2.5 times greater than that of the nailmaker: see Statistique générale, *Résultats généraux de l'enquête effectuée dans les années 1861–1865* (Nancy 1873), pp. 318–23.

42 Theodore Hershberg, Harold Cox and Dale Light, 'The journey to work: an empirical investigation of work, residence, and transportation: Philadelphia 1850–1880' (paper delivered to the 89th annual meeting of the American Historical Association, Chicago, December 1974), pp. 9 and 28.

43 If official estimates are correct, in 1901 there may have been as many as 280 children from outside the commune working in the bolt industry of Le Chambon: ADL 91/M/140. In that same year 7.6 per cent of the work-force in the Claudinon plant which employed almost 800 workers lived at least 4 to 5 kilometres from the plant.

44 Rolande Trempé, *Les mineurs de Carmaux 1848–1914*, vol. 1 (Paris 1971), p. 155.
    Similarly long journeys to work have been found in a small Belgian working-class town, the Cockerill plant in Seraing, see Caulier Mathy, 'La composition d'un prolétariat industriel: le cas de l'entreprise Cockerill', in *Revue d'histoire de la sidérurgie*, no. 4 (1963), pp. 207–32.

45 In 1891 25.1 per cent of those employed in Saint-Chamonnais textiles were women living in dormitories: manuscript census, Saint-Chamond, 1891.

46 In 1906, 140 of the belt-workers were children, 18 per cent of the work-force: ADL 92/M/140.

47 The index of segregation for Saint-Chamonnais turners was 13.9, for adjusters 19.3. These figures were not appreciably different from those of all metal-worker heads of household in Saint-Chamond, 16.3.

48 On the wages of urbanized Stéphanois industrial workers: ADL 10/M/102.

49 See Hanagan, *The Logic of Solidarity.*

50 Ward, 'Victorian cities: how modern?' To support his argument, Ward relies on two studies of the early nineteenth-century English industrial town of Chorley by A. M. Warnes, 'Residential patterns in an emerging industrial town', in B. D. Clark and M. B. Gleave (eds.), *Social Patterns in Cities*, Institute of British Geographers Special Publication No. 5 (1973), pp. 169–87, and 'Early separation from work places and the Urban Structure of Chorley, 1780–1850', in *Transactions of the Historic Society of Lancashire and Cheshire*, no. 122 (1970), pp. 105–35. The layout of Chorley strongly resembles that of Le Chambon-Feugerolles.

51 See Ward, 'Environs and neighbors in the "Two Nations"'.

Chapter 10: Socialist municipalities confront the French state

1 Research in France in 1978 was made possible by a grant-in-aid from the American Council of Learned Societies. Preparation of this article was begun at the Institute for Advanced Study, Princeton, NJ, 1978–9. I am grateful to Leon Fink and Alan Dawley who offered important suggestions and to Donald M. Scott for all his help.

2 Alexandre Zévaès, *Le Socialisme en France depuis 1871* (Paris 1908), pp. 106–33.

3 Brochure of the Parti Ouvrier, signed by Ferroul, Lefargue and Guesde, in *Le 19e Siècle*, 15 March 1892. The plan for the day was discussed at the Congress of Lyon, November 1891. A report on the discussion is contained in AN F7 12490.

4 Archives of the Prefecture of Police of Paris, BA 46.

5 M. J. McQuillen, 'The development of municipal socialism in France, 1880–1914' (unpublished Ph.D dissertation, University of Virginia 1973), pp. 77–9.

6 Aaron Noland, *The Founding of the French Socialist Party* (Cambridge, Mass. 1956) pp. 27, 32, 48.

7 Jules Guesde, 'Suffrage universel et prolétariat', *Quatre ans de lutte de classe à la Chambre (1893–1898)*, vol. 1 (Paris 1901), p. 191.

8 'Liberté communale et collectivisme', in Guesde, ibid., pp. 154–5.

9 'Reform and revolution, far from contradicting each other, complement one another and we are reformists because we are revolutionaries': Guesde in 1892, quoted in Claude Willard, *Le Mouve-*

ment socialiste en France: Les Guesdistes 1893–1905 (Paris 1965), p. 191.

10 Michelle Perrot, 'Les Socialistes français et les problèmes du pouvoir', in M. Perrot and A. Kriegel, *Le Socialisme français et le pouvoir* (Paris 1966), p. 38. See also discussion in Robert Baker, 'Socialism in the Nord 1880–1914: a regional view of the French socialist movement', *International Review of Social History*, vol. 12 (1967), p. 360.

11 Willard, *Le Mouvement socialiste en France*, pp. 192–3.

12 Eric Hobsbawm, 'Labor history and ideology', *Journal of Social History*, no. 7 (Summer 1974), p. 376; Georges Haupt, *La Deuxième Internationale, 1889–1914*; *Étude critique des sources*, (Paris–Hague 1964).

13 Noland, for example, sees the municipal victories as a step on the road to the creation of a unified socialist party in 1905. Harvey Goldberg, *The Life of Jean Jaurès* (Madison, Wis. 1963) treats the municipal victory in Carmaux in terms of its impact on the election of Jaurès. Willard discusses the Guesdist leadership's infatuation with parliamentary politics. A brilliant treatment in a local context is Roland Trempé, *Les Mineurs de Carmaux 1848–1914*, 2 vols. (Paris 1971).

14 Paul Brousse, *La Propriété collective et les services publiques* (Paris 1883).

15 Jules Guesde, *Services publics et socialisme* (Paris 1883).

16 For the texts of the different groups' programmes see A. Veber, *Le socialisme municipal* (Paris 1908). See McQuillen, 'Development of municipal socialism in France', pp. 76, 85 for an interpretation of the Guesdists' decision to support a municipal programme in 1891.

17 Veber, *Le socialisme municipale*, p. 19.

18 ibid., pp. 40–2.

19 Edward Shorter and Charles Tilly, *Strikes in France* (Cambridge, 1974), pp. 172–3.

20 Paul Lafargue, *Le Citoyen*, 11 May 1882, quoted in Noland, *Founding of the French Socialist Party*, p. 27, n. 50. See also A. Marpaux, 'L'oeuvre des municipalités socialistes: Dijon', *Le Mouvement Socialiste*, 1 April 1900.

21 In this period the Guesdists, for example, left specific propaganda measures to local initiative. See Willard, *Le Mouvement socialiste en France*, p. 136.
  The socialist municipal victories gave rise to a national co-ordinating effort, an annual congress of socialist municipalities, initiated by Edouard Vaillant. Early agreement gave way to factional disputes and to Guesdist withdrawal in 1896: McQuillen, 'Development of municipal socialism in France', pp. 92–99. See also *Mai*

1896, Le Banquet des municipalités socialistes (Paris 1896); *Deux-ième Congrès des Conseillers Municipaux Socialistes de France* (St Denis 1893); *Troisième Congrès des Conseillers Municipaux Socialistes* (Paris 1895). Accounts of the third and fourth (Commentry 1896) Congresses are in AN F7 12494. The fifth congress (Dijon 1897) is reported in AN F7 12494 and AN F7 13071. A description of a 1900 banquet in Paris is in the Archives of the Prefecture of Police of Paris, BA 122.

22 This certainly was the case with Jaurès and Guesde, both of whom were elected as socialist deputies in 1893, following the success of socialists in the municipalities of Carmaux and Roubaix in 1892. Yet some preliminary analysis also suggests voting rates were consistently higher in local than in national elections.

23 An example of this process in glass bottle-making is Joan W. Scott, *The Glassworkers of Carmaux* (Cambridge, Mass. 1974).

24 Shorter and Tilly, *Strikes in France*, pp. 23, 25. The other side of these laws, of course, permitted greater regulation of working-class activity by the state. The law of 1884, for example, required unions to submit to officials their statutes and lists of those responsible for enforcing them. Complete membership lists were sometimes made a requirement for authorization as well.

25 Scott, *The Glassworkers of Carmaux*, p. 109.

26 Quoted in Willard, *Le Mouvement socialiste en France*, p. 187.

27 The reformist posture of French socialism and its municipal strategy needs also to be seen in an international or Western European context of advanced industrial capitalism and powerful nation-states. See note 11 and also Daniel Tarschys, *Beyond the State: The Future Polity in Classical and Soviet Marxism* (Stockholm 1971), chs. 1 and 2. An important discussion of the question of electoral politics as it applies to the Knights of Labour in the US is Leon Fink, 'The uses of political power: towards a theory of the labor movement in the era of the Knights of Labor', (unpublished paper 1979).

28 See Willard, *Le Mouvement socialiste en France*, p. 159: 'L'étude de la doctrine est-elle inseparable de celle de la propagande et de l'action collectiviste?' See also Guesde, *Quatre ans*, vol. 1, p. 122: '... Dans les municipalités socialisées ... il y aurait là une de ces propagandes par le fait.'

29 McQuillen, 'Development of municipal socialism in France', p. 114; M. Gaucheron, *L'oeuvre économique des municipalités* (Paris 1906); Veber, *Le Socialisme municipal*; L. Stehelin, *Essais de Socialisme Municipal* (Paris 1901).

30 H. Ghesquière, 'L'action des municipalités socialistes: Lille', *Le Mouvement Socialiste*, 1 February, 1 May, 15 July, 1 October 1899; A. Marpeaux, 'L'action des municipalités socialistes: Dijon', 1, 15

April and 1, 15 May 1900, *Le Mouvement Socialiste*; G. Siauve, *Roubaix socialiste ou 4 ans de gestion municipale ouvrière (1892–6)* (Lille 1896); G. Rougeron, *Le Mouvement socialiste en Bourbonnais* (Montluçon 1942), p. 19.

31 AN BB18 1969, doss. 995 A94 (6 April 1894).
32 AN BB18 1966 (6 February 1894).
33 AN BB18 1969 (19 March 1894).
34 AN F7 12495 (Albi, 1 September 1895).
35 AN BB18 1948, doss. 2360 A 93 (29 December 1893).
36 ibid. For examples of other incidents in other cities see AN BB18 1969, doss. 1049 A94 (22 March 1894) on Narbonne; BB18 2045, doss. 2472 A96 (30 September 1896), and BB18 2040, doss. 1933 A96 (20 July 1896) on Carmaux; AN F7 12490, report on the Congrès de Lyon (1891). In Carmaux, the mayor is reported wearing his mayoral sash during these conflicts over public authority.
37 AD Tarn, IV M2 74.
38 Marpaux, 'L'action des municipalités socialistes', p. 387; Stehelin, *Essais de socialisme municipal*, pp. 28, 47–8.
39 C. Verenque, 'Children of the working class', *International Socialist Review*, no. 2 (September 1901), p. 175.
40 Siauve, *Roubaix socialiste*, p. 52.
41 An important theoretical statement on the issue of the working-class family is Jane Humphries, 'Class struggle and the persistence of the working-class family', *Cambridge Journal of Economics*, no. 1 (1977), pp. 241–58.
42 Willard, *Le Mouvement socialiste en France*, p. 162.
43 Quoted in R. Pierreuse, 'L'ouvrier roubaisien et la propagande politique 1890–1900', *Revue du Nord*, no. 51 (April–June 1969), p. 260. On consolation as a theme in English working-class culture in the 1890s see Gareth Stedman-Jones, 'Working-class culture and working-class politics in London, 1870–1900: notes on the remaking of the working class', *Journal of Social History*, vol. 7, no. 4 (Summer 1974), p. 499.
44 Willard, *Le Mouvement socialiste en France*, p. 162; McQuillen, 'Development of municipal socialism in France, p. 139; AN BB18 1969, doss. 1049 A94.
45 AN BB18 2033, doss. 1119 A96 (1896–9).
46 AN BB18 2045, doss. 2472 A96. Other examples include the suspension of Vaillandet, mayor of Bourges, in 1901 for making an anti-militarist speech to young army recruits. Vaillandet claimed that he was really suspended because of government fears that Bourges was becoming a militant socialist municipality: see Jolyon Howorth, 'Edward Vaillant and the French socialist movement' (unpublished Ph.D thesis, University of Reading 1973), p. 240. See also

pp. 311–29 on the general question of socialist political strategy in the municipalities. I am grateful to Jolyon Howorth for sharing this material with me.

47 Rolande Trempé, *Les Mineurs de Carmaux*, vol. 2, pp. 884, 888.

Select bibliography

The following bibliography is intended to be suggestive; as such it is somewhat arbitrary and incomplete. Countless articles of some use may also be found in the French regional journals. For a European perspective, see *A Selected Bibliography of European Urbanization*, compiled by Charles Tilly (Ann Arbor, Mich.: Centre for Western European Studies 1975). See also Philippe Dollinger and Philippe Wolff, *Bibliographie des villes de France* (Paris 1967). The relevant volume in the excellent series, *Histoire de la France urbaine*, is forthcoming.

An overview

Ariès, Philippe, *Histoire des population françaises*, Paris 1971

Bédarida, François, 'The growth of urban history in France: some methodological trends', in H. J. Dyos (ed.), *The Study of Urban History*, London 1968

Bergeron, Louis and Roncayolo M., 'De la ville pre-industrielle à la ville industrielle', *Quaderni Storici* (1975), pp. 827–76

Castells, Manuel, 'Structures sociales et processus d'urbanisation,' *Annales, ESC*, no. 25 (1970), pp. 1155–199

Davis, Kingsley, 'The urbanization of the human population', in Charles Tilly (ed.), *An Urban World*, Boston 1974

Dupeux, Georges, 'La croissance urbaine en France au XIXe siècle', *Revue d'histoire économique et sociale*, no. 52 (1974), pp. 73–89

Dyos, H. J. (ed.), *The Study of Urban History*, London 1968

Friedmann, Georges (ed.), *Villes et campagnes; civilisation urbaine et civilisation rurale en France*, Paris 1953

Gravier, J. F., *Paris et le désert français*, Paris 1947

Leroy, Maxime, *La ville française*, Paris 1927

Mumford, Lewis, *The City in History*, New York 1961

Roche, Daniel, 'Urban history in France: achievements, tendencies, and objectives', *Urban History Yearbook* 1980

Thernstrom, Stephan, and Sennett, Richard (eds.), *Nineteenth-Century Cities: Essays in the New Urban History*, New Haven, Conn. 1969

Tilly, Charles (ed.), *An Urban World*, Boston 1974

Tréanton, Jean-Réné, 'Quelques travaux récents d'histoire et de sociologie urbaine', *Revue française de sociologie*, no. 12 (October–December 1971), pp. 589–96

Van de Walle, Étienne, *The Female Population of France in the Nineteenth Century*, Princeton, NJ 1973

Weber, Adna Ferrin, *The Growth of Cities in the Nineteenth-Century*, Ithaca, NY 1899

Weber, Eugen, *Peasants into Frenchmen: The Modernization of Rural France, 1870–1914*, Stanford, Ca. 1976

Wrigley, E. A., *Population and History*, New York 1969

Population and structure

Châtelain, Abel, *Les migrants temporaires en France de 1800 à 1914*, Paris, n.d.

Chevalier, Louis, *La formation de la population parisienne au XIXe siècle*, Paris 1949

Codaccioni, F., *Lille, 1850–1914: Contribution à une étude des structures sociales*, Lille 1971

Daumard, Adeline, *Les bourgeois de Paris au XIXe siècle*, Paris 1970

Daumard, Adeline (ed.), *Les fortunes francaises au XIXe siècle*, Paris 1973

Daumard, Adeline, *Maisons de Paris et propriétaires pariseins au XIXe siècle*, Paris 1964

Duveau, Georges, *La vie ouvrière en France sous le Second Empire*, Paris 1946

Guerrand, Roger H., *La répartition de la population, les conditions de logement des classes ouvrières à Paris au dix-neuvième siècle*, Paris 1976

Guillaume, Pierre, *La population de Bordeaux au XIXe siècle*, Paris 1972

Hohenberg, P., 'L'exode rural en France au XIXe siècle', *Annales, ESC*, vol. 29, no. 2 (March/April 1974), pp. 461–97

Lachivier, M., *La population de Meulan du XVII au XIXe siècle (vers 1600–1870)*, Paris 1969

Murard, Lion, and Zylberman, Patrick (eds.), *Le petit travailleur infatigable ou le prolétaire régénéré*, Fontenay-sous-Bois 1976

Pouthas, Charles, *La population française pendant la première moitié du XIXe siècle*, Paris 1956

Raison-Jourde, F., *La colonie auvergnate de Paris au XIXe siècle*, Paris 1976

Tilly, Louise A., and Scott, Joan W., *Women, Work and Family*, New York 1978

Vidalenc, Jean, *La société française de 1815 à 1848*, vol. 2: *Le peuple des villes et des bourgs*, Paris 1973

The social movement and urban politics

Agulhon, Maurice, *La République au village*, Paris 1970

Bezucha, Robert J., *The Lyon Uprising of 1834*, Cambridge, Mass. 1974

Cazals, Rémy, *Avec les ouvriers de Mazamet*, Paris 1978

Dalotel, Alain, Faure, Alain, and Freiermuth, Jean-Claude, *Aux origines de la Commune: le mouvement des réunions publiques à Paris, 1868–1870*, Paris 1980

Duveau, Georges, *1848: The Making of a Revolution*, New York 1969

Edwards, Stewart, *The Paris Commune, 1871*, New York 1971

Gaillard, Jeanne, *Communes de province, commune de Paris, 1870–1871*, Paris 1971

Girault, Jacques, *La Commune et Bordeaux (1870–1871)*, Paris 1971

Gossez, Rémi, *Les ouvriers de Paris*, Paris 1971

Greenberg, Louis, *Sisters of Liberty: Marseille, Lyon, Paris and the Reaction to a Centralized State, 1868–1871*, Cambridge, Mass. 1971

Guin, Yannick, *Le mouvement ouvrier nantais*, Paris 1976

Hanagan, Michael P., *The Logic of Solidarity: Artisans and Industrial Workers in Three French Towns, 1871–1914*, Urbana, Ill., 1980

Margadant, Ted W., *Peasants in Revolt: The French Insurrection of 1851*, Princeton, NJ 1979

Merriman, John M., *Agony of the Republic: The Repression of the Left in Revolutionary France, 1848–1851*, New Haven, Conn. 1978

Merriman, John M. (ed.), *Consciousness and Class Experience in Nineteenth Century Europe*, New York 1979

Merriman, John M. (ed.), *1830 in France*, New York 1975

Perrot, Michelle, *Les ouvriers en grève*, 2 vols., Paris 1974

Pinkney, David H., *The French Revolution of 1830*, Princeton, NJ 1972

Rougerie, Jacques, *Paris libre 1871*, Paris 1971

Rouland, Norbert, *Le conseil municipale marseillais et sa politique de la IIe à la IIIe République*, Aix-en-Provence 1974

Scott, Joan W., *The Glassworkers of Carmaux*, Cambridge, Mass. 1974

Tilly, Charles, 'The Chaos of the Living City', in Herbert Hirsch and David Perry (eds.), *Violence and Politics*, New York 1973

Tilly, Charles, 'The changing place of collective violence', in Melvin Richter (ed.), *Essays in Theory and History*, Cambridge, Mass. 1970

Tilly, Charles, 'How protest modernized in France, 1845–55', in William O. Aydelotte, Allan G. Bogue and Robert W. Fogel (eds.), *The Dimensions of Quantitative Research in History*, Princeton, NJ 1972

Tilly, Charles, *From Mobilization to Revolution*, Reading, Mass., 1978

Tilly, Charles, 'Food supply and public order in modern Europe', in Charles Tilly (ed.), *The formation of National States in Western Europe*, Princeton, NJ 1975

Tilly, Charles, and Lees, Lynn, 'The people of June 1848', in Roger Price (ed.), *Revolution and Reaction: 1848 and the Second French Republic*, London 1975

Urban space, geography and planning

Arbos, Philippe, *Étude de géographie urbaine – Clermont Ferrand*, Clermont Ferrand 1930

Bastié, Jean, *La croissance de la banlieu parisienne*, Paris 1964

Benevolo, Leonardo, *The Origins of Modern Town Planning*, London 1967

Blanchard, Raoul, *Grenoble: Étude de géographie urbaine*, Grenoble 1911

Chabot, Georges, *Les villes*, Paris 1978

Chapman, Joan Margaret, and Chapman, Brian, *The Life and Times of Baron Haussmann: Paris in the Second Empire*, London 1957

Chevalier, Louis, *L'Assassinat de Paris*, Paris 1977

Choay, Françoise (ed.), *L'Urbanisme: utopies et réalités*, Paris 1965

Cobb, Richard, *Promenades*, Oxford 1980

Demangéon, A., *Paris, la ville, et sa banlieu*, Paris 1938

Dugrand, Raymond, *Villes et campagnes en Bas-Languedoc*, Paris 1963

Evenson, Norma, *Paris, A Century of Change, 1878–1978*, New Haven, Conn. 1979

Gauchat, Roger, 'L'urbanisme dans les villes anciennes, les faubourgs de Dijon', *Mémoires de la Commission des Antiquités du département de la Côte-d'or*, vol. 23 (1947–53), pp. 280–343

George, Pierre, *Précis de géographie urbaine*, Paris 1969

Giedion, Siegfried, *Space, Time and Architecture*, Cambridge, Mass. 1967

Girard, Louis, *La politique des travaux publics du Second Empire*, Paris 1952

Halbwachs, Maurice, *Les expropriations et le prix des terrains à Paris, 1860–1900*, Paris 1909

Halbwachs, Maurice, *La population et les tracés des voies à Paris depuis un siècle*, Paris 1928

Herbert, Robert L., 'City vs. country: the rural image in French painting from Millet to Gauguin', *Artforum*, February 1970, pp. 44–55

Johnson, James J., *Urban Geography: An Introductory Analysis*, New York 1967

Lavedan, Pierre, *Histoire de l'urbanisme (Époque contemporaine)*, Paris 1952

Léon, Pierre, *Géographie de la fortune et structures sociales à Lyon au XIXe siècle (1815–1914)*, Lyon 1974

Leonard, Charlene-Marie, *Lyon Transformed: The Public Works of the Second Empire*, Berkeley, Ca. 1961

Levainville, Jacques, *Rouen: Étude d'une agglomération urbaine*, Paris 1913

Merlin, Pierre, *Les transports parisiens: étude de géographie économique et sociale*, Paris 1966

Murard, Lion, and Zylberman, Patrick (eds.), *L'Haleine des faubourgs: ville, habitat et santé au XIXe siècle*, Fontenay-sous-Bois 1978

Ozouf, Mona, *Fête révolutionnaire*, Paris 1977

Pinkney, David H., *Napoleon III and the Rebuilding of Paris*, Princeton, NJ 1958

Rochefort, Michel, *L'organisation urbaine de l'Alsace*, Paris 1960

Saalman, Howard, *Haussmann: Paris Transformed*, New York 1971

Sutcliffe, Anthony, *The Autumn of Central Paris*, Paris 1970

Zunc, O., 'Étude d'un processus d'urbanisation: le quartier du Gros-Cailloux à Paris', *Annales*, vol. 25, no. 4 (July–August 1970), pp. 1024–65

Studies of individual cities and regions

Agulhon, Maurice, *Une ville ouvrière au temps du socialisme utopique, Toulon de 1815 à 1851*, Paris 1971

Armengaud, André, *Les populations de l'Est acquitain au début de l'époque contemporaine*, Paris 1961

Bentier de Sauvigny, Guillaume de, *Nouvelle histoire de Paris: la Restauration*, Paris 1977

Brunet, Jean-Paul, *Saint-Denis, La ville rouge, 1890–1939*, Paris 1980

Cobb, Richard, *Death in Paris, 1795–1801*, New York 1978

Cobb, Richard, *Paris and its Provinces*, London 1975

Desgraves, Louis, and Dupeux, Georges (eds.), *Bordeaux au XIXe siècle*, Bordeaux 1969

Ducamp, Maxime, *Paris: ses organs, ses fonctions et sa vie dans la seconde moitié du XIXe siècle*, 6 vols, Paris 1883

Dupeux, Georges, *Aspects de l'histoire sociale et politique du Loir-et-Cher*, Paris 1962

Faure, Alain, *Paris, Carême prenant: Du Carnival à Paris au XIXe siècle*, Paris 1978

Gaillard, Jeanne, *Paris, la ville, 1852–1870*, Paris 1977

Le Gallo, Yves, *Brest et sa bourgeoisie sous la monarchie de juillet*, 2 vols., Paris 1968

Lequin, Yves, *Les ouvriers de la région lyonnaise (1848–1914)*, 2 vols., Lyon, n.d.

Pierrard, Pierre, *La vie ouvrière à Lille sous le Second Empire*, Paris 1965

Poëte, Marcel, *Une vie de cité: Paris de sa naissance à nos jours*, 3 vols., Paris 1931

Singer-Kerel, Jeanne, *Le coût de la vie à Paris de 1840 à 1954*, Paris 1961

Sewell, William H., Jnr. 'La classe ouvrière de Marseille sous la Seconde République: structure sociale et comportement politique', *Mouvement social*, no. 76 (July 1971), pp. 27–63

Shattuck, Roger, *The Banquet Years*, New York 1968
Trempé, Rolande, *Les mineurs de Carmaux, 1848–1914*, 2 vols., Paris 1971
Vigier, Philippe, *La Seconde République dans la région alpine*, 2 vols., Paris 1963

Note should also be made of the series of histories of individual cities organized by Privat publishers in France. Volumes to date, of varying quality, include studies of Angers, Le Mans, Brest, Grenoble, Lyon and Rennes.

Contemporary impressions

Audiganne, Armand, *Les populations ouvrières et les industries de la France: Études comparatives*, Paris 1860
Balzac, Honoré de, *La comédie humaine*, Paris 1976–
Becker, George (ed.), *Paris under Siege, 1870–71: From the Goncourt Journal*, Ithaca, NY 1969
Becker, George, and Philips, Edith (eds.), *Paris and the Arts, 1851–1896: From the Goncourt Journal*, Ithaca, NY 1971
Chevalier, Louis, *Laboring and Dangerous Classes in Paris*, New York 1973
Gelu, Victor, *Marseille au XIXe siècle*, Paris 1971
Hugo, Victor, *Les Misérables*, 2 vols., Harmondsworth 1980
Legoyt, M. A., *Du propos des agglomérations urbaines et de l'émigration rurale en Europe et particulièrement en France*, Marseille 1867
Meuriot, Paul, *Des agglomérations urbaines dans l'Europe contemporaine*, Paris 1897
Nadaud, Martin, *Léonard maçon de la Creuse*, Paris 1976
Tristan, Flora, *Le Tour de France: journal inédit, 1843–44*, Paris 1973
Villermé, Louis, *L'État physique et moral des ouvriers employés dans les manufacturers de coton, de laine et de soie*, Paris 1840
Zola, Émile, *Les Rougon-Macquart*, Paris 1960

Other related studies

Bernard, Leon, *The Emerging City: Paris in the Age of Louis XIV*, Durham, NC 1970
Bettleheim, Charles, and Frère, Suzanne, *Auxerre en 1950, une ville française moyenne: étude de structure sociale et urbaine*, Paris 1950
Cobb, Richard, *The Police and the People*, London 1970
Deyon, Pierre, *Amiens, capitale provinçiale*, Paris 1967
El Kordi, Mohamed, *Bayeux aux XVIIe et XVIIIe siècles*, Paris 1970

Farge, A. (ed.), *Vivre dans la rue à Paris au XVIIIe siècle*, Paris 1979

Ford, Franklin L., *Strasbourg in Transition, 1648–1789*, Cambridge, Mass. 1958

Garden, Maurice, *Lyon et les lyonnais au XVIIIe siècle*, Paris 1970

Hemmings, F. W. J., *Culture and Society in France, 1848–1898*, New York 1971

Hufton, Owen H., *Bayeux in the Late Eighteenth-Century*, Oxford 1967

Hufton, Owen H., *The Poor of Eighteenth Century France, 1750–1789*, Oxford 1974

Hunt, Lynn, *Revolution and Urban Politics in Provincial France: Troyes and Reims, 1786–1790*, Stanford, Ca. 1978

Kaplan, Stephen L., *Bread, Politics and Political Economy in the Reign of Louis XVI*, The Hague 1976

Kaplow, Jeffrey, *The Names of Kings*, New York 1972

Perrot, Jean-Claude, *Genèse d'une ville moderne: Caen au XVIIIe siècle*, 2 vols., Paris 1975

Landes, David S., *The Unbound Prometheus: Technological Change and Industrial Development in Western Europe from 1750 to the Present*, Cambridge 1969

Pourcher, Guy, *Le peuplement de Paris*, 1964

Ranum, Orest A., *Paris in the Age of Absolutism*, New York 1968

Rudé, George, *The Crowd in the French Revolution*, New York 1959

Shorter, Edward, and Tilly, Charles, *Strikes in France, 1830–1968*, New York 1968

Tilly, Charles, *The Vendée*, Cambridge, Mass. 1976

Williams, Alan, *The Police of Paris*, Baton Rouge, La 1979

Index

Abbessaille quarter, Limoges,
43–4
Aciéries de Firminy, 130
agriculture, 93, 210, 212
'agro-towns', 102
Aix-les-Bains, 24
Ajain commune, tax revolt in,
115–16
Allemane, Jean (*Allemanisme*),
205, 231, 234
Alliance républicaine, 267 n. 48
Alluaud, François, 49–50, 57, 60,
65, 70–1, 72
Alluaud, Victor, 59, 71
Alsace, urban population in, 96,
98–9
Amélie-les-Bains, 24
ancien régime, 45, 92, 94, 117, 168
Angers, collective violence in, 87
Anjou, collective violence in, 86,
88, 89
Annales de la Haute Vienne, 43, 45,
51–2, 53, 58–9
Apollinaire, Guillaume, 12
arbitration, law on (*1892*), 235
Ardouin-Dumazet, 184, 213, 214
Argenteuil, Monet's paintings of,
35, 149–59
arms industry, 127, 129, 210
art history, role of, 139–40
articles de Paris, 213
artisans: artisanal production, 22,
23, 47, 107, 111, 117, 118, 119,
120, 124, 133, 210, 213; urban
settlement patterns and social
protest, 209, 214–21, 224,
226–9
Asnières, 11
Aubin, *1869* strike in, 201
Aubry-Vitet, Madame, 155

Audiganne, Armand, 177
Auvergne, urban population in, 96,
98–9
Auvers, Van Gogh's paintings of,
163
Avesnes-les-Aubert, 187

Bac, Théodore, 67, 69
Bains-les-Bains, 24
Balay, Francisque, 133
Balzac, Honoré de, 11, 37, 44
Barbès, Armand, 149
Barthelémy, trial of, 51
Bastide, Pierre Hippolyte Martin
de la, mayor of Limoges, 48, 56,
57, 58, 60, 72
Baud, Lucie, 180, 273 n. 74
Beaubourg (Centre National d'Art
et de Culture Georges
Pompidou), Paris, 39
Beauregard, Desalles, 49
Bédarida, François, 15
belle époque, 11, 12
Belleville, 36, 37
Bercé, Yves-Marie, 74–5, 85
Bergeron, Louis, 15
Berri, Duchesse de, 48
Besançon, 28
Bessemer steel, 129
Béziers, 23; armed insurrection in,
109–10
Biterrois, *1851* insurrection in, 110
Blanchard, Raoul, 247–8 n. 4
Bordeaux, population, 14, 22
Bos, mayor of Decazeville, 205
Boulanger, General, 33, 201
Boulogne–Billancourt, 11
Bourdeau, Pierre Alpinien, 49
Bourdeau-Lajudie, 59
Bourdeaux (Drôme), 111

bourgeoisie, 94; anti-Republican electoral campaigns by (*1849*), 108; distribution of wealth, 122–4; industrial paternalist, 136–7; industrial v. mercantile, 117, 118–19, 120, 127, 132, 137; opposition to government, 119–20, 132; political mobilization in Paris (June Days, *1848*), in Reims and Saint-Étienne, 117–38
Bourne, François, 112
Bourse du Travail, 237; Limoges, 43
Bouvier, Jeanne, 172
Bretagne, urban population, 96, 98–9
Briant, A., 238
Brive (Corrèze), 23
Brousse, Paul, 233, 234
Buttes-Chaumont, Paris, 37

Cabet, Étienne, 39
Cabrol, François, 195, 196, 197–8, 200, 206
Cadiat, Decazeville company engineer, 196
Caen, 28; political charivari in (*1841*), 83
Caillebotte, Gustave, 159
Calvignac, Jean-Baptiste, mayor of Carmaux, 244
camelots (bolts of wool cloth), 182
canuts (Lyonnais weavers), 179, 180
'captive professionals', 218–19
Carlists, 81
Carmaux, 240, 244
cash crops, 93, 97, 102, 113
Cavaignac, General, 27, 106
Cayrade, mayor of Decazeville, 198, 200–1, 205
census, 83, 95
centralization of French state, 25–30
Cézanne, 163
Chabrol, prefect, 36–7
Chamber of Deputies, 230, 231, 235; socialists elected to (*1893*), 231, 232

Chamiot-Avanturier, Philabert, 64, 68
Champ de Foire, Limoges, 57–8, 61, 62, 63, 65
Champ de Juillet, Limoges, 42, 71
charity workshops, Limoges, 61, 65
charivaris: political, 32, 47, 50, 85, 87, 89–90; in transition, 78–84
Charles X, King, 49, 58; abdication of, 60
Châtellerault, 24
Chazelles-sur-Lyon, 214
Chevalier, Louis, 12, 31–2, 40
Chevalier, Michel, 194
child labour, 221, 235
cholera epidemics, 38
Cholet, *1826* Mardi Gras in, 73
Cirque, Limoges, 43
cités administratives, 28
Clement, Jean-Baptiste, 238
coal mining industry: Decazeville, 195, 197; Saint-Étienne, 120, 121, 126–7, 129–30; Stéphanois region, 209, 210
Cobb, Richard, 40
coercive paternalism, in Decazeville, 197–202
Colbert, Jean-Baptiste, 121
collective action, 73–91; charivaris, 32, 47, 50, 78–84, 89–90; eighteenth- and nineteenth-century repertoire of, 32, 75, 76–8; *manifestations*, 32, 83–5; a new repertoire, 84–91; popular festivals (Mardi Gras and metaphor), 73–6; violent events, 86–9
Comité central révolutionnaire, 231
Comité de l'Union démocratique, Saint-Étienne, 135
commerce and industry: in Limoges, 46–7, 49, 51, 52–3, 54; proto-urban development and, 93–104
Commune, Paris (*1871*), 12, 25, 31, 32, 37, 89, 233, 236
Communist Manifesto, 262–3 n. 5

Compagnie des fonderies et forges de Terrenoire, 129, 134
Compagnie des fonderies, forges et aciéries de Saint-Étienne, 130
company towns, *see* Decazeville
Conféderation Générale du Travail (CGT), Limoges, 42
conscription, actions against, 76, 84
Le Constitutionnel, 51
Contrexeville, 24
Le Contribuable, 52–4, 55, 56, 57, 58, 59, 65–6, 67, 254 n. 47
co-operative stores in Decazeville, 200–1, 202, 204–5
Corot, Camille, 143, 147, 154, 161; *The Belfry of Douai* (plate 1), 12, 13; *The Road to Sèvres* (plate 2), 140–2
Corps Legislatif elections, 133, 134
Cost of Living in French Towns (*1909*), 171
Coster, Baron, 49, 50, 51–2, 53, 54, 56, 58
cotton industry, 177, 182, 183, 185, 189
coup d'état of *1851* (Louis Napoleon's), 23, 32, 39–40, 95, 109–13, 137
Crédit Lyonnais, HQ transferred to Paris, 26
Le cri du peuple, 201, 203, 205
Croix Rousse (Lyon suburb), 174, 178

Daubigny, Charles, 143–9, 154, 155, 161, 162; *The Bridge between Persan and Beaumont-sur-Oise* (plate 6), 147–9; *Le Départ* (plate 7), 147, 148; *Les Deux Rivages* (plate 5), 145–7; *La Vapeur* (plate 4), 144–5
Daumard, Adeline, 12, 118
Daumier, Honoré, 12, 39
Decazes, the Duc, 195
Decazeville: the authoritarian presence, 195–7; coercive paternalism, 197–202; company control of retail trade, 200–2; company town and working-class community, 12, 33–4, 193–207; the division of control, 202–6; *1886* strike, 33, 193, 201–2, 203, 204, 208; town council elections (*1900*), 203–4, 205
Dechaume, Geoffroy, 147
Degas, Edgar, 12, 140
Déglize, Jean-Claude, 174
Delacroix, Eugène, 11
Démangéon, Albert, 24
demonstrations, *see* manifestations
department stores, women employed in, 172–3
departments: capitals, 96, 97; creation of (*1790*), 26; depopulation of, 20
La Dépêche, 203
Deseilligny, Alfred, 197, 198, 199, 202, 206–7
dévideuses, 174, 175, 176
Dieudonné, Christophe, 181–2
Dieulefit, political mobilization in, 23, 110–11
Dijon, 28, 231
district capitals, population growth, 19–20
domestic production workers, 213, 218, 221–3
domestic servants, women employed as, 169, 170, 171–2, 182, 184, 186, 190
Dorian, Frédéric, 133–4, 135, 136, 265–6 n. 36
Dormoy, Jean, mayor of Montluçon, 239–40
Douai, 12
dowry saved by working women, 175–6, 191
Du Barry, Madame, château of, 142
Duc-Quercy, Albert, 205
Dupeux, Georges, 18–19, 20
Dupont, Pierre, 149
Durkheim, Émile, 74
Duveau, Georges, *La vie ouvrière*, 12
Dyos, H. J., 15

L'Éclaireur, 134, 136, 267 n. 48, n. 49

economic depression (*1873–96*), 235
education: compulsory primary, 235; in Decazeville, 204
Elbeuf, 120
elections, 77, 86, 89, 94, 234–5; Decazeville town council (*1900*), 203–4, 205; legislative, 104, 108, 133, 134, 231; municipal (*1892*), 230–1, 232
Elias, Norbert, 75
England, urbanization in, 210–11
Expilly, L'Abbé, 174

factory production, 117, 118–19; disparity between economic growth and, 211–12; small-scale production v., 214–15; women employed in, 221, 229
fairs, see markets and fairs
'family segmented labour', 221, 222, 225
faubourg St Antoine, Paris, 168, 169
faubourg St Honoré, Paris 36
faubourg St Marceau, Paris, 168, 169
faubourgs, see suburbs
Faure, Alain, 73–4, 75, 85
Fédération des travailleurs de France, 233
festivals, popular, 73–6
file works of Le Chambon, 210, 216, 217, 219, 220
Firminy, 209, 210, 224
Flachat, Eugène, 160–1
Flament, Alexandre, 157
fonctionnaires (civil servants), 28
Fontainebleau forest, 143
food riots, 47–8, 61–3, 76, 77, 84, 86, 93, 108
Foucault, Michel, 75
Fourier, Charles, 38–9, 144
Fourmies massacre (*1891*), 230, 232, 233
Fraternité (workers' slogan), 241–2
French revolution, 37, 55, 77–8, 168, 170, 175, 232

Gachet, Dr, 163

Garden, Maurice, 176
Gare St Lazare, Paris, 35; Monet's painting of, 159–61, 162
garment industry, women employed in, 173, 221
Gastambide, Jules, 202, 203, 204
Gauguin, Paul, 163
Girardin, St Marc, 37
Giverny, Monet's home at, 35–6, 162
glassworkers, 210, 216, 219, 240
Goncourt journal, 11–12
Gourdan (Lot), tax revolt in, 115
grain markets, 100, 102
Grand-Combe (Gard), 193
Gravier, J. E., 25, 26
Great Fear (*1789*), 107
Grigny, 214
Guéret (Creuse), 115
Guesde, Jules (*Guesdisme*), 205, 231, 232, 233, 237, 238, 282 n. 21, 283 n. 22
Guizot, François, 83, 258 n. 20

halles (grain markets), 100
Les Halles, Paris, 39
Halluin, 187
handicrafts, rural, 93, 97
Harley, C. K., 214
hat-making industry, 174, 214
Haussmann, Baron, 37, 39–40, 142, 161
Haute-Garonne, collective violence in, 87
Henriet, Frédéric, 144
Hobsbawm, E. J., 118
Holden, Isaac, 133, 263–4 n. 12
Holtzer, Jules, 133
Homer, Winslow, 163–4
Hoschedé, Alice, 162
household workshops, 222–3; Lyonnais, 174, 176, 177, 178
housing, workers', 209, 215–16; Decazeville, 194, 197–8
'human' or urban geographers, 15, 247–8 n. 4
Impressionists, 35–6, 140, 142, 143, 149–63
L'Indépendent rémois, 134

industry and industrialization, 16, 34; bourgeois investment, 118–19, 120, 124–6, 130, 132; Decazeville, 193–207; development of faubourgs, 36–8; development of joint stock companies, 118–19, 125–6; impact on women's work, 22, 165–92; in the changing landscape from Daubigny to Monet, 139–64; paternalism, 136–7, 197–202; provincial bourgeois elites (in Reims and Saint-Étienne) and, 117–38; rural, 22–3, 93–104, 210, 211–13, 221–4; small-scale, 212–15; Stéphanois region, 209–10, 221–2; urbanization, urban growth and, 17–25
insurrections and rebellions, 88, 89; *1851* (Montagnards), 109–13; June Days (*1848*), 32, 95, 104, 105–8
internats (factory dormitories), women employed in, 177–8, 180, 181, 191, 192, 273 n. 74
L'Intransigeant, 201
invasion of fields and forests, 76, 77, 84

Jackson brothers, 129
Jacob Holtzer company, 129, 130, 133
jacquard looms, 178
Jacqueries, 109
Jarry, Alfred, 12
Jaurès, Jean, 206, 238
Joanne, Adolphe, 158
joint stock companies (*sociétés anonymes*), 67, 118–19, 125–6, 137, 264 n. 20
Juge, J. J., 46
Jujurieux *internat*, 177
June Days (*1848*), 32, 95, 104, 105–8
July monarchy, 42, 43, 85; bourgeois elites of Reims and Saint-Étienne under, 118, 121, 122, 124, 137

'*le juste milieu*', Limoges, 64, 66, 68

Kaplow, Jeffrey, 169–70
Keydar, Caglar, 212

labour aristocracy, distinction between artisans and, 220
labour solidarity, 215, 226–7
lacemaking in Lille, 181, 182, 185
Lachambeaudie, Pierre, 149, 161; Daubigny's illustrations to *Fables*, 144–6
La Fayette, nailmakers of, 222, 223, 224
Lafleur, J. B., 61
La Guillotière (Lyon suburb), 36, 174
La Loire, 134
land tax, 113–14
Languedoc, 93, 102; collective violence, 87, 88, 89; grain markets, 102; urban population, 96, 98–9
Laroches-Migennes (Yonne), 23
La Roche-sur-Yon, planned city of, 28–30
Lavedan, Pierre, 38
Lazerme, Madame, 79–80
Le Chambon-Feugerolles, 22, 23, 33–4, 209, 217, 224–5, 226; file-workers of, 210, 216, 219, 220
Le Creusot, 12
Legoyt, M. A., 30, 31
Le Havre, 106; population, 14, 22
Le Moniteur, 60
Le Play, Frédéric, 170–1, 177
Lequin, Yves, 23, 177, 179
Leroy-Beaulieu, Paul, 167, 178
Levainville, Jacques, 248 n. 4
Liberals: in Limoges, 48–60 *passim*, 65–7; in Reims, 132–3, 134–5, 137; in Saint-Étienne, 133–4, 135–6
Lille, 38, 179; industrial suburbs, 183, 186, 187; population, 14, 22; socialist municipality, 231, 244; textile industries, 166, 181, 182, 183–6, 187–8; women's work, 22, 165, 166, 181–9, 190

limited liability companies, 118
Limoges, 193; Bourbon monarchy
crisis and *1830* revolution,
56–60, 64–5; changing urban
politics, 34, 42–72; commerce
and industry, 46–7, 49, 51, 52–3,
54, 64, 67; commune (*1871*), 27;
development of municipal
politics, 56, 65; economic crisis
and riots, 60–4, 67; *1833* strike,
69–70; elections of *1827–8*,
48–50, 51, 52; faubourgs, 44;
grain and bread riots (*1816*),
47–8, 61–3; improvement of
urban environment, 56–8;
increasing number of *eligibles*,
53–4, 58–9, 64; liberal demands,
53–6, 58–9, 65–7; Missions,
50–1, 65; political
demonstration against
Mourgnes, 68–9; population
growth, 44; public works, 65;
religion, 45–6, 54–6, 64–5, 70,
72; republicanism (Saint-
Simonism), 67–8, 69; socialist
municipality, 231
Limousin urban population, 96,
98–9
linen industry, 177, 182, 183–4
liseuses, 175
livestock industry, 101, 102
Louis XVI, King, 25
Louis Napoleon, *see* Napoleon III
Louis Philippe, King, 27, 36, 42,
43, 60, 68, 81, 105, 197
Louveciennes, paintings of, 140,
142
Lyon, 12, 23, 169, 210;
population, 14, 21–2, 211; silk
production, 22, 166, 174–81,
214, 215, 223; and silk workers'
insurrection, 69–70; suburbs, 36,
174; women and work, 22, 165,
166, 174–81, 189, 190

Magnien, M., 231, 232, 245
Maison Centrale, Limoges, 61
Maison Nivet, Limoges, 44
Malabat (Gers), tax revolt, 114
Malon, Benoit, 234

Manet, Edouard, 140, 159
manifestations (demonstrations),
32, 77, 83–5, 86, 87, 88, 89, 90,
104
Marais (Paris), 37
Mardi Gras and metaphor, 73–6
markets and fairs, 113; rural v.
urban, 97, 100–4
Markovich, Tihomir, 125
Marmont, Marshal, 60
Marseille, 12, 95; commune
(*1871*), 27; population, 14, 22,
211; socialist municipality, 231,
244
Marshall, Alfred, 213
Martignac, minster of justice, 44
Martin, Aristide, 135–6
May Day: *1892* municipal elections
held on, 230–2; Fourmies
massacre (*1891*), 230
mayors, 236; confrontation
between police and, 238–40; and
state campaign against, 244–5;
see also municipal socialism
mechanization, 235; artisanal
production v., 214–15, 220; of
textile industry, 22–3, 119,
124–6
Meunier, Marie, 176
Meuriot, Paul, 31
Michelet, Jules, 167
Michon, Jeanne, 176
Miélan (Gers), 114
migration, *see* rural–urban
migration
Millet, J. F., 147, 161, 162; *In the
Garden* (plate 12), 157–8
Missions (Limoges, *1828*), 50–1,
55
monarchie censitaire (*1815–48*),
118, 122
Monet, Claude, 35–6, 140,
149–63, 164; *La Gare St Lazare*
(plate 13), 159–61, 162;
Gladiolas (plate 11), 155, 157;
Railroad Bridge (plate 9), 152–3,
154, 159; *The Railroad Bridge at
Argenteuil* (plate 8), 150, 152,
159; *Sailboats on the Seine at
Argenteuil* (plate 10), 155

Montagnards, 105, 109–13
montagnards, 221
Montbrison, 20, 121
Montceau-les-Mines, 12, 193, 201
Montluçon, 231, 237; mayor's confrontation with police (*1893*), 238–40; and suspension of mayor, 244
Montmartre, 11
Montpellier, charivari in (*1860*), 83–4
Monts du Lyonnais, 210
Mourgnes, Jean Scipion, 68–9
Mulhouse, 120
Mumford, Lewis, *The City in History*, 28
municipal elections, 234, 235–6; Decazeville (*1900*), 203–4, 205; *1892*, 230–1, 232; Roubaix (*1896*), 242
municipal organization, law on (*1884*), 235–6
municipal services in Decazeville, 197–8, 203
municipal socialism, 30, 205, 220, 230–45; creation of enterprises, 237; *1892* election victories, 230–1, 232; finances, 237; public assistance and welfare, 237, 240–2; working-class activities supported by, 237–40
mutation après décès (national probate of wills), 118, 119, 122, 124, 262 n. 3, 263 n. 10, n. 11
mutual aid associations, 38, 69

Nadar, photographer, 12
Nadaud, Martin, 33
nailmakers, 222–3, 224
Nancy Manifesto (*1866*), 27
Nantes population, 14, 22
Napoleon Bonaparte I, Emperor, 26, 38, 181
Napoleon III, Emperor (Louis Napoleon Bonaparte), 27, 74, 118, 119, 142, 144, 161, 197, 236; resistance to coup d'état of (*1861*), 23, 32, 39–40, 95, 109–13

Narbonne, 23, 27, 28, 231, 244
National Guard: Decazeville, 195–6; Limoges, 42, 48, 60, 61, 62, 65, 68, 70, 71; mobilizations against Parisian workers (June Days, *1848*), 104, 105–8
national workshops, Paris, 105, 106
naturalism, 142, 159
new towns, *see villes champignons*
Niort, 39
Nord, urban population, 96, 98–9
notables, 117, 118, 121, 126, 136, 263 n. 11; distribution of wealth at Reims of, 122–4

O'Brien, Patrick, 212

Paris and environs, 11–12, 21, 93, 95, 104; cholera epidemics, 38; collective violence in, 88–9; Commune (*1871*), 12, 25, 31, 32, 37, 233; department stores, 172–3; domination over provinces, 25–7, 30, 93; *1848* revolution, 74; Haussmannization, 37, 39–40; June Days (*1848*), 95, 104, 105–8; Monet's paintings of Argenteuil, 149–59; Monet's paintings of the Gare St Lazare, 159–62; popular politics, 30, 31–2; population, 11, 14, 96, 98–9, 211; social segregation, 37, 38; suburbs, 11, 35, 36–7, 140, 142, 143, 149–59; women and work, 22, 165, 166, 168–73, 189, 190
Parti Ouvrier Français (POF), 231, 232, 233–4
Parti ouvrier socialiste révolutionnaire, 205
Parti socialiste de France, 205–6
Parti socialiste français, 206
'Party of Order', triumph in *1949* legislative elections, 104, 108
peasant markets, urban networks and, 95–104
peasant politics, *see* political mobilization

peasant proprietors, small-scale industry and, 212
peasant solidarity, 112–13, 115
peasant tax revolts (*1848–9*), 95, 113–16
Père Lachaise cemetery, Wall of the Fédérés, 37
Perier, Casimir, 27, 68
periodic marketing, *see* markets and fairs
Perpignan, 23, 28; political charivari in, 79–81, 82
Perrot, Jean-Claude, 15
Perrot, Michelle, 74, 232
Petin and Gaudet company, 129
Pierrard, Pierre, 183–4
Pissarro, Camille, 163
Place de la Liberté, Limoges, 72
Place des Bancs, Limoges, 46
poissardes (market women), 170
Poitiers, 24
police, socialist confrontation with, 238–40, 244
Polignac, Jules, 51, 53, 54
political associations, repressive law on (*1834*), 67
political meetings, 86, 88, 89
political mobilization: proto-urban development and, 92–5, 104–16; urbanization, workers' settlement patterns and, 208–29; working-class collective action (*1880–1914*), 234–5; *see also* municipal socialism; provincial politics; urban politics
Pont de la Révolution, Limoges, 42, 65, 72
population: growth of twelve largest cities in France, 14; Limoges, 44; Paris, 11, 14, 96, 98, 211; rural growth, 97; spatial influence and, 96; urban, 96, 98–9, 210–11
porcelain industry, Limoges, 46, 47, 60, 63, 69, 70
Possibilists, 231, 233, 234, 237
post office women employees, 173
Poubelle, 38
Pouthas, Charles, 18, 19
Printemps department store, 173

printmaking, Daubigny's, 143–4, 147
proto-urban development, 23, 35, 92–116; political mobilization and, 104–16; urban networks and peasant markets, 95–104; urban population by region (*1841*), 98–9
Proust, Marcel, 12
Provence: grain markets, 102; urban population, 96, 98–9
'provincial', definition of word, 25
provincial communes of *1871*, 27
provincial politics (in Reims and Saint-Étienne) and industrialization, 118, 119–20, 127, 132–8
public assistance, socialist municipalities' extension of, 237, 240–2

quincaillerie industry, 121, 122, 127, 129

railroads, 24, 26, 36, 129, 130
Ramadier, Paul, mayor of Decazeville, 205
Rambuteau, 38
Rancayolo, Camille, 15
Reclus, Elisée, 158–9
redoubleuses, women employed as, 182
Reims: artisans, 120, 124–5; bourgeois elite, 117–38; cathedral, 121; industrial–political relationship, 34; political opposition, 132–3, 134–5; population, 14, 22; press, 134; textile (woollen) industry, 22–3, 34, 120, 121, 122, 124–6, 130, 133
religion (the church): Decazeville, 196–7, 203–4; Limoges, 45–6, 50–1, 54–6, 64–5, 70
Rennes, 28
repertoires of collective action, 32, 75; eighteenth-and nineteenth-century, 76–8; a new repertoire, 84–91

Republicans, 81, 104–5, 108, 113, 129–30, 144, 236–7; Decazeville, 198, 202, 203, 204, 205, 207; insurrections against *1851* coup d'état, 23, 32, 39–40, 95, 109–13; Limoges, 67–8, 69; *see also* Second Republic; Third Republic
Restif de la Bretonne, N. E., 169
La Revanche Prolétarienne, Decazeville, 204
revolution (*1830*), 32, 42, 43, 58–60, 64–5, 68, 73, 81, 118
revolution (*1848*), 32, 42, 73–4, 77, 118, 196; *see also* French revolution
revolutionary syndicalists, 205, 236
Reybaud, Louis, 178, 194, 197–8
ribbon industry, Saint-Étienne, 21, 22, 120, 121–2, 126, 127, 128, 130, 133, 135, 136, 138, 210, 222, 223, 264 n. 2
Rive-de-Gier, 209, 226; glassworkers, 210, 216, 219, 220
Roanne, 231, 244
Roche, Daniel, 15–16
Rochechouart, 51
Rogelot, Victor, 133
Roubaix, 12, 120, 213, 238; municipal council, 231, 241; municipal election campaign song, 242; population, 14, 22; woollen industry, 189
Rouen, 14, 22, 38, 105, 106, 120, 162
Rousseau, Jean-Jacques, 169
Rousseau, Théodore, 143, 147
Roussillon, Montagnard insurrection in, 112
Rue de la boucherie, Limoges, 56–7
rural industry, 22–3, 93–104, 210, 211–13, 229; industrial worker mobilization and, 221–4; *see also* proto-urban development
rural–urban migration, 196–7, 210, 211; of women workers, 169, 171–2, 175–6, 178–9, 183, 185, 190

rural–urban relations, *see* proto-urban development

St Bonnet (Charente-Inférieure), tax revolt in, 114–15
Saint-Chamond, 209, 210, 225
Saint-Étienne, 193, 209, 210, 224; bourgeois elite, 117–38; coal and steel industries, 120, 121, 126–7, 129–30; commune (*1871*), 27; housing and amenities, 122; political opposition, 133–4, 135–7; *quincaillerie* industry, 121, 127, 129; relationship between industry and politics, 34; ribbon industry, 21, 22, 120, 121, 126, 127, 128, 130, 133, 210; urban growth and industrialization, 20–1, 22
Saint-Genest-Malifaux, 222, 223
St Germain-des-prés, Paris, 36
St Michel-les-Lions, Limoges, 43, 45, 72
St Priest, Dumont, 49, 50, 59, 60, 62, 63, 64, 68
St Sauveur (Yonne), 111
Saint Saveur (Lille suburb), 182, 183
Saint-Simonism, 67–8, 69, 144, 161
Saint-Symphorien d'Ozon, 214
Saint-Symphorien-sur-Coise, 214
saleswomen, 172–3
Sauget, Juliette, 171
SCF (SCFD), 203, 204, 205, 206, 207
Schneider, Eugène, 197
seamstresses, 169, 172, 174, 181
Second Empire, bourgeois elites of Reims and Saint-Étienne under, 117–38; *see also* Napoleon III
Second Republic, 27, 42, 43, 74, 85, 118, 137; proto-urbanization and political mobilization during, 92–116
Segantini, Giovanni, 164
'self-employed' workers, 213
Septennial Ostensions, Limoges, 46
serenades, 78, 79, 82

sewing threads production, 183
SHFA in Decazeville, 195–7, 199, 200, 203, 204, 206
shirt-makers, women employed as, 184–5
Shorter, Edward, 234
silk industry (Lyon), 22, 102, 166, 214, 215, 223, 224; women employed in, 174–81
Simon, Jules, 134; *L'Ouvrière*, 167
Sisley, Alfred, *The Sèvres Road* (plate 3), 140, 142–3
skilled workers, *see* artisans; workers
small-scale industry, 212–15
SNHFA in Decazeville, 197–200, 202–3, 204, 206, 207
'the social family', 241–2
social protest, influence of urbanization and worker settlement patterns on, 208–29
social segregation in French cities, 37–8
socialism and socialists, 68; in Decazeville, 203–4, 205–6, 207; municipal, 230–45
Société Industrielle, Reims, 132–3
sociétés anonymes, *see* joint-stock companies
space, urban form and planning, 35–40
spinning, *see* textile industries
steel industry, 127, 129–30, 136
Stendhal (Henri Beyle), 44
Stéphanois region, urban development and working-class protest in, 209–10, 216, 217, 218, 219, 220, 221–4, 226, 227
street market women, 170, 173, 182
strikes, 32, 74, 77, 86, 87, 88, 89, 208, 234, 235, 236, 237; artisans' role, 219–20, 226; Aubin (*1869*), 201; Decazeville (*1886*), 33, 193, 201–2, 203, 204, 208; Limoges (*1833*), 69–70; Stéphanois region, 226
suburbs (faubourgs), 35; industrial, 36–8, 182, 183; Lille, 182, 183, 186, 187; Limoges, 44; Lyon,

36, 174, 178; Paris, 11, 35, 36–7, 140, 142, 143, 168–9, 171; pre-Impressionist v. Impressionist portrayal of, 140, 142, 143–59
La Syndicale, Decazeville, 204–5

taxes, 122, 237; land, 113–14; protests/revolts against, 61, 63–4, 68, 76, 77, 84, 93, 95, 105, 113–16
telephone operators, female, 173
Ternyck, Sophie, 184
textile industry, 93, 102, 189; Dieulefit, 110–11; Lille (cotton, linen, etc.), 166, 181–6, 187–8; Limoges, 46–7; Lyon (silk), 22, 166, 174–81, 189; mechanization, 22–3, 119, 124–6; Reims (woollen), 22–3, 120, 121, 122, 124–6, 127; rural, 212–13; women employed in, 174–81, 221; woollen industry (in Roubaix and Tourcoing), 189
thermal towns, 24
Thiers, Adolphe, 27–8, 266 n. 45
Third Republic, 92, 94, 117, 138, 194, 204, 206, 230, 236
Thompson, E. P., 165, 192
Tillac (Gers), tax revolt in, 114
'time segmented labour', 221
'time-thrift', concept of, 165
tireuses, 174, 175
Tocqueville, Alexis de, 26, 107
Toulouse, 23; collective violence in, 86–7, 88; political charivaris, 81–3; population, 14, 22
Tourcoing, 189, 213
Tournefort, Bishop Prosper de, 54, 55–6, 64
town planning, space and urban form, 35–40
trade unions, 138, 238; in Decazeville, 204, 205, 206; legalization of, 235
Trempé, Rolande, 244
Tristan, Flora, 20, 30, 122
Truquin, Norbert, 178–9
Turgan's *Grandes usines*, 126

universal suffrage, introduction of, 122
urban networks and peasant markets, 95–104
urban (popular) politics, 30–5; charavaris, 32, 47, 50, 78–84, 89–90; collective violence, 86–9; eighteenth- and nineteenth-century repertoires, 76–8, 84–91; Limoges, 42–72; *manifestations*, 32, 83–5; Mardi Gras and metaphor, 73–6
l'urbanisme constructeur, 38
l'urbanisme démolisseur, 39
urbanization, 11, 12, 15–16, 40–1; evolution of social protest and, 208–29; industrialization, urban growth and, 17–25, 211–15; space, urban form and planning, 35–40; women's work and, 165–92; *see also* proto-urban development
'urbanized villages', 102
utopian socialists, 38–9, 68

Vacher, Antoine, 248 n. 4
Vaillant, Edouard, 230, 234, 282 n. 21
Van Gogh, Vincent, 163
Vance, James, Jnr, 221
Vendée uprising, 28–9
Vergniaud, Girondin, 27
Victorine B, 170
Vienne, 39
Vigier, Philippe, 32
Villegoureix, François, 64
Villeminot-Huard, industrialist, 132
Villermé, Louis, 166–7
villes champignons (new towns), 193; *see also* Decazeville
villes parlementaires, 29

wage-labour, women's, 166–92 *passim*
Wagner–Marsan company, 126

Walter, Rodolphe, 155
Ward, David, 226, 227
Warnier, Jules, 132–3, 134, 135
Watrin, Jules (*watrinade*), 193, 199–200, 201
Weber, Eugen, 34–5, 79, 85, 257 n. 5
Werlé, Edouard, 134
white-collar workers, women employed as, 186–7
Wildenstein, Daniel, 155
wine industry, 22, 23, 93, 102, 109–10, 122, 123
women workers, 22, 165–92, 221; in Lille, 181–9; in Lyon, 174–81; in Paris, 168–73
woollen industry: Nord, 189; Reims, 120, 121, 122, 124–6, 130, 133, 137
workers and the working class: 'captive professionals', 218–19; in Decazeville, 193–207; *fraternité* as slogan of, 241–2; housing for, 215–16; in Limoges, 47, 63, 69–70; May Day demonstrations by, 230; move to socialism from republicanism, 236; occupational pride, 216–17; Paris uprising of (June Days, *1848*), 95, 104, 105–8; political mobilization (*1880–1914*), 234–5, 237; settlement patterns and social protest of, 208–29; skilled, 47, 63, 69, 214, 215–18; 'the social family', 241–2; songs of, 216–17 242; women, 165–92, 221; *see also* artisans

Young, Arthur, 54

Zeldin, Théodore, 120
Zola, Émile, 11, 17, 173; *L'Assommoir*, 170; *Germinal*, 33, 193, 201